Microsoft®

EXCEL FOR

WINDOWS® 95

Step by Step

Other titles in the Step by Step series:

For Microsoft Windows 95

(available in Fall 1995)

Integrating Microsoft Office Applications Step by Step, for Windows 95

Microsoft Access for Windows 95 Step by Step

Microsoft Access/Visual Basic Step by Step

Microsoft Excel/Visual Basic Step by Step

Microsoft PowerPoint for Windows 95 Step by Step

Microsoft Project for Windows 95 Step by Step

Microsoft Visual Basic 4 Step by Step

Microsoft Windows 95 Step by Step

Microsoft Word for Windows 95 Step by Step

Microsoft Works for Windows 95 Step by Step

More Microsoft Windows 95 Step by Step

Upgrading to Microsoft Windows 95 Step by Step

For Microsoft Windows 3.1

(available now)

Microsoft Access 2 for Windows Step by Step

Microsoft Excel 5 for Windows Step by Step

Microsoft Excel Visual Basic for
   Applications Step by Step, version 5 for Windows

Microsoft Mail for Windows Step by Step, versions 3.0b and later

Microsoft Office for Windows Step by Step, version 4

Microsoft PowerPoint 4 for Windows Step by Step

Microsoft Project 4 for Windows Step by Step

Microsoft Visual FoxPro 3 for Windows Step by Step

Microsoft Word 6 for Windows Step by Step

Microsoft Works 3 for Windows Step by Step

Microsoft®

EXCEL FOR WINDOWS® 95
Step by Step

Microsoft Press

PUBLISHED BY
Microsoft Press
A Division of Microsoft Corporation
One Microsoft Way
Redmond, Washington 98052-6399

Library of Congress Cataloging-in-Publication Data
Microsoft Excel for Windows 95 step by step / Catapult, Inc.
     p.   cm.
   Includes index.
   ISBN 1-55615-825-4
    1. Microsoft Excel for Windows   2. Business--Computer programs.
   3. Electronic spreadsheets.   I. Catapult, Inc.
   HF5548.4.M523M525   1995
   005.369--dc20
                             95-31430
                                CIP

Printed and bound in the United States of America.

1 2 3 4 5 6 7 8 9 QMQM 9 8 7 6 5

Distributed to the book trade in Canada by Macmillan of Canada, a division of Canada Publishing Corporation.

A CIP catalogue record for this book is available from the British Library.

Microsoft Press books are available through booksellers and distributors worldwide. For further information about international editions, contact your local Microsoft Corporation office. Or contact Microsoft Press International directly at fax (206) 936-7329.

For Catapult, Inc.
Managing Editor: Donald Elman
Writer: Julia Kelly
Project Editor: Ann T. Rosenthal
Production/Layout Editor: Jeanne K. Hunt
Technical Editor: Brett R. Davidson

For Microsoft Press
Acquisitions Editor: Casey D. Doyle
Project Editor: Brenda L. Matteson

Catapult, Inc. & Microsoft Press

Microsoft Excel for Windows 95 Step by Step has been created by the professional trainers and writers at Catapult, Inc., to the exacting standards you've come to expect from Microsoft Press. Together, we are pleased to present this self-paced training guide, which you can use individually or as part of a class.

Catapult, Inc., is a software training company with years of experience in PC and Macintosh instruction. Catapult's exclusive Performance-Based Training system is available in Catapult training centers across North America and at customer sites. Based on the principles of adult learning, Performance-Based Training ensures that students leave the classroom with confidence and the ability to apply skills to real-world scenarios. *Microsoft Excel for Windows 95 Step by Step* incorporates Catapult's training expertise to ensure that you'll receive the maximum return on your training time. You'll focus on the skills that increase productivity the most while working at your own pace and convenience.

Microsoft Press is the independent—and independent-minded—book publishing division of Microsoft Corporation. The leading publisher of information on Microsoft software, Microsoft Press is dedicated to providing the highest quality end-user training, reference, and technical books that make using Microsoft software easier, more enjoyable, and more productive.

Contents at a Glance

Table of Contents

Table of Contents

Table of Contents

Table of Contents

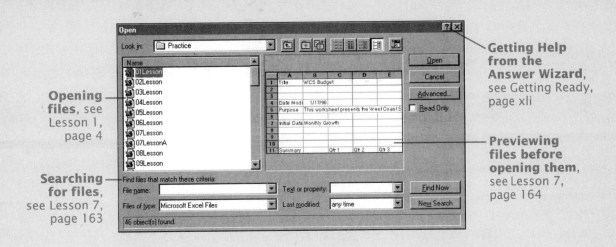

Opening files, see Lesson 1, page 4

Searching for files, see Lesson 7, page 163

Getting Help from the Answer Wizard, see Getting Ready, page xli

Previewing files before opening them, see Lesson 7, page 164

Naming cell ranges, see Lesson 2, page 32

Writing simple formulas, see Lesson 2, page 28

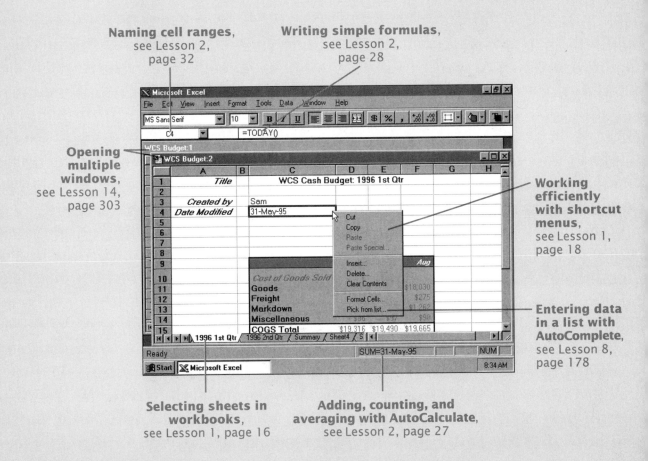

Opening multiple windows, see Lesson 14, page 303

Working efficiently with shortcut menus, see Lesson 1, page 18

Entering data in a list with AutoComplete, see Lesson 8, page 178

Selecting sheets in workbooks, see Lesson 1, page 16

Adding, counting, and averaging with AutoCalculate, see Lesson 2, page 27

*Quick*Look Guide

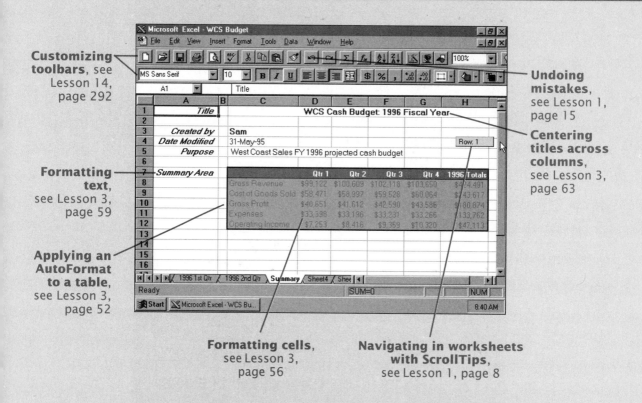

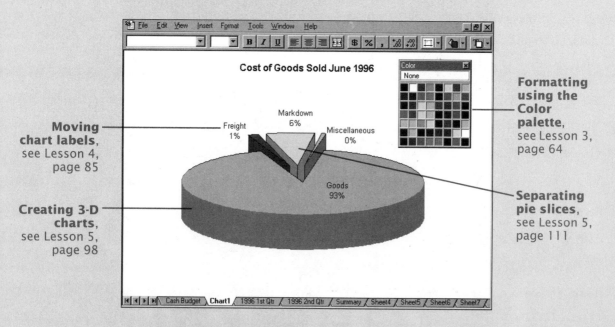

Combining chart types, see Lesson 4, page 91

Creating charts with the ChartWizard, see Lesson 4, page 78

Formatting legends, see Lesson 5, page 101

Changing series order, see Lesson 4, page 89

Changing the chart type using the Chart Type palette, see Lesson 5, page 96

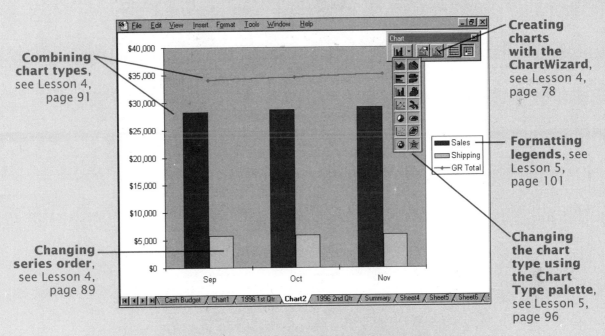

Summarizing data with pivot tables, see Lesson 10, page 202

Formatting pivot table numbers, see Lesson 10, page 220

Editing pivot table text, see Lesson 10, page 206

Printing worksheets without their embedded charts, see Lesson 6, page 138

Creating charts from pivot tables, see Lesson 10, page 222

Creating embedded charts, see Lesson 4, page 78

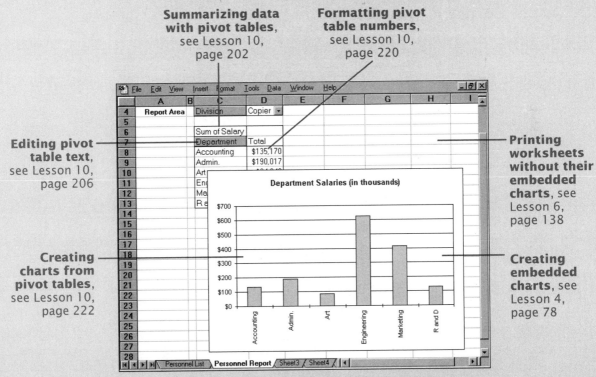

QuickLook Guide

Printing custom headers, see Lesson 6, page 134

Printing part of your worksheet, see Lesson 6, page 138

Using data or graphics from other applications, see Lesson 13, page 268

Printing with or without gridlines, see Lesson 6, page 139

Printing custom footers, see Lesson 6, page 134

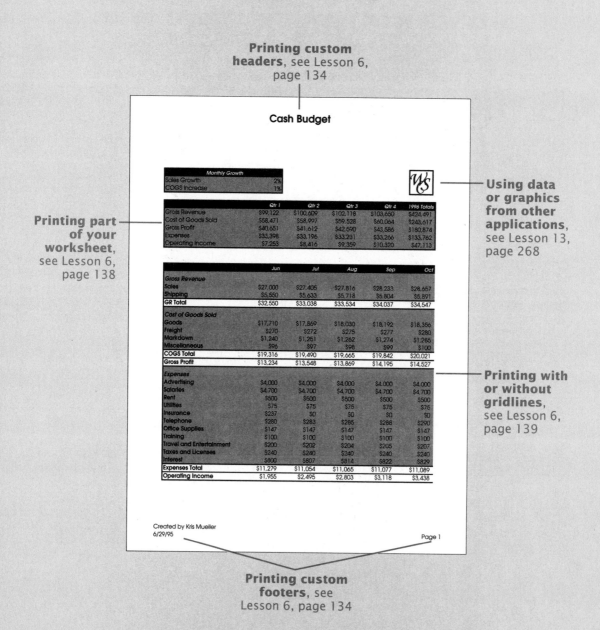

About This Book

In "About This Book" you will learn how to:

- Find your best starting point in this book based on your level of experience.
- Learn what the conventions in this book mean.
- Learn where to get additional information about Windows 95.

Microsoft Excel for Windows 95 is a powerful spreadsheet program that you can use for managing, analyzing, and charting your data. *Microsoft Excel for Windows 95 Step by Step* shows you how to use Microsoft Excel to simplify your work and increase your productivity. With this book, you can learn Microsoft Excel at your own pace and at your own convenience, or you can use it in a classroom setting.

IMPORTANT   This book is for use with Microsoft Excel for the Windows 95 operating system. To determine what software you are running, you can check the software documentation, the installation disk labels, or the exterior product packaging.

You get hands-on practice by using the practice files on the disk located in the back of this book. Each lesson explains when and how to use the appropriate practice files. Instructions for copying the practice files to your computer hard disk are in "Getting Ready," the next chapter in this book.

Finding the Best Starting Point for You

This book is designed both for new users learning Microsoft Excel for the first time and for experienced users who want to learn and use the new features in Microsoft Excel for Windows 95. Either way, *Microsoft Excel for Windows 95 Step by Step* will help you get the most out of Microsoft Excel.

This book is divided into five major parts, each containing several related lessons. Each lesson takes approximately 20 to 45 minutes, with an optional practice exercise, titled "One Step Further," at the end of each lesson. At the end of each part is a Review & Practice section that gives you the opportunity to practice the skills you learned in that part. Each Review & Practice section allows you to test your knowledge and prepare for your own work.

Use the following table to determine your best path through the book.

If you are	Follow these steps
New to a computer or graphical environment, such as Microsoft Windows 95	Read "Getting Ready," the next chapter in this book, and follow the instructions to install the practice files. Carefully read the section "If You Are New to Microsoft Windows 95." Next, work through Lessons 1 through 3 in order for a basic introduction to Microsoft Excel. Work through Lessons 4 through 15 in any order.
Familiar with the Microsoft Windows 95 graphical computer environment, but new to using Microsoft Excel	Follow the instructions for installing the practice files in "Getting Ready," the next chapter in this book. Next, work through Lessons 1 through 3 in order for a basic introduction to Microsoft Excel. Work through Lessons 4 through 15 in any order.
Experienced with Microsoft Excel	Follow the instructions for installing the practice files in "Getting Ready," the next chapter in this book. Next, read through "New Features in Microsoft Excel," following "Getting Ready," for summary of the new features in this version that are covered in this book. Complete the lessons that best fit your needs.

Using This Book As a Classroom Aid

If you're an instructor, you can use *Microsoft Excel for Windows 95 Step by Step* for teaching computer users. You might want to select certain lessons that meet your students' particular needs and incorporate your own demonstrations into the lessons.

If you plan to teach the entire contents of this book, you should probably set aside up to three days of classroom time to allow for discussion, questions, and any customized practice you might create.

Conventions Used in This Book

Before you start any of the lessons, it's important that you understand the terms and notational conventions used in this book.

Procedural Conventions

- Hands-on exercises that you are to follow are given in numbered lists of steps (1, 2, and so on). An arrowhead bullet (➤) indicates an exercise with only one step.

- Characters or commands that you type appear in **bold lowercase** type.

Print

- You can carry out many commands by clicking a button at the top of the program window. If a procedure instructs you to click a button, a picture of the button usually appears in the left margin, as the Print button does here.

Mouse Conventions

- If you have a multiple-button mouse, it is assumed that the left mouse button is the primary mouse button. Any procedure that requires you to press the secondary button will refer to it as the right mouse button.

- *Click* means to point to an object and then press and release the mouse button. For example, "Click the Cut button on the Standard toolbar." *Use the right mouse button to click* means to point to an object and then press and release the right mouse button.

- *Drag* means to point to an object and then press and hold down the mouse button while you move the mouse. For example, "Drag the window edge downward to enlarge the window."

- *Double-click* means to rapidly press and release the mouse button twice. For example, "Double-click the Microsoft Excel icon to start Microsoft Excel."

Keyboard Conventions

- Names of keyboard keys that you are instructed to press are in small capital letters, for example, TAB and SHIFT.

- A plus sign (+) between two key names means that you must press those keys at the same time. For example, "Press ALT+TAB" means that you hold down the ALT key while you press TAB.

- Procedures generally emphasize use of the mouse, rather than the keyboard. However, you can choose menu commands with the keyboard by pressing the ALT key to activate the menu bar, and then sequentially pressing the keys that correspond to the highlighted or underlined letter of the menu name and then the command name. For some commands, you can also press a key combination listed in the menu.

Notes

- Notes or Tips that appear either in the text or the left margin provide additional information or alternative methods for a procedure.

- Notes labeled "Important" alert you to essential information that you should check before continuing with the lesson.

- Notes labeled "Warning" alert you to possible data loss and tell you how to proceed safely.

Other Features of This Book

- The "One Step Further" exercise at the end of each lesson introduces new options or techniques that build on the commands and skills you used in the lesson.

- Each lesson concludes with a Lesson Summary that lists the skills you have learned in the lesson and briefly reviews how to accomplish particular tasks.

- References to Microsoft Excel online Help at the end of each lesson direct you to Help topics for additional information. The Help system provides a complete online reference to Microsoft Excel. You'll learn more about Help in "Getting Ready," the next chapter in this book.

- The "Review & Practice" activity at the end of each part provides an opportunity to use the major skills presented in the lessons for that part. These activities present problems that reinforce what you have learned and demonstrate new ways you can use Microsoft Excel.

- In the Appendix, "Matching the Exercises," you can review the options used in this book to get the results you see in the illustrations. Refer to this section of the book when your screen does not match the illustrations or when you get unexpected results as you work through the exercises.

Getting Ready

In "Getting Ready" you will learn how to:

- Copy the practice files to your computer hard disk.
- Start Microsoft Windows 95 and use the mouse.
- Use basic Windows 95 features such as windows, menus, dialog boxes, and Help.
- Start Microsoft Excel and get acquainted with some of its tools.

This chapter of the book prepares you for your first steps into the Microsoft Excel for Windows 95 environment. You will learn how to install the practice files that come with this book and how to start both Microsoft Windows 95 and Microsoft Excel. You will also get an overview of some useful Windows 95 techniques, and you'll get an introduction to some terms and concepts that are important to understand as you learn Microsoft Excel.

If you have not yet installed Windows 95 or Microsoft Excel, you'll need to do that before you start the lessons. To install Windows 95, see your Windows 95 documentation. To install Microsoft Excel for Windows 95, see your Microsoft Excel documentation.

IMPORTANT   Before you break the seal on the practice disk in the back of this book, be sure that you have the correct version of the software. This book is designed for use with Microsoft Excel, an application that runs on the Windows 95 operating system. To determine what software you are running, you can either check the software documentation, the setup disk labels, or the exterior product packaging.

Installing the Step by Step Practice Files

The disk attached to the inside back cover of this book contains practice files that you'll use to perform the exercises in the lessons. For example, the lesson that teaches you how to find documents stored on your computer instructs you to find and open one of the practice files. Because the practice files simulate tasks you'll encounter in a typical business setting, you can easily transfer what you learn from this book to your own work.

NOTE If you would like an introduction to using the mouse before you set up your Step by Step practice files, refer to the section "If You Are New to Microsoft Windows 95" later in this chapter. When you are finished practicing with the mouse, return to this section and copy the practice files to your hard disk.

Copy the practice files to your hard disk

You must have Microsoft Windows 95 installed on your computer in addition to Microsoft Excel for Windows 95 to use the practice files. Follow these steps to copy the practice files to your computer hard disk so that you can use them with the lessons.

If you do not know your user name or password, contact your system administrator for further help.

1 If your computer isn't already on, turn it on now. If you see a dialog box asking for your user name and password, type them in the appropriate boxes and then click OK. If you see the Welcome dialog box, click the Close button.

Windows 95 starts automatically when you turn on your computer.

My Computer icon

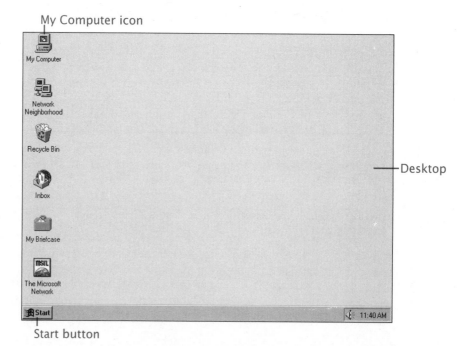

Desktop

Start button

2 Remove the disk from the package on the inside back cover of this book.

3 Put the disk in drive A or drive B of your computer.

4 On the taskbar at the bottom of your screen, click the Start button.

5 On the Start menu, click Run.

...and then click Run.

Click Start...

6 In the Run dialog box, type **a:setup** (or **b:setup** if the disk is in drive B), and then click the OK button. Do not type a space anywhere in the command.

7 Follow the directions on the screen.

The setup program window appears with recommended options preselected for you. For best results in using the practice files with this book, accept the recommendations made by the program.

8 After the files are copied, remove the disk from your computer and replace it in the envelope on the inside back cover of the book.

The Step by Step setup program copies the practice files from the floppy disk onto the hard disk in a subfolder called Excel SBS Practice. The setup program makes use of the Windows 95 Favorites folder. Follow the steps as presented in each lesson to open or save your practice files.

Using the Practice Files

The text in each lesson in this book explains when and how to use the practice file for that lesson. The installation doesn't create any icons—when it's time to use a practice file in a lesson, the book will list instructions for how to open the file.

Be sure to follow the directions for saving the files and giving them new names. Renaming the practice files allows you to use the renamed copy of a file to complete a lesson while leaving the original file intact. That way, if you want to start a lesson over or repeat a lesson later, you can reuse the original file.

Most lessons begin by opening a new practice file whose name corresponds to the lesson number. Be sure to close any open practice files and then open the correct practice file when you are directed in a lesson. Using a practice file from another lesson might not give you the correct results.

Filenames in Windows 95

Windows 95 allows much greater flexibility in naming files than did previous versions of Windows. Instead of the MS-DOS filename limitation of eight characters with a three-character extension (such as BUDG0595.XLS), you can use longer, more meaningful names in Windows 95 (such as "Budget for May 1995"), consisting of one or more words with spaces in between.

NOTE Long filenames are displayed in uppercase and lowercase letters as originally typed, but Windows 95 does not distinguish filenames according to case. For example, a file named "Letter 23" is considered the same as both "LETTER 23" and "letter 23" in this operating system.

Lesson Background

The practice files and exercises are designed to represent typical types of work you might carry out with Microsoft Excel in a business setting. For these lessons, imagine that you work for a company called West Coast Sales, which builds and sells printers, copiers, and fax machines. Throughout these lessons, you use Microsoft Excel to assist you in your daily tasks.

If You Are New to Microsoft Windows 95

Microsoft Windows 95 is an easy-to-use work environment that helps you handle the daily work that you perform with your computer. It provides a common look and functionality among the many different programs you might use—both in the way they share data and in the way you use the programs. This makes it easy for you to learn and use different programs in Windows 95. In this section, you'll get an introduction to Windows 95. If you are already familiar with Windows 95, you can skip to the next section, "Working with Microsoft Excel."

Start Windows 95

Starting Windows 95 is as easy as turning on your computer.

If you do not know your user name or password, contact your system administrator for further help.

 If your computer isn't already on, turn it on now. If you see a dialog box asking for your user name and password, type them in the appropriate boxes and then click OK. If you see the Welcome dialog box, click the Close button or press ENTER.

Windows 95 starts automatically when you turn on your computer. Your screen looks similar to the following illustration.

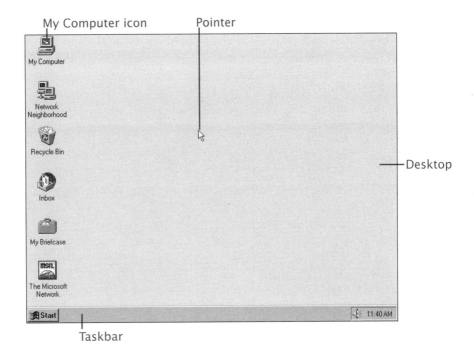

Using the Mouse

Windows 95 is designed for use with a mouse. Although you can use the keyboard for most actions in Windows 95, many of these actions are easier to do with a mouse.

The mouse controls a pointer on the screen, as shown in the preceding illustration. You move the pointer by sliding the mouse over a flat surface in the direction you want the pointer to move. If you run out of room to move the mouse, lift it up and then put it down in a more comfortable location. The pointer moves only when the mouse is touching a flat surface.

Moving the mouse pointer across the screen does not affect the information that you see; the pointer simply indicates a location on the screen. When you press the mouse button, an action occurs at the location of the pointer. You will use four basic mouse actions throughout the lessons in this book.

Pointing Moving the mouse to place the pointer on an item is called *pointing*.

Clicking Pointing to an item on your screen and then quickly pressing and releasing the mouse button is called *clicking*. You select items on the screen by clicking. Occasionally there are operations you perform by pressing the right mouse button, but unless you are instructed otherwise, press with the left mouse button.

Double-clicking Pointing to an item and then quickly pressing and releasing the mouse button twice is called *double-clicking*. This is a convenient shortcut for many tasks. Whenever you are unsure of the command to use for an operation, try double-clicking the item you want to affect. This often displays a dialog box in which you can make changes to the item you double-clicked.

Dragging Pointing to an item and then holding down the mouse button as you move the pointer is called *dragging*. You can use this action to select data and to move and copy text or objects.

Try the mouse

Take a moment to test drive the mouse.

1 Slide the mouse pointer over the Windows 95 Desktop.

The pointer is a left-pointing arrow.

2 Move the mouse pointer on top of the Start button at the bottom of the screen, and then press the left mouse button to open the Start menu.

3 Move the mouse pointer outside the Start menu, and click the Desktop.

The Start menu closes.

4 Point to the My Computer icon, and then double-click the left mouse button.

The My Computer window opens, where you can view the disk drives and folders stored there.

My Computer

5 Move the mouse pointer over the bottom edge of the My Computer window until the pointer changes to a double-headed arrow.

When you move the mouse pointer over different parts of the Windows 95 Desktop or different areas in a program window, the pointer can change shape to indicate what action is available at that point.

6   Hold down the left mouse button and move (*drag*) the mouse pointer downward.

7   Release the mouse button.

The My Computer window is resized.

Using Windows-Based Programs

After you become familiar with the basic operation of Windows 95, you can apply these skills to learn and use Windows-based programs—programs that are designed for use with Windows 95.

All Windows-based programs have similar characteristics in how they appear on the screen and how you use them. All the windows in Windows-based programs have common controls that you use to scroll, size, move, and close a window.

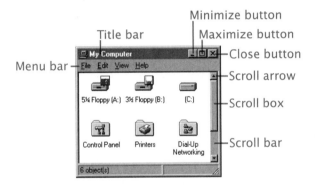

To	Do this
Scroll through a window	Click a scroll bar or scroll arrow, or drag the scroll box.
Enlarge a window to fill the screen	Double-click the title bar, or click the Maximize button.
Restore a window to its previous size	Double-click the title bar, or click the Restore button. When a window is maximized, the Maximize button changes to the Restore button.
Reduce a window to a button on the taskbar	Click the Minimize button. To display a minimized window, simply click its button on the taskbar.
Move a window	Drag the title bar.
Close a window	Click the Close button.

You'll try out these Windows techniques and learn more about them in the following sections.

Using Menus

To choose a command on a menu, you click the menu name to open the menu, and then you click the command name on the menu. When a command name appears dimmed, either it doesn't apply to your current situation or it is unavailable. For example, the Paste command on the Edit menu appears dimmed if the Copy or Cut command has not been used first.

Some commands have a *shortcut key* combination shown to the right of the command name. Once you are familiar with the menus and commands, you might prefer to use these shortcut keys to save time if your hands are already at the keyboard.

To close a menu without choosing a command, you can click the menu name again or click anywhere outside of the menu. You can also press ESC to close a menu.

Open the Edit menu

To make menu selections with the keyboard, press ALT, and then type the underlined character in the menu or command name.

1   In the My Computer window, click Edit in the menu bar.

The Edit menu appears. Notice which commands are dimmed and which have shortcut key combinations listed.

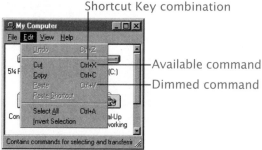

Shortcut Key combination

Available command

Dimmed command

2   Click the Edit menu name to close the menu.

The menu closes.

Make menu selections

Commands on a menu are grouped by common functions. Commands that are in effect are indicated by a check mark or a bullet mark to the left of the command name. A check mark indicates that multiple items in this group of commands can be in effect at the same time. A bullet mark indicates that only one item in this group can be in effect at the same time.

1   Click View in the menu bar.

The View menu looks like the following illustration.

Check mark

Bullet mark —

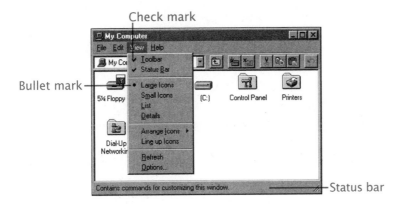

Status bar

2　On the View menu, click Toolbar.

The View menu closes, and a toolbar appears below the menu bar.

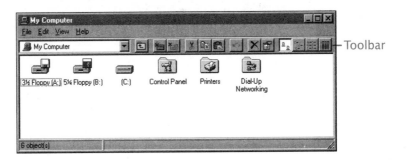

Toolbar

3　On the View menu, click List.

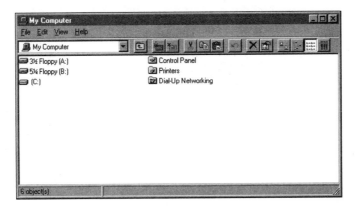

The items in the My Computer window are now displayed in a list, instead of by icons.

Large Icons

4 On the toolbar, click the Large Icons button.

If you do not see the button, drag a corner of the window to enlarge it until you see the button. Clicking a button on a toolbar is a quick way to select a command.

5 On the View menu, point to Arrange Icons.

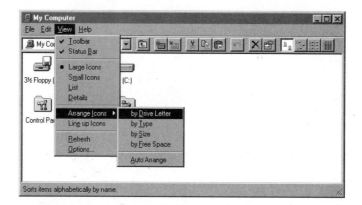

A cascading menu appears listing additional menu choices. When a right-pointing arrow appears after a command name, it indicates that additional commands are available.

6 To close the menu, click the menu name or anywhere outside the menu.

7 On the menu bar, click View, and then click Toolbar again.

The View menu closes, and the toolbar is now hidden.

Close

8 Click the Close button in the upper-right corner of the My Computer window to close the window.

Using Dialog Boxes

When you choose a command name that is followed by an ellipsis (...), Windows-based programs display a dialog box in which you can provide more information about how the command should be carried out. Dialog boxes consist of a number of standard features as shown in the following illustration.

Text box   Tab

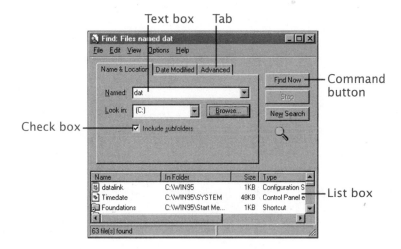

Check box

Command
button

List box

To move around in a dialog box, you click the item you want. You can also hold down ALT as you press the underlined letter. Or, you can press TAB to move between items.

After you enter information or make selections in a dialog box, you choose the OK button in the dialog box or you press the ENTER key on the keyboard to carry out the command. Click the Cancel button or press ESC to close a dialog box and cancel the command.

Display the Taskbar dialog box

Some dialog boxes provide several categories of options displayed on separate tabs, like folders in a filing cabinet. You click the top of a tab to bring it forward and display additional options in the dialog box.

1   On the taskbar, click the Start button. On the Start menu, point to Settings, and then click Taskbar to display the Taskbar Properties dialog box.

2   Click the Start Menu Programs tab.

Click here.

On this tab, you can customize the list of programs that appears on your Start menu.

3 Click the Taskbar Options tab, and then click Show Small Icons In Start Menu.

Clicking a check box that is selected (that displays a check mark) turns the option off.

4 Click the check box a couple of times, and observe how the display in the dialog box changes.

Clicking any check box or option button will turn the option off or on.

5 Click the Cancel button in the dialog box.

This closes the dialog box without changing any settings.

Getting Help with Windows 95

When you need information about a procedure or how to use a particular feature on your computer, the online Help system is one of the most efficient ways to learn. The online Help system for Windows 95 is available from the Start menu, and you choose the type of help you want from the Help dialog box.

For instructions on broad categories, you can look at the Help contents. Or, you can search the Help index for information on specific topics. The Help information is short and concise, so you can get the exact information you need quickly. There are also shortcut buttons in many Help topics that you can use to directly switch to the task you want to perform.

Viewing Help Contents

The Help Contents tab is organized like a book's table of contents. As you choose top-level topics, or "chapters," you see a list of more detailed topics from which to choose. Many of these chapters have special "Tips and Tricks" subsections that can help you work more efficiently.

If you are new to Windows 95, you might be interested in the Help topic under "Introducing Windows 95" named "Ten minutes to using Windows."

Find Help on general categories

In this exercise, you'll look up information in the online Help system.

1 Click Start. On the Start menu, click Help.

The Help dialog box appears.

2 If necessary, click the Contents tab to make it active.

3 Double-click "Introducing Windows."

The book icon opens to display a set of subtopics.

4 Double-click "Using Windows Accessories."

5 Double-click "For General Use."

6 Double-click "Calculator: for making calculations."

A Help topic window appears.

Maximize

7 Click the Maximize button on the Help window.

The Help topic window fills the entire screen.

Minimize

8 Click the Minimize button to reduce the Help window to a button on the taskbar.

Whenever you minimize a window, its button appears on the taskbar.

Finding Help on Specific Topics

There are two methods for finding specific Help topics: the Index tab and the Find tab. The Index tab is organized like a book's index. Keywords for topics are organized alphabetically. You can either scroll through the list of keywords, or you can type the keyword you want to find. One or more topic choices are then presented.

With the Find tab, you can also enter a keyword. The main difference is that you get a list of all Help topics in which that keyword appears, not just the topics that begin with that word.

Find Help on specific topics using the Help index

In this exercise, you use the Help index to learn how to change the background pattern of your Desktop.

1 Click the Windows Help button on the taskbar.

The Help dialog box appears as you left it.

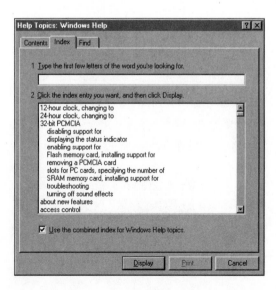

Restore

2 Click the Restore button so that you can see both the Help window and the Desktop.

3 Click the Help Topics button at the top of the Help dialog box, and then click the Index tab.

The Help index appears.

4 In the text box, type **display**

A list of display-related topics appears.

5 Double-click the topic named "background pictures or patterns, changing."

The Topics Found window appears.

6 Double-click the topic named "Changing the background of your Desktop."

7 Read the Help topic if you like.

8 Click the jump button in Step 1 of the Help topic.

The Properties For Display dialog box appears. If you want, you can immediately perform the task you were looking up in Help.

9 Click the Close button on the Display Properties dialog box.

10 Click the Close button on the Windows Help window.

Jump

Close

 NOTE You can print any Help topic. Click the Options button in the upper-left corner of any Help topic window, click Print Topic, and then click OK. To continue searching for additional topics, you can click the Help Topics button in any open Help topic window.

Find Help on specific topics using the Find tab

In this exercise, you'll use the Find tab to learn how to change your printer's settings.

1 Click Start. On the Start menu, click Help to display the Help dialog box.

2 Click the Find tab to make it active.

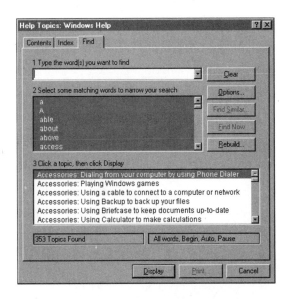

3 If you see a wizard, select the best option for your system, and then click Next. Click Finish to complete and close the wizard.

The wizard creates a search index for your Help files. This might take a few minutes. The next time you use Find, you won't have to wait for Windows 95 to create a topic list.

4 In the text box under step 1, type **print**

All topics pertaining to printing appear in the list box at the bottom of the tab.

5 In the list box under step 3, click the topic "Changing printer settings," and then click Display.

6 Read the Help topic if you want, using the scroll bar as necessary.

Close

7 Click the Close button on the Windows Help window.

 NOTE You can also get help about the controls in a dialog box by clicking the question mark button in the upper-right corner of the dialog box. When you click this button and then click any dialog box control, a ScreenTip pops up that explains what the control is and how to use it.

Working with Microsoft Excel

Now that you are familiar with the Windows 95 operating environment, you can start Microsoft Excel. The easiest way to start Excel is from the Programs menu, but you can also use My Computer.

Start Microsoft Excel from the Programs menu

 NOTE If you do not see Microsoft Excel listed on the Programs menu when you do step 1 in the following exercise, skip to the exercise, "Start Microsoft Excel from My Computer" to use an alternate way to start the program.

1 Click Start. On the Start menu, point to Programs, and then click Microsoft Excel.

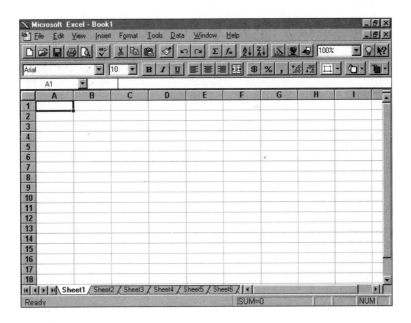

2   If you see the Welcome dialog box, click OK.

Maximize

3   If the window is not already maximized, as shown in the above illustration, click the Maximize button.

Start Microsoft Excel from My Computer

If Microsoft Excel is not listed on the Windows 95 Programs menu, you can start the program from My Computer.

1   Double-click the My Computer icon.

2   In the My Computer window, double-click the Drive C icon.

3   Find and then double-click the Excel folder to open it.

You will have to double-click the MSOffice folder to find the Excel folder.

4   Double-click the Microsoft Excel program file called Excel to start the program.

A Microsoft Excel file consists of a workbook that contains one or more worksheets. A worksheet is like an accountant's ledger sheet, with rows and columns that intersect to form cells that hold data. The data can be numbers or text that you enter, or formulas that calculate values based on references to other numbers in the workbook.

The worksheet area that you see in your Microsoft Excel window is just a small part of a very large worksheet, which is 16,384 rows long and 256 columns wide. You can think of the Microsoft Excel window as a camera lens focused on one small "picture" in a large worksheet "landscape."

You can use worksheets to store numeric data and then use Microsoft Excel commands and tools to perform calculations on your data. You can sort, rearrange, analyze, and present your data easily by using Microsoft Excel features such as copying, moving, sorting, consolidating, charting, and pivot tables. You can also use Microsoft Excel to create business forms, such as invoices that calculate totals and add sales tax for you.

Using Toolbars

The first row of buttons below the Microsoft Excel menu bar is the *Standard toolbar*. This toolbar contains buttons for performing basic operations for working with the program, such as opening, closing, and printing a file. The following illustration identifies the buttons on the Standard toolbar.

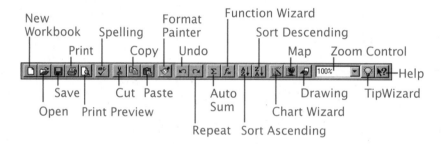

There are several toolbars specific to Microsoft Excel that you can display or hide depending on your needs. Each toolbar is composed of buttons that perform related tasks. For example, you'll use the Formatting toolbar to enhance the appearance of your document, including the style and size of your type. It is generally much faster to click a button on a toolbar than to select a command from a menu.

When you click a button on a toolbar, Microsoft Excel carries out the corresponding command using the command's default options. If you want to specify different options for carrying out a command, use the command from the menu. The instructions in this book emphasize using the toolbar for almost all Microsoft Excel operations.

Take a quick tour of the Standard toolbar

Take a moment to get acquainted with the buttons on the Standard toolbar. If you accidentally click a button, you can press the ESC key or click the Undo button on the Standard toolbar.

If you do not see the button name, click Toolbars on the View menu, and then click the Show Tool Tips check box.

 Move the pointer over a button, and wait.

After a moment, the name of the button appears.

ToolTip

Using Wizards

Wizards are built-in assistants that guide you through the steps of performing specific tasks, such as creating charts or pivot tables from your data. When you run a wizard, you are asked to make selections and enter information that will be incorporated into your workbook. Wizards might also make suggestions to help you work more effectively. Various wizards will be used or described throughout this book.

The *Answer Wizard,* available through the Microsoft Excel Help menu, can assist you to find online information about a topic of your choice. In this wizard, you type a topic or question. The wizard then presents you with a list of related topics from which you can choose. After you choose a topic, the wizard displays a Help window or guides you through the task.

Find Help on specific topics using the Answer Wizard

In this exercise, you use the Answer Wizard to learn how to copy a cell.

1   On the Help menu, click Answer Wizard.

   The Help dialog box opens, with the Answer Wizard tab displayed.

2   In box number 1, type **copy a cell** and then click the Search button.

   In box number 2, a list of topics related to your question appears.

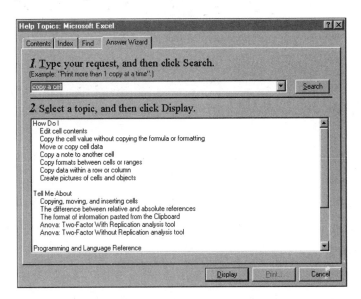

3   Under "Tell Me About," double-click the topic "Copying, moving, and inserting cells."

   An illustrated Help window appears.

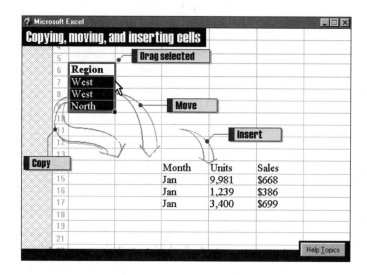

4 Click a topic, such as "Copy," and then read the ScreenTip.

You can click the minimize button on the Help window to keep the topic available as you work.

Close

5 Click the Close button on the Help window.

Quitting Microsoft Excel and Windows 95

Now that you are introduced to Windows 95 and Microsoft Excel, you can proceed to Lesson 1. If you would like to quit Microsoft Excel or Windows 95 for now, follow these steps.

Quit Microsoft Excel

1 Hold down the ALT key and press F4.

2 If you see a message box asking whether you want to save changes, choose the No button.

Quit Windows 95

1 Close all open windows by clicking the Close button in the upper-right corner of each window.

2 Click Start, and then click Shut Down.

3 When you see the message dialog box, click the Yes button.

⚠ WARNING To avoid loss of data or damage to Windows 95, always quit Windows 95 using the Shut Down command on the Start menu before you turn your computer off.

New Features in Microsoft Excel for Windows 95

The following table lists the major new features in Microsoft Excel for Windows 95 that are covered in this book. The table shows the lesson in which you can learn about each feature. For more information about new features, you can search the Help Answer Wizard.

To learn how to	See
Open files using the new Open dialog box	Lesson 1
Correct typing mistakes with AutoCorrect	Lesson 1
Navigate through your worksheet with new ScrollTips	Lesson 1
Drag cells between worksheets in the same workbook	Lesson 2
Sum, count, or average selected cells with AutoCalculate	Lesson 2
Open the new Microsoft Excel templates	Lesson 3
Format numbers using the new number formatting dialog box	Lesson 3
Display your data geographically and demographically with Data Map	Lesson 4
Display cell notes with new CellTips	Lesson 7
Search for files using the new Open dialog box	Lesson 7
Quickly enter data in a list with AutoComplete	Lesson 8

To learn how to	See
Filter data with the new "Top 10" option in AutoFilter.	Lesson 8
Share workbooks among multiple users with Shared Lists.	Lesson 8

Getting Started with Microsoft Excel

Entering Data

Estimated time
45 min.

In this lesson you will learn how to:

- Open and save a workbook file.
- Enter and edit data in a worksheet.
- Work with workbooks.

The basic working environment in Microsoft Excel is a workbook file that can contain one or more worksheets. A worksheet is similar to an accountant's ledger, with numbers and calculations lined up in columns and rows. Unlike an accountant's ledger, you type in the numbers and let Microsoft Excel perform the calculations for you electronically.

With Microsoft Excel, it's easy to enter information into a worksheet and then change, delete, or add to the information. You don't need to worry about entering your data perfectly or completely the first time. You can always edit your data later. You can arrange multiple worksheets within a workbook and name them so that you can locate the information you need quickly. In this lesson, you'll learn how to work with worksheets and workbooks; open, save, and close a file; and enter and edit data in a worksheet.

Starting the Lesson

If you have not yet started Microsoft Excel or set up the Excel SBS practice files, refer to the instructions in "Getting Ready," earlier in this book.

In the following exercises, you'll open the practice file called 01Lesson and then save the file with a different name, Lesson01. This process creates a duplicate of the file that you can work on and modify during the lesson. The original file, 01Lesson, will remain unchanged in case you want to start the lesson again.

Open a practice file

Open

Depending on how your system is configured, your dialog box might look different from this illustration.

1 On the Standard toolbar, click the Open button.

The Open dialog box appears. In this dialog box, you select the folder and the document you want to open. The text box labeled Look In shows the folder that is currently selected.

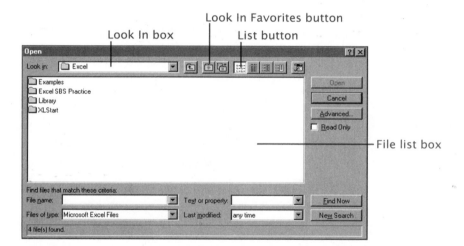

2 Click the Look In Favorites button.

The names of all folders and files that are contained within the selected folder are listed in the file list box.

3 Be sure that the Excel SBS Practice folder appears in the list of folders, as shown in the previous illustration.

4 In the file list box, double-click the folder named Excel SBS Practice.

The practice files appear in the file list box.

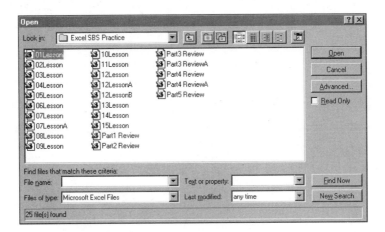

5 In the file list box, double-click the file named 01Lesson.

The dialog box closes, and the file 01Lesson appears in the document window.

Save the practice file with a new name

When you save a file, you give it a name and specify where you want to store it. For each file you use in this book, you'll usually save it in the Step by Step practice files folder with a new name so that the original practice file will remain unchanged.

1 On the File menu, click Save As to display the Save As dialog box.

Save In box

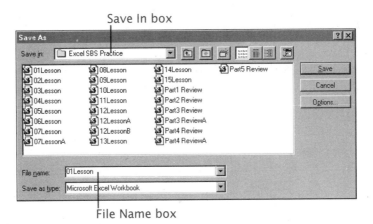

File Name box

2   Be sure that Excel SBS Practice appears in the Save In box.

If the Excel SBS Practice folder does not appear, follow the suggestions under step 2 of the previous exercise to select the folder.

3   Double-click in the File Name box, and then type **Lesson01**

4   Click the Save button, or press ENTER, to close the dialog box and save the file.

Your file is saved with the name Lesson01 in the Excel SBS Practice folder.

Moving Around in a Worksheet

A worksheet consists of *columns* and *rows*. Columns run vertically and are identified by letters across the top; rows run horizontally and are identified by numbers down the left side. The intersection of a column and a row is called a *cell*. Cells are named by their positions in the rows and columns. This combination of the column letter and row number for a cell is called a *cell reference*. The cell in column A and row 1 is called A1. The cell one column to the right is called B1. The cell one row down from A1 is A2, and so on.

 NOTE   If your columns are identified by numbers instead of letters, it is because your reference style option is set to R1C1 style instead of A1 style. For this book, all references are in A1 style. To change to the A1 reference style, choose the Options command on the Tools menu, and click the General tab. In the Reference Style box, select A1, and then click OK.

When you select a cell with the mouse or with the arrow keys, that cell becomes the *active cell*. When you make a cell active, you can type new data into it or edit the data it contains. The active cell has a border around it. You can always determine the reference for the active cell by looking in the Name box on the Formula bar.

In the following illustration, cell A1 is the active cell. The border around the cell and the reference in the Name box indicate that the cell is active.

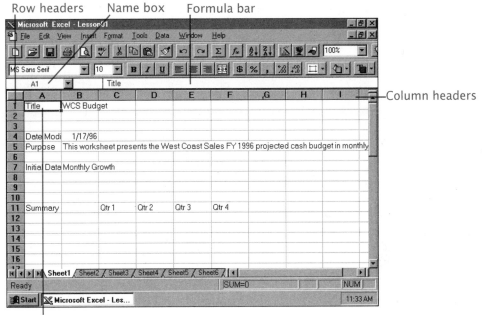

Row headers   Name box   Formula bar

Column headers

Active cell with border

To change the active cell by using the mouse, simply click a new cell. To change the active cell with your keyboard, use the arrow keys. The following table lists the keys you can use.

To move	Press
Left one cell	LEFT ARROW
Right one cell	RIGHT ARROW
Up one cell	UP ARROW
Down one cell	DOWN ARROW
Up one screen	PAGE UP
Down one screen	PAGE DOWN
To the beginning or end of the next block of data to the left	CTRL+LEFT ARROW
To the beginning or end of the next block of data to the right	CTRL+RIGHT ARROW
To the start of the worksheet	CTRL+HOME
To the cell at the intersection of the last row and column that contains data	CTRL+END

You can also use the scroll bars, scroll boxes, or scroll arrows to move to other areas in your worksheet. When you scroll through your worksheet, however, the cell that was active before you began scrolling remains the active cell.

Select cells in a worksheet

In this exercise, you use the keyboard commands to move around in your worksheet and select specific cells.

1 Press the RIGHT ARROW key.

The active cell changes to cell B1, one cell to the right of A1.

2 Click cell B11.

3 Press CTRL+RIGHT ARROW, and then press CTRL+RIGHT ARROW again.

The active cell changes to the first cell in the next block of data on the right and then to the last cell in that block of data. If you press CTRL+RIGHT ARROW a third time, the active cell changes to the last cell in the row, cell IV11.

4 Press CTRL+END.

The active cell changes to the cell at the intersection of the last row and column that contain data (the cell marks the lower-right corner of the worksheet, which might or might not contain data).

5 Press PAGE UP.

The active cell changes to the cell one screen up from the previous active cell.

6 Press CTRL+HOME.

The active cell changes to the first cell in the sheet, cell A1.

 NOTE To view a specific row (for example, row 24) without moving the active cell, drag the scroll box in the vertical scroll bar downward until the ScrollTip reads Row: 24. When you release the mouse button, row 24 will be at the top of your screen, and the active cell will still be where you left it. To view the active cell again, press SHIFT+BACKSPACE.

Selecting Multiple Cells

You can select several cells at once by pressing and holding down either the SHIFT or CTRL key while you press the mouse button. To select several adjacent cells, click the first cell in the set, press and hold down SHIFT, and then click the last cell in the set. Or, using the mouse only, click the first cell and drag to the last cell. Either way, every cell between the first and last cell is selected. When you select more than one adjacent cell, you are selecting a *range* of cells. To select several nonadjacent cells, click the first cell, then press and hold down CTRL, and click the next cell that you want.

 NOTE You can also select a range of cells on several sheets at once. You will learn more about working with sheets in your workbooks later in this lesson.

Select multiple cells in a worksheet

In this exercise, you practice selecting multiple cells using the SHIFT and CTRL keys.

1 Click cell A1.

2 Press and hold down SHIFT and click cell B5.

All of the cells between cell A1 and cell B5 are selected.

3 Press CTRL+HOME.

Pressing CTRL+HOME makes cell A1 active again.

4 Press and hold down CTRL and click cell B5.

By holding down CTRL and clicking cell B5, you select only cells A1 and B5, and not the cells between them.

5 Click cell A1.

Cell A1 becomes the active cell again.

6 Drag from cell A1 to cell B5.

All of the cells between A1 and B5 are selected.

7 Click cell A1.

Entering and Editing Data

You can enter text, numbers, and formulas into any cell on a worksheet. You simply select a cell and then type. You'll start your projected budget worksheet for West Coast Sales (WCS) by entering text in column A to label the rows of your budget sheet. You will label the rows with descriptions, such as Created by, Budget Model Area, and so on. When you add labels to your worksheets, you and others are able to understand each of your worksheet's purpose, logic, and assumptions, making your worksheets easier to use.

Whatever you type appears in both the active cell and the formula bar. After typing, the data must be entered in the cell. You can enter your data in the active cell by pressing ENTER or by clicking on another cell. You can cancel the entry before you enter it by pressing ESC. If you make a mistake while you're typing in a cell, you can use the BACKSPACE key or the arrow keys to move the *insertion point*, the blinking vertical line that indicates where you can enter text.

If the active cell does not change when you press ENTER, on the Tools menu click Options, and select Move Selection After Enter on the Edit tab. See the Appendix, "Matching the Exercises," for more information.

Enter the heading information

As you type the row titles, a long entry will either spill into the next column, or the entry will appear to be cut off if the next column contains data. You'll learn how to correct this by changing column widths in Lesson 3, "Formatting Your Data."

1 Select cell A3, type **Created by** and then press ENTER.

2 Select cell B3.

3 Type your name, and then press ENTER.

4   Select cell A18.

5   Type **Budget Model Area** and then press ENTER.

Your worksheet should look like the following.

	A	B	C	D	E	F	G	H	I
1	Title	WCS Budget							
2									
3	Created by	Kris Mueller							
4	Date Modi	1/17/96							
5	Purpose	This worksheet presents the West Coast Sales FY 1996 projected cash budget in monthly							
6									
7	Initial Data	Monthly Growth							
8									
9									
10									
11	Summary		Qtr 1	Qtr 2	Qtr 3	Qtr 4			
12									
13									
14									
15									
16									
17									
18	Budget Model Area								
19									
20		Gross Revenue							

Sheet1 / Sheet2 / Sheet3 / Sheet4 / Sheet5 / Sheet6 /

You can save time when entering data in a range of cells if you select all of the cells in the range first. As you enter data in each cell and then press ENTER or TAB, the next cell in the range becomes the active cell. The ENTER key moves the active cell top-to-bottom in the column and then to the top of the next column in the selected range. The TAB key moves the selected cell left-to-right within the selected range and then down to the next row.

NOTE   Ranges are usually referred to by listing the first cell reference in the range, followed by a colon, and then the last cell reference in a range. For example, the range of cells from cell B8 to cell C9 would be referred to as B8:C9.

Select a cell range and enter data

In this exercise, you select the range B8:C9, where you will enter the initial data for your budget sheet. The first cell you select remains the active cell. If you make a typing mistake and want to move backward through the selection, press and hold down the SHIFT key and press TAB or ENTER.

1   Drag from cell B8 to cell C9.

2   Type **Sales Growth** TAB **1.50** TAB **COGS Increase** TAB **0.90** TAB.

When you reach the last cell in the range and press TAB or ENTER, the active cell returns to the beginning of the range. Your document should look like the following.

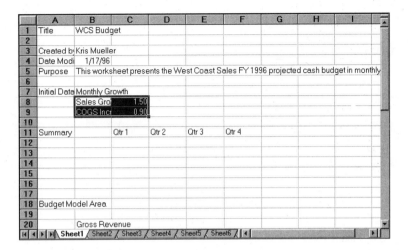

Editing Data in a Cell

You can edit data in two different ways. You can select the cell and then click in the formula bar to edit there, or you can edit the data right in the cell. To edit data in the cell, double-click the cell and then click to place the insertion point wherever you need it. You can then either type the new information or delete the information that's incorrect. Editing directly in the cell is useful when you're editing text in a cell, and it's even more useful when you're working with formulas, as you will see in Lesson 2.

Edit data in a cell

In this exercise, you edit the title of the worksheet.

1 Double-click cell B1.

Cell B1, which contains the title of the worksheet, is opened for editing in the cell.

2 In cell B1, click just before the word "Budget," and then type **Cash** followed by a space.

3 Click just after the word "Budget," type a colon followed by a space, and then type **1996 Fiscal Year**

4 Press ENTER.

Your new title appears in cell B1. Your worksheet should look like the following.

	A	B	C	D	E	F	G	H	I
1	Title	WCS Cash Budget: 1996 Fiscal Year							
2									
3	Created by	Kris Mueller							
4	Date Modi	1/17/96							
5	Purpose	This worksheet presents the West Coast Sales FY 1996 projected cash budget in monthly							
6									
7	Initial Data	Monthly Growth							
8		Sales Gro	1.50						
9		COGS Incr	0.90						
10									
11	Summary		Qtr 1	Qtr 2	Qtr 3	Qtr 4			
12									
13									
14									
15									
16									

Sheet1 / Sheet2 / Sheet3 / Sheet4 / Sheet5 / Sheet6 /

Using AutoCorrect to Make Corrections

A new feature in Microsoft Excel 95 is AutoCorrect, which is similar to AutoCorrect in Microsoft Word 6 and Microsoft Word 95. When you mistype a word, Microsoft Excel can automatically correct it for you. AutoCorrect has a built-in list of commonly mistyped words, such as "teh" for "the" and "adn" for "and."

You can customize AutoCorrect by adding words you commonly mistype to the AutoCorrect list. You can also use AutoCorrect as a kind of shorthand to finish typing out long words that you use repeatedly. In addition to adding your own commonly mistyped words to the list, you can add abbreviations for long words or phrases. To customize AutoCorrect, you choose the AutoCorrect command on the Tools menu and then type the abbreviation or misspelled word along with the correct spelling in the dialog box.

Correct commonly mistyped words

In this exercise, you use AutoCorrect to correct mistyped words.

1   Click cell B14.

2   Type **teh** followed by a space, then **adn** followed by a space.

    When you press the SPACEBAR, the spelling of the word you just typed is corrected.

3   Press ENTER.

Customize AutoCorrect to type long words

In this exercise, you customize AutoCorrect to type out the name West Coast Sales from an abbreviation.

1   On the Tools menu, click AutoCorrect.

2   In the Replace box, type **wcs**.

3   In the With box, type **West Coast Sales**, and click OK.

    If you have more words to add to the list, click Add, and then click OK to close the dialog box when you are finished.

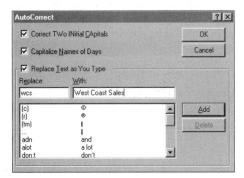

4 Click cell B14.

5 Type **wcs** and then press ENTER.

West Coast Sales is typed in the cell.

 NOTE You can turn off AutoCorrect by clearing the Replace Text As You Type check box in the AutoCorrect dialog box.

Entering a Series of Data into Cells

As you saw in the last exercise, you can select a range of cells and enter data into each of them. You can also enter a series of data, either numbers or text, into several cells. To do this, type the first two numbers or text entries in the series and then use AutoFill to enter the rest of the series. For example, you can type 1 into the first cell, 2 in the second cell, and then use AutoFill to quickly fill in 3, 4, 5, and 6.

If you are entering a series, such as the months of the year or the days of the week, you can type the first item in the series and then fill in the rest of the series without typing anything else. For example, if you want to enter the months of the year into a row, you simply type "Jan" and then use AutoFill to fill in the rest. These are built-in lists provided in Microsoft Excel. You can also create custom lists, such as lists of personnel names or department titles (see "One Step Further" at the end of this lesson).

Use AutoFill to enter a series of numbers

You can use AutoFill by dragging the fill handle on the cell border to fill your series in quickly. In this exercise, you add a series of numbers to your budget sheet by using AutoFill.

To select a range of cells, see the previous section, "Selecting Multiple Cells."

1 Select cells C19:D19.

2 Type **1** ENTER **2**

3 With both cells still selected, move your pointer over the black box (the fill handle) in the lower-right corner of cell D19 until the pointer changes to a solid plus sign. Your pointer should look like the following.

Fill handle

4 Drag the fill handle to cell L19.

Use AutoFill to enter a series of months

You can enter month or day names either in full (January) or short (Jan) form. When you fill the series into the other cells, the rest of the series follows the same format that you entered.

1 Select cell C19.

2 Type **Jun** and press ENTER.

3 Click cell C19 again, and then drag the fill handle to cell N19.

The rest of the series is entered into the cells.

4 Press CTRL+HOME.

The active cell changes to cell A1.

Removing Data from Cells

If you need to remove data from a cell, you can easily delete the information and replace it with new information by typing the new information into the cell. You can also remove data from a cell either by selecting the cell and pressing DEL, or by pressing the right mouse button and choosing the Clear Contents command on the shortcut menu. Usually, however, selecting a cell and typing the new information over the old data is the quickest method.

Clear a cell and enter new information

In this exercise, you enter new information by typing over the old data.

1 Select cell B4.

This cell reflects the date on which the budget sheet was last modified.

2 Type the current date in the form *mm/dd/yy*, and then press ENTER.

The old date is removed from the cell, and the new date is entered. Your worksheet should look similar to the following.

In Lesson 2, "Writing Formulas," you'll learn how to create a formula that automatically displays the current date.

	B5	▼	This worksheet presents the West Coast Sales FY 1996 projected cash budget
	A	B	in monthly detail and quarterly summaries.
1	Title	WCS Cash Budget: 1996 Fiscal Year	
2			
3	Created by	Kris Mueller	
4	Date Modi	06/03/95	
5	Purpose	This worksheet presents the West Coast Sales FY 1996 projected cash budget in monthly	
6			
7	Initial Data	Monthly Growth	
8		Sales Gro	1.50
9		COGS Incr	0.90
10			
11	Summary		Qtr 1	Qtr 2	Qtr 3	Qtr 4
12			
13			
14		West Coast Sales	
15			
16			

Sheet1 / Sheet2 / Sheet3 / Sheet4 / Sheet5 / Sheet6

Undoing Changes

The Redo command acts on the cell or range in which the previous action took place. The Repeat command acts on the current active cell or range.

You can always correct mistakes while you are typing by pressing the BACKSPACE key and retyping the correct letters or numbers. But what if you select a cell and either clear it or replace its contents by mistake? You can recover from such mistakes by using either the Undo command on the Edit menu or the Undo button on the toolbar. If you decide that you want to keep the change after all, you can use either the Redo command on the Edit menu or the Repeat button on the toolbar.

Undo previous actions

In this exercise, you delete the contents of a cell and then restore them.

1 Select cell B4.

2 Press DEL.

The date is removed from the cell.

3 On the Edit menu, click Undo Clear.

Undo

You can also click the Undo button on the toolbar. The data is restored. The name of the Undo command changes to reflect the specific action that you need to Undo. If you had typed new text, the Undo command would have been the Undo Entry command instead of the Undo Clear command.

4 On the Edit menu, click Redo (u) Clear, or press CTRL+Z.

Repeat

You can also click the Repeat button on the toolbar. The Undo command changes to Redo since you've just used Undo. CTRL+Z is the shortcut key for both Undo and Redo. The date you typed in the last exercise is cleared from cell B4.

NOTE In some instances, the Undo command is not available. If you have just saved your workbook, for example, and you open the Edit menu, you will see Can't Undo in the place of the Undo command.

Working with Workbooks

In Microsoft Excel, files are called *workbooks*. Workbooks can contain multiple worksheets, chart sheets, and Visual Basic modules. You'll learn more about charts and chart sheets in Lessons 4 and 5, "Charting Your Data" and "Modifying Your Charts." You'll learn more about Visual Basic modules in Lesson 15, "Automating Repetitive Tasks." For now, you'll work mostly with worksheets.

In Microsoft Excel workbooks, you can switch between sheets easily, enter data in more than one sheet at a time, and give the sheets logical names. All of the sheets are accessible at all times, and saving the file saves the entire workbook at once.

Moving Around in a Workbook

You can select different sheets in a workbook by clicking the tabs at the bottom of the sheets. You can use the arrow buttons (the *sheet tab scroll buttons*) at the lower-left corner of the screen to move to the first tab in the workbook, one tab backward, one tab forward, or to the last tab in the workbook. You can also use keyboard shortcuts to move between sheets. If you press CTRL+PAGE DOWN, you'll select the next sheet. If you press CTRL+PAGE UP, you'll select the previous sheet. The following illustration shows the tabs and arrows you can use to move around in a workbook.

Sheet tab scroll buttons   Sheet tabs

You can also select several sheets at a time in the same way that you select several cells at a time. You can select several adjacent sheets by pressing and holding down SHIFT and clicking the tabs of the first and last sheets that you want, or you can select several nonadjacent sheets by pressing and holding down CTRL and clicking the individual sheet tabs.

When you select several sheets in a workbook, you can enter the same data on all sheets simultaneously. You simply select all the sheets that you want the data to appear on and then type the data on one of the sheets. The data appears in the same cell on each selected sheet.

Move to other sheets and enter data

In this exercise, you select different sheets in the workbook and enter data in them.

1 Click the tab for Sheet4.

Sheet4 becomes the active sheet.

2 Click the tab for Sheet5.

Sheet5, the next sheet in the workbook, becomes the active sheet.

3 Press and hold down SHIFT and click the tab for Sheet3.

Sheets 3 through 5 are selected, but Sheet5 remains the active sheet. When multiple sheets are selected, Microsoft Excel is in group edit mode, and the word (Group) appears in the title bar.

4 On Sheet5, select cell B3.

5 Type **Kris Mueller** and press ENTER.

6 Click the tab for Sheet4.

Sheet4 becomes the active sheet. Your screen should look like the following.

The name appears on Sheet4, even though you typed it only in Sheet5. When you select several sheets and then enter data in one, the data is entered in each selected sheet in the corresponding cells. Sheet3 and Sheet5 are still selected, even though Sheet4 is now the active sheet.

7 Click the Sheet2 tab.

Clicking this tab clears the other sheet selections. Sheet2 becomes the active sheet.

Inserting, Deleting, Renaming, and Moving Sheets

When you open a new workbook, you have 16 blank sheets named Sheet1, Sheet2, and so on. You can leave these sheets in place, or you can customize your workbook by adding, removing, or renaming the sheets. You can have any number of sheets in a workbook. You can use the Worksheet command on the Insert menu to insert a new worksheet and use the Delete Sheet command on the Edit menu to remove a sheet. You can also rename sheets to describe their purpose or contents.

Remove, add, and rename sheets within a workbook

In this exercise, you remove a sheet and insert a new one. Then, you rename a sheet to make its purpose clearer.

To change the default number of sheets in a new workbook, click Options on the Tools menu, click the General tab, and then change the Sheets In New Workbook setting.

1 Use the right mouse button to click the Sheet2 tab, and then click Delete on the shortcut menu.

A dialog box opens, informing you that the sheet will be deleted permanently.

2 Click OK.

The dialog box closes, and the sheet is deleted. Sheet2 is gone, and Sheet3 now follows Sheet1.

3 Use the right mouse button to click the Sheet3 tab, and then click Insert on the shortcut menu.

The Insert dialog box opens.

4 Be sure the Worksheet icon is selected, and then click OK.

A new sheet is inserted to the left of the selected sheet.

Last Tab Scroll

5 Click the Last Tab Scroll button.

The sheet tabs scroll so that you can see the tab for Sheet16. Scrolling through sheet tabs does not change the active sheet; it just makes other tabs visible so that other sheets can be selected.

 NOTE There are two right arrows and two left arrows for scrolling through the sheet tabs in your workbook. The arrows with the bar (Last Tab Scroll and First Tab Scroll buttons) scroll to the beginning or end of the sheet tabs. The arrows without the bar scroll forward or backward through the workbook tabs one at a time.

18

First Tab Scroll

*You can also
select a sheet
by using the
right mouse
button to click
the tab scroll
buttons, and
then select a
sheet name
from the
shortcut menu.*

6 Click the First Tab Scroll button.

The sheet tabs scroll so that you can see the tab for Sheet1.

7 Double-click the Sheet1 tab.

The Rename Sheet dialog box opens.

8 In the Name box, type **1996 Budget** and then press ENTER.

Sheet1 is renamed to 1996 Budget. Your worksheet should look like the following.

*Sheet names
are limited to
a length of 31
characters,
including
spaces.*

	A	B	C	D	E	F	G	H	I
1	Title	WCS Cash Budget: 1996 Fiscal Year							
2									
3	Created b	Kris Mueller							
4	Date Mod	ified							
5	Purpose	This worksheet presents the West Coast Sales FY 1996 projected cash budget in monthly							
6									
7	Initial Data	Monthly Growth							
8		Sales Gro	1.50						
9		COGS Incr	0.90						
10									
11	Summary		Qtr 1	Qtr 2	Qtr 3	Qtr 4			
12									
13									
14		West Coast Sales							
15									
16									

1996 Budget / Sheet2 / Sheet3 / Sheet4 / Sheet5 / Sh

Move sheets within a workbook

In this exercise, you move a sheet to a new position in the workbook.

1 Select Sheet5.

2 Drag the sheet tab to the left, and release the mouse button when the small triangle appears to the left of the 1996 Budget sheet.

Sheet5 is moved to the front of the workbook, to the left of the 1996 Budget sheet.

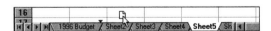

One Step Further: Customizing AutoFill

In this lesson, you learned that you can automatically enter a series of data into a series of cells. Microsoft Excel recognizes several standard series, such as 1, 2, 3; Qtr1, Qtr2, Qtr3; and the series of months that you used earlier. You can also define custom series. By using the Options command on the Tools menu, you can create a custom list that you can fill into cells in your worksheets. The custom list will be available for use in any of your workbooks.

Create a custom list of data

In this exercise, you create a custom list.

1   On the Tools menu, click Options.

The Options dialog box opens.

2   Click the Custom Lists tab.

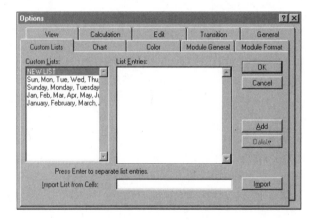

3   In the Custom Lists list, be sure NEW LIST is selected.

4   In the List Entries box, type **Gross Revenue** ENTER **Cost of Goods Sold** ENTER **Gross Profit** ENTER **Expenses** ENTER **Operating Income**

5   Click the Add button.

Your new custom list is added to the Custom Lists in the dialog box.

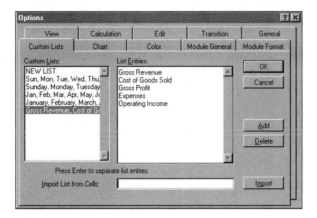

6   Click OK.

7   On Sheet5, select cell B12.

8   Type **Gross Revenue** ENTER.

9   Select cell B12, and then drag the fill handle downward four rows to cell B16.

     The series labels are automatically filled in.

Import a custom list of data

If a list already exists in a workbook, you do not have to retype it in the Custom Lists dialog box. You can save time by selecting the existing list and importing it into the Custom Lists dialog box.

1   On the 1996 Budget sheet, select the range B31:B44.

2   On the Tools menu, click Options and then click the Custom Lists tab.

     The selected range appears in the Import List From Cells box.

3   Click the Import button, and then click OK.

4   Select Sheet5.

5   Select cell B5, and then type **Gross Profit** ENTER.

6   Select cell B5, and then drag the fill handle to O5.

     Again, the series labels are automatically filled in.

If You Want to Continue to the Next Lesson

1 On the File menu, click Save.
2 On the File menu, click Close.

If You Want to Quit Microsoft Excel for Now

➤ On the File menu, click Exit.
    If you see the Save dialog box, click Yes.

Lesson Summary

To	Do this	Button
Open a workbook	On the toolbar, click the Open button. Select the folder and filename, and click Open.	
Save a workbook with a new name	On the File menu, click Save As. In the File Name box, type the filename, and click Save.	
Enter data	Select a cell and type the data, and then press ENTER or click another cell.	
Edit data	Double-click in the cell that contains the data. Place the insertion point where you want to edit, and either type over the data or use the backspace key to delete data.	
Fill a series of numeric data into cells	Enter the data for the first two cells in the series, and then drag the AutoFill handle to fill in the rest of the series.	
Clear a cell	Select the cell, and then press DEL. *or* On the Edit menu, point to Clear, then click Contents.	
Undo a change	On the Edit menu, click Undo, if it is available. *or* On the toolbar, click the Undo button.	
Repeat a change	On the Edit menu, click Redo or Repeat, if it is available. *or* On the toolbar, click the Repeat button.	

To	Do this	Button
Delete a worksheet from a workbook	Use the right mouse button to click the tab of the sheet you want to delete, and then click Delete on the shortcut menu.	
Insert a worksheet into a workbook	Use the right mouse button to click a sheet tab, and then click Insert on the shortcut menu. Select the type of sheet you want to enter, and then click OK.	
Rename a sheet	Double-click the sheet tab. Type the new name in the Name box, and click OK.	
Close a workbook	On the File menu, click Close. *or* Click the Close button in the upper-right corner of the workbook.	

For online information about	Use the Answer Wizard to search for
Opening, saving, and closing a workbook	**open** *or* **save** *or* **close** *or* **workbook**
Entering data	**enter**
Editing data	**edit**
Filling a series of data into cells	**fill**
Clearing cells	**clear**
Undoing changes	**undo**
Inserting, deleting, and renaming sheets	**insert sheet** *or* **delete sheet** *or* **rename**
Creating custom lists and sort orders	**custom list**

Preview of the Next Lesson

In the next lesson, you'll learn how to copy, paste, and move information into other cells on a worksheet. You'll learn how to use simple formulas to perform mathematical and other kinds of operations and how to use cell references in formulas to point to the cells you need. You'll also learn more about ranges and naming them so that you can quickly find and use the information you need.

Writing Formulas

Estimated time
50 min.

In this lesson you will learn how to:

- Total rows and columns automatically.
- Create simple formulas.
- Create formulas with the Function Wizard.
- Name ranges of cells.
- Copy and paste data between cells.
- Move data between cells and worksheets.
- Create formulas with relative and absolute references.

You can perform calculations with your data using *formulas,* which are made up of *arithmetic operators* (such as =, +, and –), and often *functions*, which are built-in formulas. Microsoft Excel comes with hundreds of functions that you can use in formulas. The AutoSum feature uses the SUM function to total data in rows or columns, and the Function Wizard makes it easy to create formulas.

In this lesson, you'll learn how to total data in rows and columns, create simple formulas, and name ranges to make formulas and references easy to understand. You'll learn how to copy, paste, and move data with ease. You'll also learn the difference between relative and absolute references, and why the difference is important when you copy or move data.

Start the lesson

Follow the steps below to open the practice file called 02Lesson, and then save it with the new name Lesson02.

Open

To select the folder containing your practice files, refer to "Open a practice file" near the start of Lesson 1.

1 On the Standard toolbar, click the Open button.

2 In the Look In box, be sure that the Excel SBS Practice folder appears.

3 In the file list box, double-click the file named 02Lesson to open it.

4 On the File menu, click Save As.

The Save As dialog box opens. Be sure the Excel SBS Practice folder appears in the Save In box.

5 Double-click in the File Name box, and then type **Lesson02**

6 Click the Save button, or press ENTER.

If you share your computer with others who use Microsoft Excel, the screen display might have changed since your last lesson. If your screen does not look similar to the illustrations as you work through this lesson, see the Appendix, "Matching the Exercises."

Totaling Rows and Columns Automatically

One of the tasks that you will probably do frequently in Microsoft Excel is total rows and columns. You could create a new formula every time you needed to total a row or a column, but Microsoft Excel provides an easier way. The AutoSum button on the Standard toolbar automatically creates a formula to total rows and columns for you.

You can use AutoSum in one of three ways—to locate and total the rows or columns in the range nearest to the current cell, to total any range that you select, or to add grand totals to a range containing other totals. To automatically total the nearest range, click the AutoSum button and check that the selected range is correct (you can drag to select a new range if you need to). When the range is correct, you can either click the AutoSum button again, or press ENTER. When you click the AutoSum button once, the formula is created, and then you have the option of accepting the formula or modifying the formula. To total a selected range, select the range and then click the AutoSum button. When you use the AutoSum button, the Sum formula is created and entered.

Total the cost of goods sold

In this and the next exercises, you use AutoSum to total the cost of goods sold data for June and then to total the summary data on your budget sheet.

1 Be sure that the 1996 Budget sheet is the active sheet.

2 Select cell C29.

You will use AutoSum to enter a total for the range C25:C28.

AutoSum

3 Click the AutoSum button on the Standard toolbar once.

The range C25:C28 on the worksheet is surrounded by a *marquee* (a *moving border*), and a sum formula, =SUM(C25:C28), appears in the formula bar. When you click the AutoSum button once, you can decide whether the selected range is the range that you want totaled. Your worksheet should look like the following.

	A	B	C	D	E	F	G	H
14		Gross Profit	40651	41612	42590	43586		
15		Expenses	33398	33196	33231	33266		
16		Operating Income	7253	8416	9359	10320		
17								
18	Budget Model Area							
19			Jun	Jul	Aug	Sep	Oct	Nov
20		Gross Revenue						
21		Sales	27000	27405	27816	28233	28657	2908
22		Shipping	5550	5633	5718	5804	5891	597
23		GR Total	32550	33038	33534	34037	34547	3506
24		Cost of Goods Sold						
25		Goods	17710	17869	18030	18192	18356	1852
26		Freight	270	272	275	277	280	28
27		Markdowns	1240	1251	1262	1274	1285	129
28		Miscellaneous	96	97	98	99	100	10
29		COGS Total	=SUM(C25:C28)					
30		Gross Profit						

I◄ ◄ ► ►I\ **1996 Budget** / 1996 1st Qtr / Sheet4 / Sheet5 / Sheet6 | ◄

4 Press ENTER, or click the AutoSum button again.

The result is entered into cell C29.

Total the other summary ranges

A new feature in Excel, called AutoCalculate, displays the sum of the currently selected cells in a box on the Status Bar. To change the calculation function, use the right mouse button to click the AutoCalculate box, and then click the function you want.

1 Select the range C12:G16.

This range contains the summary data and the totals column.

2 Click the AutoSum button.

The totals for the rows appear in cells G12:G16.

	B	C	D	E	F	G	H	I
6								
7	Monthly Growth							
8	Sales Growth	1.50%						
9	COGS Increase	0.90%						
10								
11		Qtr 1	Qtr 2	Qtr 3	Qtr 4	1996 Totals		
12	Gross Revenue	99122	100609	102118	103650	405499		
13	Cost Of Goods Sold	58471	58997	59528	60064	237060		
14	Gross Profit	40651	41612	42590	43586	168439		
15	Expenses	33398	33196	33231	33266	133091		
16	Operating Income	7253	8416	9359	10320	35348		
17								
18	Area							
19		Jun	Jul	Aug	Sep	Oct	Nov	Dec	Ja
20	Gross Revenue							
21	Sales	27000	27405	27816	28233	28657	29087	29523
22	Shipping	5550	5633	5718	5804	5891	5979	6060

I◄ ◄ ► ►I\ **1996 Budget** / 1996 1st Qtr / Sheet4 / Sheet5 / Sheet6 | ◄

Creating Simple Formulas

When you need to perform a calculation in Microsoft Excel, you use a formula. You can create formulas to perform calculations as simple as adding the values in two cells, or as complex as finding how much a particular value deviates from other values in a set. To tell Microsoft Excel that you're entering a formula in a cell, you must begin the entry with an arithmetic operator such as an equal sign (=). A simple formula, such as adding, subtracting, multiplying, or dividing cells, has two parts: an operator to begin the formula and at least one cell reference.

When you create formulas that perform calculations or generate information from your data, you need to tell Microsoft Excel where to find the data. You can either type a cell reference or a range name, or you can click on the cells while you are creating the formula. The cells you click are surrounded by a dotted line called a moving border, so you can see which cells are selected while you work with the formula.

Calculate the gross profit

Suppose you need to create a formula that calculates the gross profit for June. In this exercise, you use the pointing method to create the formula in cell C30.

1　Select cell C30.

2　Type =, then click cell C23.

3　Type –, then click cell C29.

4　Press ENTER.

The formula is entered, and the gross profit amount appears in cell C30.

C30	▼	=C23-C29					
	A	B	C	D	E	F	G	H
18	Budget Model Area							
19			Jun	Jul	Aug	Sep	Oct	Nov
20		Gross Revenue						
21		Sales	27000	27405	27816	28233	28657	2908
22		Shipping	5550	5633	5718	5804	5891	597
23		GR Total	32550	33038	33534	34037	34547	3506
24		Cost of Goods Sold						
25		Goods	17710	17869	18030	18192	18356	1852
26		Freight	270	272	275	277	280	28
27		Markdowns	1240	1251	1262	1274	1285	129
28		Miscellaneous	96	97	98	99	100	10
29		COGS Total	19316					
30		Gross Profit	13234					
31								
32		Expenses						
33		Advertising	4000	4000	4000	4000	4000	400

1996 Budget / 1996 1st Qtr / Sheet4 / Sheet5 / Sheet6

Using the Function Wizard to Create Formulas

A simple formula can consist of only arithmetic operators and cell references. More complex formulas can also include numbers and functions. Microsoft Excel has hundreds of worksheet functions to help you perform specialized calculations easily. A worksheet function is a special built-in formula that performs an operation on the values you provide. For example, the formula =SUM(C22:C26) uses a function to add the values in the cell range C22:C26. It gives you the same result as the following formula, which adds the individual values: =(C22+C23+C24+C25+C26).

Functions can be used alone or nested within other functions. You can enter functions by typing them in the cell along with the other information needed for the formula, or you can use the Function Wizard to enter a function automatically.

Certain functions are complete on their own; you do not need to include any cell references or other information for them to work. For example, the TODAY function enters the current system date into a cell, and the NOW function enters both the current date and the current time.

Display the current date

In this exercise, you use the TODAY function to display the current date.

1 Select cell B4 and press DELETE.

2 In cell B4, type **=today( )**

Typing functions in lowercase will help you to locate typing errors. If a function does not convert to uppercase when you press ENTER, it is because the function name has been spelled incorrectly.

You can type function names in either uppercase or lowercase type. When you press ENTER, the names are converted automatically to uppercase if they are spelled correctly.

3 Press ENTER.

The formula is entered, and the current system date appears in the cell.

	B4	▼		=TODAY()					
	A	**B**	**C**	**D**	**E**	**F**	**G**	**H**	
1	Title	WCS Cash Budget: 1996 Fiscal Year							
2									
3	Created by	Kris Mueller							
4	Date Modified	6/3/95							
5	Purpose	This worksheet presents the West Coast Sales FY 1996 projected cash budget in mo							
6									
7	Initial Data	Monthly Growth							
8		Sales Growth	1.50%						
9		COGS Increase	0.90%						
10									
11	Summary		Qtr 1	Qtr 2	Qtr 3	Qtr 4	1996 Totals		
12		Gross Revenue	99122	100609	102118	103650	405499		
13		Cost Of Goods Sold	58471	58997	59528	60064	237060		
14		Gross Profit	40651	41612	42590	43586	168439		
15		Expenses	33398	33196	33231	33266	133091		
16		Operating Income	7253	8416	9359	10320	35348		

1996 Budget / 1996 1st Qtr / Sheet4 / Sheet5 / Sheet6

Most formulas that you create will require more than just a function name. You might need to include cell references and/or values to complete the formula. These additional elements in a formula are called *arguments*. For example, in the summary formulas you entered with the AutoSum button, the formula was broken down into the function (=SUM) that determines what the formula does and the argument (C25:C28) that determines which cells are used.

You can also use values in certain formulas, such as some financial functions that determine loan payments or future values of investments. Arguments usually appear within parentheses, such as in the sum formula =SUM(C25:C28). In fact, whenever you use a function, you must have parentheses, even if you don't need any arguments, such as when you entered the TODAY function, =TODAY( ). Some functions, such as many statistical or financial functions, require more than one argument. In these cases, individual arguments are separated by commas.

For more information about specific functions, search in online Help for the function name.

When you work with a function that requires arguments, it can become difficult to keep track of the information that you need. Microsoft Excel has a Function Wizard that prompts you for any arguments that are required to complete a formula. For example, suppose you want to calculate the average monthly sales over the fiscal year.

Average the sales for the entire year

In this exercise, you use the Function Wizard to create a formula that averages the sales for the entire year.

1 Select cell C50, and then click the Function Wizard button on the Standard toolbar. The Function Wizard opens.

Function Wizard

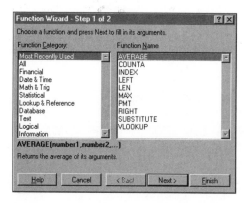

2   In the Function Category list, select Statistical.

A list of statistical functions appears in the Function Name box.

3   In the Function Name box, select AVERAGE, and then click the Next button.

The next step in the Function Wizard appears.

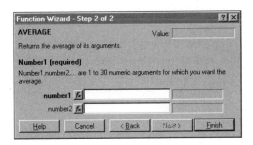

4   Click the title bar of the Function Wizard dialog box, and drag the dialog box downward to the bottom of your screen.

You need to move the dialog box out of the way so that you can select the range you want to average on the budget sheet.

5   Click in the Number1 box.

6   Scroll upward in your budget sheet until you can see row 21.

You can drag the vertical scroll box upward until the ScrollTip reads Row:21.

7   Drag to select cells C21:N21 in the budget sheet.

As you drag to select the cells, the value in the Value box in the Function Wizard dialog box changes to reflect your selection. The references C21:N21 appear in the Number1 box.

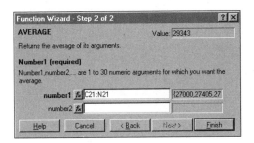

8   Click the Finish button, and scroll downward in the budget sheet until you can see cell C50.

The average of the year's sales, 29343, appears in cell C50.

Naming Ranges

Any rectangular group of cells on a worksheet is called a *range*. As you saw in the AutoSum section of this lesson, you can refer to a range by listing the cell reference for the first cell in the range, followed by a colon, followed by the last cell in the range, for example C20:C46. Often, you use ranges to refer to a group of similar data that falls within a rectangular area on the worksheet, such as the sales data for a particular project or the year's data for the freight category in the budget. When you need to refer to a range in a formula (as you will learn a little later in this lesson), you can either identify the range by its cell references, or you can name the range and then use the name in the formula. Naming ranges can save you time and effort, since a name is easier to remember than the beginning and ending cell references for a range. Names also make formulas much easier to read and understand, which you will see in Lesson 11, and named ranges can help preserve the integrity of workbook links, which you will learn about in Lesson 12.

Creating Names

Creating names for a range is easy. You can select the range and then use the name box on the formula bar to define a name, or you can create names automatically based on row or column headings. You can also use the Name command on the Insert menu to define names.

Range names can be as long as you need them to be, provided that you don't use any spaces or commas. Usually, a range name consists of either one word or a few words separated by underscore characters or periods between words. For example, the names "PrinterSales" and "Printer_Sales" and "Printer.Sales" are acceptable range names. However, "Printer Sales" is not. In general, use names that you can easily remember and type.

A cell reference, such as FY 1996, is not a valid name, since it is a specific cell reference, as in A1 or ET121.

If you have a range with row and column labels, you can name all of the rows and columns in the range, using the labels as names, with the Create command.

Create range names

In this exercise, you define a range with a name you type, and then you create names for a larger range using the Create command.

1   Select the range C20:C46.

The first cell reference appears in the name box.

2   Click in the name box on the formula bar, and then type **June96_Budget**

3   Press ENTER.

The range C20:C46 is named June96_Budget.

4   Select the range B19:N46.

This range contains the headings and all of the data in your budget.

5   On the Insert menu, point to Name, and then click Create.

The Create Names dialog box opens. The options to use the headings in the top row and left column are already selected.

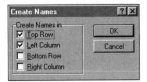

6   Click OK, and then click the down arrow next to the name box to view the list of range names.

Each row becomes a range named with the row title, and each column becomes a range named with the column title.

Editing Names

With the Name command, you can edit the range name or change the specific cells included in a named range after you create it. Suppose you want to change the range you have just named to Jun_Budget.

Expand a range and edit a name

In this exercise, you expand the range to include additional cells and then edit the range name.

1   On the Insert menu, point to Name, and then click Define.

The Define Name dialog box opens, and all of your new names are listed in the Names In Workbook list.

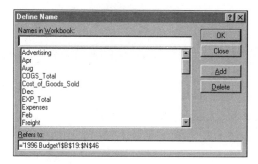

2 Scroll downward in the list, if necessary, and select the name June96_Budget.

This is the first range that you named.

3 In the Refers To box, select 20, and type **19**

This expands the range to include cell C19.

4 In the Names In Workbook text box, select the text "e96" in the June96_Budget name and press DEL.

Your dialog box should look like the following.

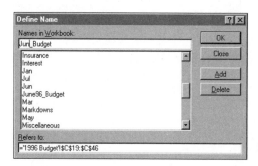

5 Click the Add button.

Clicking the Add button adds your modified name, Jun_Budget, to the list of ranges. The name June96_Budget is still on the list. To change a range name, you must add the new name and delete the old name.

6 Select the range June96_Budget, and click the Delete button in the dialog box.

The range name is deleted from the list.

7 Click OK.

The dialog box closes.

Going to Ranges

You can move around in your worksheet more quickly now that you have named your ranges. Instead of scrolling or moving to another area on the worksheet to select a range, you can use the name box on the formula bar to move to and select a range in one step. You do this by selecting the range name from the list in the name box.

Select ranges using the name box

In this exercise, you use the name box to move around in your worksheet.

1   Click the down arrow next to the name box.

A list of named ranges opens for you to select from.

You can also use the name box to move to a specific cell by typing a cell reference in the name box, such as N56.

2   Scroll downward, and select the Jun_Budget range.

Cells C19:C46 are selected.

3   Click the down arrow again, and then scroll downward and select Sales.

Sales is a range name that was created automatically when you used the Create command. The Sales range, cells C21:N21, is selected.

Select ranges using the F5 key

Another way to move around your worksheet is to use the Go To function key.

1   Press the F5 key.

The Go To dialog box appears, containing a list of all the cell and range names in the workbook.

2   In the Go To list, click Jun_Budget, and then click OK.

The Jun_Budget range is selected.

Using Names in Formulas

You can use range names in place of cell references in formulas. Instead of listing the reference for the range C20:C46, you can use the name "Jun" that you created earlier in this lesson. Names can make your formulas much easier to understand if you ever need to backtrack and figure out exactly what a formula is calculating. For example, the formula MAX(Sales) is more meaningful than MAX(C21:N21).

Find the maximum and minimum sales values

In this exercise, you'll use the Function Wizard to find the maximum sales value, and then you'll type a formula to find the minimum sales value in your budget data.

Function Wizard

1 Select cell C51 and then click the Function Wizard button on the Standard toolbar.

The Function Wizard opens.

2 In the Function Category box, be sure that Statistical is selected, and then in the Function Name box, scroll downward and select MAX.

This function finds the maximum value in a selected range.

3 Click the Next button.

The next step in the Function Wizard appears.

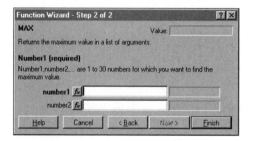

4 Click in the Number1 box.

5 Click the down arrow next to the name box on the formula bar.

The list of range names in the sheet opens.

6 Scroll downward in the list, and select Sales.

The range name "Sales" appears in the Number1 box in the Function Wizard dialog box.

7 Click the Finish button.

The formula is completed, and the value 31804.62 appears in cell C51.

8 Select cell C52.

9 Type **=min(Sales)**

This finds the minimum value in the range "Sales." Instead of typing **Sales**, you can also select it from the name box list.

10 Press ENTER.

The value 27000 appears in cell C51. Your worksheet should look like the following.

	A	B	C	D	E	F	G	H
45								
46		Operating Income	1955	-11054	-11066	-11079	-11092	-1134
47								
48								
49								
50		Average Sales	29343					
51		Maximum Sales	31804.62					
52		Minimum Sales	27000					
53								
54								
55								
56								
57								
58								
59								
60								

1996 Budget / 1996 1st Qtr / Sheet4 / Sheet5 / Sheet6

Rearranging Cell Contents

After you enter data in worksheet cells—whether it is text, numbers, or formulas—you are not locked into this arrangement. You can always rearrange the data if you need to, although you should use some caution if you are rearranging formulas. You can copy and paste data between cells; insert and delete cells, rows, and columns; and even move data between cells.

Copying and Pasting Data Between Cells

If you need to copy information to another place on the worksheet, you can either use the Copy and Paste buttons on the toolbar, use the Copy and Paste commands on the Edit menu, or use the mouse to drag the data to a new location. Copying with the mouse is the quickest method if you are copying onto the same sheet, especially if the distance between the cells is short. If you need to copy to another sheet, you can use the menu commands, you can drag using the ALT key, or you can use multiple windows (you'll learn about using multiple windows in Lesson 14, "Customizing Your Workspace").

Copy data using the menu and the mouse

In this exercise, you'll use the mouse to copy data on the budget sheet and use the Edit menu commands to copy data onto another sheet.

1 Select cells M19:N46.

2 Position the pointer over any part of the range border, and then press and hold down CTRL.

When you hold down CTRL with your pointer positioned over the range border, your pointer displays a small plus sign near its tip, as shown on the left. This plus sign indicates that contents of the range are being copied.

3 Drag the border surrounding the range to the new range O19:P46, release the mouse button, and then release CTRL.

A copy of the information is pasted into the new cell range.

4 On the Edit menu, click Undo Drag And Drop.

The information is removed from the new cell range.

Pointer

TIP You can also copy data from one cell or range into an adjoining cell or range with another method. If your data is not a series that can be filled automatically into cells (such as the months of the year, days of the week, or consecutive numbers), you can copy the data by dragging the fill handle. Simply select the cell or the range, drag the fill handle to the adjoining cell or range, and release. The data or series of data is copied into the new cells.

Copying Formulas

You can copy (or fill) formulas into a range of cells just as you can fill data into a range. To fill a formula into a range, select the cell that contains the formula and then drag the fill handle downward, upward, right, or left as far as you need. The formula is automatically copied into the new cells. For example, suppose you want to fill your Cost of Goods Sold formula across the row.

Fill a formula into a range

1 Select cell C29.

2 Drag the fill handle to cell N29 and release.

The Cost of Goods Sold sum formula is filled into cells D29:N29. Your worksheet should look like the following.

COGS_Total			=SUM(C25:C28)				
	B	C	D	E	F	G	H	I

	B	C	D	E	F	G	H	I
21	Sales	27000	27405	27816	28233	28657	29087	29523
22	Shipping	5550	5633	5718	5804	5891	5979	6069
23	GR Total	32550	33038	33534	34037	34547	35066	35592
24	Cost of Goods Sold							
25	Goods	17710	17869	18030	18192	18356	18521	18688
26	Freight	270	272	275	277	280	282	285
27	Markdowns	1240	1251	1262	1274	1285	1297	1308
28	Miscellaneous	96	97	98	99	100	100	101
29	COGS Total	19316	19490	19665	19842	20021	20201	20383
30	Gross Profit	13234						
31								
32	Expenses							
33	Advertising	4000	4000	4000	4000	4000	4000	4000
34	Salaries	4700	4700	4700	4700	4700	4700	4700
35	Rent	500	500	500	500	500	500	500
36	Utilities	75	75	75	75	75	75	75

1996 Budget / 1996 1st Qtr / Sheet4 / Sheet5 / Sheet6

Copying and Pasting Specific Aspects of a Cell

When you copy and paste, you can paste every aspect of the cell as you did in the last exercise, or you can paste only certain aspects of the data in the cell. For example, if the cell contains a formula, you can paste only the value, or the result, of the formula to the new cell. You can also paste only the formatting of a cell, as you will learn in Lesson 3, "Formatting Your Data."

To copy and paste specific aspects of a cell selectively, use the Copy command or button as usual, but use the Paste Special command on the Edit menu instead of the Paste command. The Paste Special command allows you to choose which aspects of the cell you want to paste. For example, if a particular cell contains a formula, but you want to copy only the value that results from the formula, you can copy the cell and then use the Paste Special command to paste only the value into the new cell.

Copy only the values of the first quarter budget data to another sheet

In this exercise, you copy the totals information from the budget area and paste only the values into a summary area.

1 Select B19:E30.

2 Click the Copy button on the toolbar.

Copy

3 Switch to the 1996 1st Qtr sheet, and select cell B9.

Cell B9 indicates the upper-left corner of the paste area.

4 Use the right mouse button to click cell B9, and then click Paste Special on the shortcut menu.

The Paste Special dialog box opens.

You can also drag cells using the right mouse button and then click Copy Values on the shortcut menu when you drop the cells.

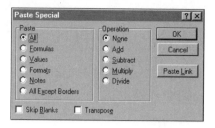

5   Under Paste, select the Values option and then click OK.

The dialog box closes, and only the values are pasted into the new cell range.

Moving Data Between Cells

Just as you can copy data by dragging with the mouse or by using menu commands, you can also move data by either method. When you use the Cut and Paste commands on the Edit menu, you can cut data from one cell and paste it into another. With the mouse, you simply select a cell and drag the cell by its border to a new location. When you move data, you do not need to hold down CTRL or any other keys while you drag.

Move cells on the same worksheet

In this exercise, you move cells from one location to another within the budget sheet.

1   Switch back to the 1996 Budget sheet, and select the range B30:C30.

2   Position the mouse pointer over part of the range border, press and hold down the mouse button, and drag the range border to B31:C31.

Be sure that you do not select the lower-right corner; doing so will automatically fill the data from cells B30:C30 into cells B31:C31, rather than moving the data.

3   Release the mouse button.

The data is dropped into place in the new location. Your worksheet should look like the following.

	B	C	D	E	F	G	H	I	
19		Jun	Jul	Aug	Sep	Oct	Nov	Dec	Ja
20	Gross Revenue								
21	Sales	27000	27405	27816	28233	28657	29087	29523	
22	Shipping	5550	5633	5718	5804	5891	5979	6069	
23	GR Total	32550	33038	33534	34037	34547	35066	35592	
24	Cost of Goods Sold								
25	Goods	17710	17869	18030	18192	18356	18521	18688	
26	Freight	270	272	275	277	280	282	285	
27	Markdowns	1240	1251	1262	1274	1285	1297	1308	
28	Miscellaneous	96	97	98	99	100	100	101	
29	COGS Total	19316	19490	19665	19842	20021	20201	20383	
30									
31	Gross Profit	13234							
32	Expenses								
33	Advertising	4000	4000	4000	4000	4000	4000	4000	
34	Salaries	4700	4700	4700	4700	4700	4700	4700	

1996 Budget / 1996 1st Qtr / Sheet4 / Sheet5 / Sheet6

Move cells to another worksheet

In this exercise, you move cells from the budget sheet to Sheet4.

1   On the 1996 Budget sheet, select the range B50:B52.

2   Press and hold down ALT, and then drag the cells onto the Sheet4 tab.

3   When Sheet4 is the active sheet, release the ALT key, drag the cells up to A1:A3, and then release the mouse button.

The data is dropped into place in the new worksheet.

Inserting and Deleting Cells, Rows, and Columns

You can copy cells to rearrange the data in your worksheet, but what if you just need more room in one particular area? You can insert or delete cells, rows, or columns easily. When you delete a cell, you are not just clearing the contents. You are removing the entire cell from the sheet, and other cells must move into the deleted cell's place, either from the right or below the deleted cell. To insert a cell, row, or column, you can use the Cells, Rows, or Columns commands on the Insert menu. To delete a cell, row, or column, you use the Delete command on the Edit menu.

When you insert or delete a row or column, you must select the entire row or column, not just part of it. To select an entire row or column, you click the header at the left of a row or the top of a column.

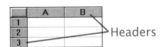
Headers

When you insert a cell, column, or row, you need to select the cell, column, or row immediately to the right or below where you want the new cell, column, or row to appear. When you use the menu commands to insert a cell, you can decide which cells will move to make space for the new cell. When you delete a cell, you can decide which cells will move to take the place of the deleted cells.

You can also insert or delete entire columns or rows and then move them around, just as you can insert, delete, and move cells.

Insert a column

Suppose you want to have a blank column to the right of your labels. In this exercise, you insert a new column into your budget.

1   Select the 1996 Budget sheet, and then press CTRL+HOME.

2   Use the right mouse button to click the column header for column A.

All of column A is selected, and a shortcut menu appears.

3 Click Insert.

A new column is inserted to the left of the selected column, and the new column is selected.

Rearrange columns

In this exercise, you move your columns so that there is a blank column between the area labels and the data.

1 Click the column header for column B.

2 Position the pointer on the right range border of the selected column and drag to column A.

The data from column B moves to column A. You now have a blank column (Column B) between the labels and the data. Your worksheet should look like the following.

	A	B	C	D	E	F	G	H
1	Title		WCS Cash Budget: 1996 Fiscal Year					
2								
3	Created by		Kris Mueller					
4	Date Modified		6/3/95					
5	Purpose		This worksheet presents the West Coast Sales FY 1996 projected cash bu					
6								
7	Initial Data		Monthly Growth					
8			Sales Growth	1.50%				
9			COGS Increase	0.90%				
10								
11	Summary			Qtr 1	Qtr 2	Qtr 3	Qtr 4	1996 Tot
12			Gross Revenue	99122	100609	102118	103650	40549
13			Cost Of Goods Sold	58471	58997	59528	60064	23706
14			Gross Profit	40651	41612	42590	43586	16843
15			Expenses	33398	33196	33231	33266	13309
16			Operating Income	7253	8416	9359	10320	3534
17								

1996 Budget / 1996 1st Qtr / Sheet4 / Sheet5 / Sheet6

Creating Formulas with Relative and Absolute References

An absolute reference contains dollar signs (for example, $A$1) to identify it as an absolute reference. A relative reference has no dollar signs (for example, A1). So far, you have used only relative references in your formulas.

A relative reference describes the location of a cell in terms of its distance, in rows and columns, from another cell. Relative references are analogous to giving directions, such as "one street over and two houses down." In your 1996 Budget worksheet, the formula in cell D23 totals the values in cells D21:D22. Because D21:D22 are relative references, the formula in D23 is actually adding the two cells above D23. If you copy that formula to F18, the formula will add the two cells above F18.

When you copied the formula for totaling the Cost of Goods Sold from cell C29 to D29:N29, the cell references used in the formulas were automatically adjusted to reflect the column that the formula was in. The formula in C29 totaled C25:C28, the four cells above C29. The formula in D29 totaled the four cells above D29, and so on. References that change automatically when you copy them to a new cell are called *relative references*. When you copy a formula containing relative references, the references are adjusted to reflect the new location of the formula. However, you can also use formulas with *absolute references*, references that always refer to the same cells, regardless of the location of the formula.

An absolute cell reference describes a specific cell address. Absolute references are analogous to giving a fixed address, such as "405 Mason Street." In your 1996 Budget sheet, the formulas in cells E21:O21 calculate the sales increase between months based on a fixed percentage. However, each of these formulas refers to cell $D$8, the cell that contains the sales growth rate (1.50%). The dollar signs ($) indicate an absolute reference to cell $D$8. No matter where the sales growth formula is copied, it always refers to cell $D$8.

	E21		=D21+(D21*$D$8)						
	C	D	E	F	G	H	I	J	
7	Monthly Growth								
8	Sales Growth	1.50%							
9	COGS Increase	0.90%							
10									
11		Qtr 1	Qtr 2	Qtr 3	Qtr 4	1996 Totals			
12	Gross Revenue	99122	100609	102118	103650	405499			
13	Cost Of Goods Sold	58471	58997	59528	60064	237060			
14	Gross Profit	40651	41612	42590	43586	168439			
15	Expenses	33398	33196	33231	33266	133091			
16	Operating Income	7253	8416	9359	10320	35348			
17									
18									
19		Jun	Jul	Aug	Sep	Oct	Nov	Dec	Ja
20	Gross Revenue								
21	Sales	27000	27405	27816	28233	28657	29087	29523	
22	Shipping	5550	5633	5718	5804	5891	5979	6069	

1996 Budget / 1996 1st Qtr / Sheet4 / Sheet5 / Sheet6

The type of reference you use will depend on what you are calculating, and you can use both relative and absolute references in the same formula. For example, in the following illustration, the formula in cell D3 uses a relative reference to cell C6, three rows down and one column to the left of cell D3. The formula also uses an absolute reference to cell C2.

	D3		=$C$2+C6	
	B	C	D	E
1				
2		5	absolute	
3			13	
4			relative	
5				
6		8		
7				
8				

43

If you copy the formula one cell to the right, as in the following illustration, the formula's relative reference will continue to look for data in the cell three rows down and one column to the left of its new location. But your data remains in the same spot, which is now three rows down and two columns to the left of the formula. Now the formula is in cell E3, and the relative reference refers to cell D6, three rows down and one column to the left, while the data remains in cell C6.

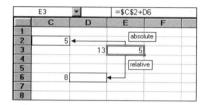

The absolute reference still refers to cell C2, even after the formula has been copied to a new location. You can change a relative reference to an absolute reference, so even if you copy the formula, the reference will always point to the same cell.

You can also create mixed references, which have a relative column and an absolute row, or a relative row and an absolute column. $A1 and A$1 are examples of mixed references.

NOTE   If you move a formula, instead of copying it, the references will not change—they will continue to point to the original data, whether the references are relative or absolute.

Copy a formula and change it to an absolute reference

In this exercise, you copy a formula made up of relative references and see how the references change. Then you'll change the references to absolute references and see whether they change.

1   Select cell O23.

This cell contains a formula with relative references.

2   Copy cell O23 to cell P23.

The formula moves to the new cell. Look at the formula in P23—the references have changed, and you now get a result of 0 instead of the original value. This is because the relative references now point to blank cells. Your worksheet should look like the following.

P23	▼		=SUM(P21:P22)						
	K	**L**	**M**	**N**	**O**	**P**	**Q**	**R**	**S**
17									
18									
19	Jan	Feb	Mar	Apr	May				
20									
21	29966	30415	30872	31335	31805				
22	6160	6252	6346	6441	6538				
23	36125	36667	37217	37776	38342	0			
24									
25	18856	19026	19197	19370	19544				
26	287	290	293	295	298				
27	1320	1332	1344	1356	1368				
28	102	103	104	105	106				
29	20566	20751	20938	21127	21317				
30									
31									
32									

|◄| ◄| ►| ►|\ **1996 Budget** / 1996 1st Qtr / Sheet4 / Sheet5 / Sheet6 |◄|

3 On the Edit menu, click the Undo command.

The command may be Undo Paste or Undo Drag And Drop or Undo AutoFill, depending on the copy method you used in step 2.

4 Select cell O23.

5 In the formula bar, select "O21:O22."

You can select individual references quickly by double-clicking them.

6 Press the F4 key, and then press ENTER.

This changes the references to absolute references.

7 Copy cell O23 to cell P23.

The formula is copied to the new cell, but the formula retains its value because you changed the relative references to absolute references.

NOTE You can press the F4 key repeatedly to cycle through the different types of references. You can change both the row and the column references to absolute (such as $A$1), only the row reference to absolute (such as A$1), only the column reference to absolute (such as $A1), or both to relative (such as A1).

One Step Further: Using the COUNTA Function

Microsoft Excel comes with many functions that can help with mathematical, financial, statistical, and other formulas. You already saw a few of the functions you'll probably use most often: SUM, MAX, MIN, and TODAY. Some of the others that you'll probably use often are the NOW, COUNT, and COUNTA functions. The NOW function is very similar to the TODAY function, except that it enters both the current date and time. COUNT and COUNTA count how many cells have numbers in them and how many cells have any entries in them, respectively.

For example, suppose you have a list of contributors to a company charity drive, with all employee names in one column and amounts contributed in another column. You can use the COUNT function in the amounts column to find out how many employees have contributed, and you can use the COUNTA function in the names column to count the total number of employees.

NOTE COUNT counts only numeric entries, and it ignores text and errors; COUNTA counts all entries. If you have a range with the entries *one, 2, 3, 4, 5,* and you use the COUNT function to find out how many numbers are in the range, the result will be four. If you use the COUNTA function with the same range, the result will be five.

In the next exercise, you'll use the COUNTA function to look at the information in your worksheets.

1   Switch to the 1996 1st Qtr sheet.

2   Select cell C23 and click the Function Wizard button.

Function Wizard

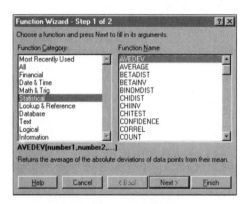

3   In the Function Category list, select Statistical, if it is not already selected.

4   In the Function Name list, scroll downward and select COUNTA, and then click the Next button.

5   In the spreadsheet, drag to select the range C11:C19.

6   Click the Finish button.

The result of the function, 8, appears in cell C23. Your worksheet should look like the following.

C23	▼		=COUNTA(C11:C19)					
	A	B	C	D	E	F	G	H	I
9			Jun	Jul	Aug				
10		Gross Revenue							
11		Sales	27000	27405	27816.08				
12		Shipping	5550	5633	5718				
13		GR Total	32550	33038	33534				
14		Cost of Goods Sold							
15		Goods	17710	17869	18030				
16		Freight	270	272	275				
17		Markdowns	1240	1251	1262				
18		Miscellaneo	96	97	98				
19		COGS Total	19316	19490	19665				
20		Gross Profit	13234						
21									
22									
23		Count	8						
24									
25									

1996 Budget \ **1996 1st Qtr** / Sheet4 / Sheet5 / Sheet6

If You Want to Continue to the Next Lesson

1 On the File menu, click Save.

2 On the File menu, click Close.

If You Want to Quit Microsoft Excel for Now

➤ On the File menu, click Exit.

If you see the Save dialog box, click Yes.

Lesson Summary

To	Do this	Button
Total a range	Select the range, and click the AutoSum button on the Standard toolbar.	Σ
Write a formula with the Function Wizard	Select a cell and click the Function Wizard button on the Standard toolbar. Select the function category, and then the function name. Click the Next button. Enter the arguments needed, and click the Finish button.	f_x
Define a name for a range	Select the range, and then click in the name box on the formula bar. Type the name, and press ENTER.	
Create several names within a range	Select the range. On the Insert menu, point to Name, and then click Create.	

To	Do this	Button
Edit a name	On the Insert menu, point to Name, and then click Define. Select the name in the list, and edit the name or the definition. Click OK.	
Go to a range	Click the arrow next to the name box on the formula bar, and select the name.	
Type a formula	Select a cell, and type an equal sign followed by the formula. Press ENTER.	
Copy and paste data between cells	Select the cell or range and on the Edit menu click Copy, or click the Copy button on the toolbar. Select the new cell and on the Edit menu click Paste, or click the Paste button on the toolbar. *or* Select the cell with the data in it, press and hold down CTRL, and drag the cell border to the new range. Release the mouse button, and then release CTRL.	
Move data between cells	Select the cell or range, and drag it by its border to the new location.	
Insert a cell, row, or column	Use the right mouse button to click on a cell, row header, or column header, and then click Insert.	
Delete a cell, row, or column	Use the right mouse button to click on a cell, row header, or column header, and then click Delete.	
Change a relative reference to an absolute reference, or vice versa	Select the reference in the formula or cell, and press the F4 key.	

For online information about	Use the Answer Wizard to search for
Totaling ranges	**total**
Naming ranges	**name**
Writing formulas	**formula**
Copying, pasting, and moving data	**copy** *or* **move** *or* **paste**
Inserting and deleting cells, rows, and columns	**insert** *or* **delete**
Using relative and absolute references	**reference**

Preview of the Next Lesson

In the next lesson, you'll learn how to format your data and make it easier to understand. You'll learn how to use AutoFormat to format your data and how to copy formats to other cells. You'll also learn how to control formatting elements individually with the buttons on the toolbar.

Formatting Your Data

Estimated time
35 min.

In this lesson you will learn how to:

■ Format your data with AutoFormat and Format Painter.

■ Format data with the buttons on the Formatting toolbar.

■ Copy formats to other cells.

When you are creating a worksheet to be used in a presentation or a report, it's important to make the information clear and easy to understand. You can format your data so that the information is more accessible and meaningful. By formatting your data, you can also integrate your sheet with the rest of the presentation or report. With AutoFormat, Format Painter, and the buttons on the Formatting toolbar, you can easily create clearer and better-looking sheets. In this lesson, you'll learn how to use AutoFormat to improve the look of your sheets and how to quickly copy your formatting to other areas of your sheets or onto other sheets in your workbook. Finally, you'll learn how to use the buttons on the Formatting toolbar to adjust formatting elements individually.

Start the lesson

Follow the steps below to open the practice file called 03Lesson, and then save it with the new name Lesson03.

Open

1   On the Standard toolbar, click the Open button.

2   In the Look In box, be sure that the Excel SBS Practice folder appears.

3   In the file list box, double-click the file named 03Lesson to open it.

To select the folder containing your practice files, refer to "Open a practice file" near the start of Lesson 1.

4 On the File menu, click Save As.

The Save As dialog box opens. Be sure the Excel SBS Practice folder appears in the Save In box.

5 Double-click in the File Name box, and then type **Lesson03**

6 Click the Save button, or press ENTER.

If you share your computer with others who use Microsoft Excel, the screen display might have changed since your last lesson. If your screen does not look similar to the illustrations as you work through this lesson, see the Appendix, "Matching the Exercises."

Formatting Data Automatically

When you prepare data to show to someone else, either as part of a presentation or by itself, you want your data to look professional and be easy to understand. You can create a professional and consistent look for data by using the AutoFormat command on the Format menu. AutoFormat lets you choose between standard table formats that include borders, shading, font colors, and other formatting options. With AutoFormat, you can easily apply a consistent format throughout a workbook.

When you format a range automatically, your data might not look exactly the way that you want. Later in this lesson, you'll learn additional formatting techniques to achieve the look you want.

To apply a format automatically, you first select a cell within a range and then use the AutoFormat command on the Format menu. You can select one of sixteen different table formats, including formats for financial data, accounting data, lists, and even colorful and three-dimensional formats. You can also use the Options button to select the exact elements of the AutoFormats that you want to use. With the Options button, you can apply predefined number, border, font, pattern, alignment, and width or height formats to your table by turning these options on or off. By default, all of these options are turned on and applied when you select an AutoFormat.

 NOTE Microsoft Excel includes several templates for sheets, such as invoices, budgets, and time cards, that include formulas as well as formatting. To create a new worksheet from a template, click New on the File menu, click the Spreadsheet Solutions tab, and then double-click the template you want.

Format data with AutoFormat

In this and the next exercise, you select ranges and then apply different table formats to them with AutoFormat.

1 Select a cell within the range C11:H16.

2 On the Format menu, click AutoFormat.

The AutoFormat dialog box opens.

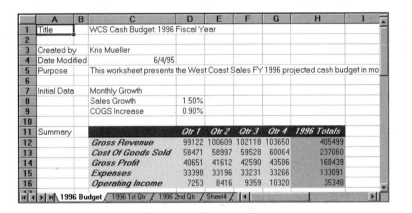

3 In the Table Format list, scroll downward and select Colorful 2, and then click OK.

Your data is formatted in the Colorful 2 style. Your worksheet should look like the following.

	A	B	C	D	E	F	G	H	I
1	Title		WCS Cash Budget: 1996 Fiscal Year						
2									
3	Created by		Kris Mueller						
4	Date Modified		6/4/95						
5	Purpose		This worksheet presents the West Coast Sales FY 1996 projected cash budget in mo						
6									
7	Initial Data		Monthly Growth						
8			Sales Growth	1.50%					
9			COGS Increase	0.90%					
10									
11	Summary			*Qtr 1*	*Qtr 2*	*Qtr 3*	*Qtr 4*	*1996 Totals*	
12			*Gross Revenue*	99122	100609	102118	103650	405499	
13			*Cost Of Goods Sold*	58471	58997	59528	60064	237060	
14			*Gross Profit*	40651	41612	42590	43586	168439	
15			*Expenses*	33398	33196	33231	33266	133091	
16			*Operating Income*	7253	8416	9359	10320	35348	

1996 Budget / 1996 1st Qtr / 1996 2nd Qtr / Sheet4

Format another range of data and turn off an option

1 Select a cell within the range C19:O46.

2 On the Format menu, click AutoFormat.

The AutoFormat dialog box opens.

3 In the Table Format list, select Classic 3, and click the Options button.

The AutoFormat dialog box expands to display the formatting options.

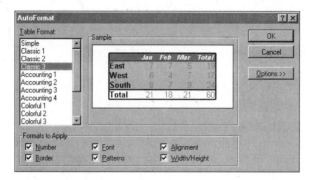

4 In the Formats To Apply box, click the Number and Width/Height check boxes.

Clearing the check marks from these boxes turns off these AutoFormat attributes and ensures that the number formats, column widths, and row heights in each cell remain as they are in the worksheet. Applying an AutoFormat changes the number format, column width, row height, font, colors, and borders for the selected area, unless you choose not to apply these attributes.

5 Click OK.

The AutoFormat dialog box closes, and the changes take effect. Your worksheet should look like the following.

	A	B	C	D	E	F	G	H	I
18	Budget Model Area								
19				*Jun*	*Jul*	*Aug*	*Sep*	*Oct*	*Nov*
20			*Gross Revenue*						
21			Sales	27000	27405	27816	28233	28657	29087
22			Shipping	5550	5633	5718	5804	5891	5979
23			GR Total	32550	33038	33534	34037	34547	35066
24			*Cost of Goods Sold*						
25			Goods	17710	17869	18030	18192	18356	18521
26			Freight	270	272	275	277	280	282
27			Markdowns	1240	1251	1262	1274	1285	1297
28			Miscellaneous	96	97	98	99	100	100
29			COGS Total	19316	19490	19665	19842	20021	20201
30			*Gross Profit*	13234	13548	13869	14195	14527	14865
31			*Expenses*						
32			*Advertising*	4000	4000	4000	4000	4000	4000
33			Salaries	4700	4700	4700	4700	4700	4700

1996 Budget / 1996 1st Qtr / 1996 2nd Qtr / Sheet4

Repeat AutoFormatting

In this exercise, you format the Summary Area to look the same as the Budget Model Area.

1 Select a cell within the range C11:H16.

2 On the Edit menu, click Repeat AutoFormat.

The Classic 3 format is applied to the summary range.

Copying Formats to Other Cells

When you want to copy the formatting used in one section of your worksheet to another, you can use the Format Painter button. The Format Painter button lets you copy formats quickly. You simply select a cell with the format that you like, click the Format Painter tool, and then select the cell or range to which you want to apply the formatting.

If you click the Format Painter button once, you can paste the format once. If you need to copy formatting from one area of the worksheet to several nonadjacent areas, you can double-click the Format Painter button to turn it on. When you are finished pasting formats, you click the Format Painter button again to turn it off.

Copy a format with the Format Painter button

In this exercise, you use the Format Painter button to copy formatting from the Summary Area to the Initial Data area.

Format Painter

1 Select the range C11:D13.

2 On the toolbar, click the Format Painter button.

The pointer changes to look like a paintbrush with a plus sign.

3 With the new pointer, select C7.

The formatting is copied to the range C7:D9. If you had selected only one row, you would have copied only one row of formatting. By selecting three rows, you'll copy the formats in each of the three rows to the three rows in the destination range. The new color applied to cell C7 is obscuring the text.

Font Color

4 Select C7, then click the down arrow next to the Font Color button on the Formatting toolbar, and click the white square on the font color palette.

The text in C7 is visible again. You can click the Bold button on the Formatting toolbar to make the text more visible. Your worksheet should look like the following.

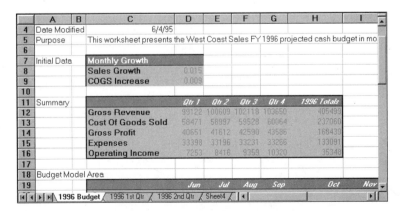

Formatting Data with the Formatting Toolbar

You might not want all of the standard settings in a table format, or perhaps you might want to emphasize a section of the sheet by applying different formats from the rest of your sheet. You can format specific cells, rows, columns, or ranges easily with the buttons on the Formatting toolbar.

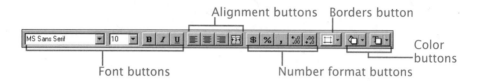

Alignment buttons   Borders button

Font buttons   Number format buttons   Color buttons

Changing Number Formats

When you change a cell's number format, the underlying cell value is not affected. To see a cell's underlying value, you can change the cell's format to General.

You can quickly apply common number formats to a cell by using the Currency Style, Percent Style, and Comma Style buttons on the toolbar. Each of these styles has a default number of decimal points that you can change with the Increase Decimal and Decrease Decimal buttons. Parts of your worksheet might be easier to understand if the cells had a format appropriate to the way the numbers are used, such as currency or percent.

Change number formats

In this exercise, you change the number formats for your budget data to currency style, and the Monthly Growth figures to percent style. You'll also adjust the number of decimal places for the budget data.

NOTE When you change to the currency format, some of the cells might display a row of number signs (#) rather than the actual values. Do not worry about losing any data; the number signs merely indicate that the columns are not wide enough to display the entire numbers. Later in this lesson, you'll change the size of the columns to make your data visible.

Currency Style

Decrease Decimal

1   Select cells D20:O45.

2   Click the Currency Style button on the Formatting toolbar.

This adds a dollar sign, a decimal point, and two decimal places to your numbers.

3   Click the Decrease Decimal button on the toolbar twice.

This removes the decimal places from your numbers. The values in the cells are not changed; only the way the values are displayed is changed.

4 Select D21 and click the Format Painter button.

5 With the Format Painter pointer, select cells D12:H16.

6 Select cells D8:D9 and click the Percent Style button on the toolbar.

The cells are formatted as percentages. Your worksheet should look like the following.

Format Painter

Percent Style

	B	C	D	E	F	G	H	I	J
7		Monthly Growth							
8		Sales Growth	2%						
9		COGS Increase	1%						
10									
11			Qtr 1	Qtr 2	Qtr 3	Qtr 4	1996 Totals		
12		Gross Revenue	#####	#####	#####	#####	$405,499		
13		Cost Of Goods Sold	#####	#####	#####	#####	$237,060		
14		Gross Profit	#####	#####	#####	#####	$168,439		
15		Expenses	#####	#####	#####	#####	$133,091		
16		Operating Income	$7,253	$8,416	$9,359	#####	$35,348		
17									
18	del Area								
19			Jun	Jul	Aug	Sep	Oct	Nov	Dec
20		Gross Revenue							
21		Sales	#####	#####	#####	#####	$28,657	$29,087	$29,523
22		Shipping	$5,550	$5,633	$5,718	$5,804	$5,891	$5,979	$6,069

1996 Budget / 1996 1st Qtr / 1996 2nd Qtr / Sheet4 /

NOTE You can also change number formats by using the shortcut menu. Select the cells you want to change, click the right mouse button, and then click Format Cells. With the Format Cells command, you have more choices of number formats than you do with the buttons on the toolbar.

Change to date format

In this exercise, you use the Format Cells command to change the format of cell C4, which contains the date the sheet was modified.

1 Select cell C4.

2 Use the right mouse button to click cell C4.

3 On the shortcut menu, click Format Cells.

The Format Cells dialog box opens.

4 In the dialog box, click the Number tab, if it is not already selected.

The Number tab opens, displaying the formatting options for numbers.

Number tab

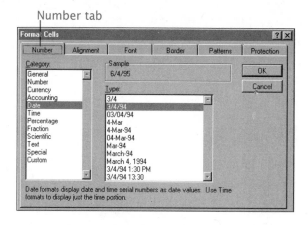

5 In the Category list, select Date.

As you can see, there are many built-in number formats to select from.

6 In the Type list, select a day-month-year format.

This type of format changes your date to display the day followed by the month and then the year, separated by hyphens. For example, July 5, 1996, would be displayed as 5-Jul-96. View the Sample box to see how your worksheet entry will appear.

7 Click OK.

The date display changes to the day-month-year format you selected. Your worksheet might look like the following, depending on which format you selected.

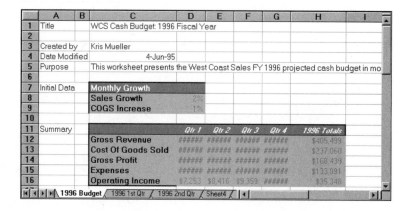

Changing Fonts

Not only can you change the number style of your data, but you can also change other aspects of your text's appearance. You can quickly change fonts and font sizes with the Font and Font Size boxes on the Formatting toolbar, or you can use the Format Cells command. You can also use the Bold, Italic, or Underline buttons on the toolbar.

Change fonts and sizes

In the next exercises, you change the font, font size, and font attributes used in your budget sheet.

1   In the upper-left corner of the worksheet grid, click the Select All button to display the entire worksheet. Or, press CTRL+SHIFT+SPACEBAR.

Select All button

Font

2   On the Formatting toolbar, click the down arrow next to the Font box.

A list of fonts appears. The available fonts will vary depending on what fonts you have installed.

3   Select MS Serif, or any other font of your choice.

Your text and numbers change to the selected font.

Font Size

4   On the Formatting toolbar, click the down arrow next to the Font Size box.

A list of font sizes appears.

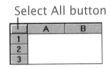

5   Select 12.

The font size changes to 12 points.

6   Click the down arrow next to the Font Size box again, and select 10 from the list.

The font size changes to 10 points. Your worksheet should look like the following.

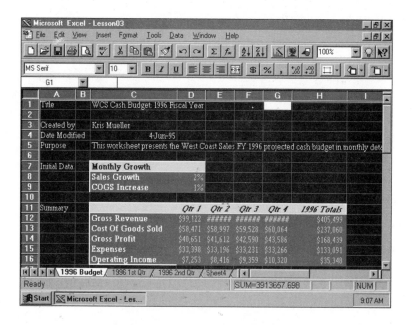

 NOTE   You can also change your font, font size, and other attributes by clicking Format Cells on the shortcut menu. Select the cells you want to change, click the selected range with the right mouse button, click Format Cells, and click the Font tab in the Format Cells dialog box. Select a font name, size, and other attributes, and then click OK.

Change font attributes

1   Click cell C1, press and hold down CTRL, and then click cell C3.

Both cells are selected.

2   On the Formatting toolbar, click the Bold button.

3   Select cell C1.

C1 becomes the active cell, and cell C3 is no longer selected.

4   On the Formatting toolbar, click the down arrow next to the Font Color button.

A palette of color choices appears, similar to the following.

Bold

Font Color

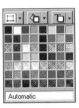

5   Select Dark Blue.

The title text is shaded Dark Blue.

6   Click the column header for column A.

The entire column is selected.

7   On the Formatting toolbar, click the Italic button.

The entries in column A are formatted in italics.

8   On the Formatting toolbar, click the Bold button.

The entries in column A are formatted bold.

9   Press CTRL+HOME.

Cell A1 becomes the active cell. Your worksheet should look like the following.

Italic

Bold

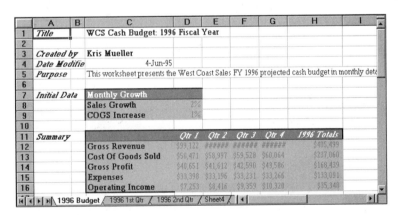

Changing Row Heights and Column Widths

Occasionally, your data will not fit within the standard column width. This is often the case when you are working with long labels, with large font sizes, or with data formatted as currency. You can easily change the column width or row height without using any menu commands or special keys. All you need is the mouse. Double-click the right border between column headers or the bottom border between row headers. The column or row will be sized to fit the width of the longest entry in the column or the height of the largest font in the row.

Change column width to best fit

In this exercise, you use the mouse to adjust column widths to fit the data within each column.

1 Select columns D through O.

2 Move the pointer over the border between any two selected column headers.

The pointer changes to a two-headed arrow.

Pointer

3 Double-click the border between the column headers.

All the selected column widths change so that each column fits the widest data in that column. Your worksheet should look like the following.

	A	B	C	D	E	F	G	H	
1	*Title*		WCS Cash Budget: 1996 Fiscal Year						
2									
3	*Created by*		Kris Mueller						
4	*Date Modifie*			4-Jun-95					
5	*Purpose*		This worksheet presents the West Coast Sales FY 1996 projected cash budget in monthly deta						
6									
7	*Initial Data*		Monthly Growth						
8			Sales Growth	2%					
9			COGS Increase	1%					
10									
11	*Summary*			*Qtr 1*	*Qtr 2*	*Qtr 3*	*Qtr 4*	*1996 Totals*	
12			Gross Revenue	$99,122	$100,609	$102,118	$103,650	$405,499	
13			Cost Of Goods Sold	$58,471	$58,997	$59,528	$60,064	$237,060	
14			Gross Profit	$40,651	$41,612	$42,590	$43,586	$168,439	
15			Expenses	$33,398	$33,196	$33,231	$33,266	$133,091	
16			Operating Income	$7,253	$8,416	$9,359	$10,320	$35,348	

1996 Budget / 1996 1st Qtr / 1996 2nd Qtr / Sheet4

NOTE You can also change column widths and row heights to any size you want by dragging the column or row header border to the desired width or height.

Changing Cell Alignments

When you open a new sheet and begin entering data, your text is automatically left-aligned and your numbers are automatically right-aligned. However, you might decide that you want labels to be right-aligned or data to be centered in the cells. Perhaps you have a title that you want to center across the top of the worksheet. You can easily align text to the right, left, or center, or center text across several columns using the buttons on the Formatting toolbar.

If you want to align a title across several columns, you can select the cells in which you want the text to be centered and use the Center Across Columns button on the Formatting toolbar.

Change cell alignments

In this exercise, you change the alignment of your label data, and then center the title across the top of the data.

Align Right

Align Left

Center Across Columns

1   Click the column header for column A.

The entire column is selected.

2   On the Formatting toolbar, click the Align Right button.

The entire column is right-aligned.

3   Double-click the column header border between column A and column B.

The column width is adjusted to fit the text in the cells.

4   Select cell C4, and then click the Align Left button on the Formatting toolbar.

5   Select cells C1:L1.

This range includes the title of the sheet.

6   On the Formatting toolbar, click the Center Across Columns button.

The title is centered across the selected columns. Your worksheet should look like the following.

	A	B	C	D	E	F	G	H
1	*Title*					WCS Cash Budget: 1996 Fiscal Year		
2								
3	*Created by*		Kris Mueller					
4	*Date Modified*		4-Jun-95					
5	*Purpose*		This worksheet presents the West Coast Sales FY 1996 projected cash budget in mo					
6								
7	*Initial Data*		Monthly Growth					
8			Sales Growth		2%			
9			COGS Increase		1%			
10								
11	*Summary*			Qtr 1	Qtr 2	Qtr 3	Qtr 4	1996 Tot
12			Gross Revenue	$99,122	$100,609	$102,110	$103,650	$405,
13			Cost Of Goods Sold	$58,471	$58,997	$59,528	$60,064	$237,
14			Gross Profit	$40,651	$41,612	$42,590	$43,586	$168,
15			Expenses	$33,398	$33,196	$33,231	$33,266	$133,
16			Operating Income	$7,253	$8,416	$9,359	$10,320	$35,

1996 Budget / 1996 1st Qtr / 1996 2nd Qtr / Sheet4 /

Adding Borders and Color

You can emphasize particular areas of the sheet or specific cells by using borders and color. Borders add lines above, below, or to either side of a cell. You can add a single line or multiple lines, along one side of a cell or around it. You can shade a cell in one of many patterns or colors. You have already changed the color of your text with the Font Color button on the toolbar. In the next exercises, you'll add borders to the Monthly Growth area on your spreadsheet and shade the cells with a light gray color to emphasize them. You'll then add a double underline to the Operating Income row.

Add borders and color

1 Select D8:D9.

Borders

2 On the Formatting toolbar, click the down arrow next to the Borders button.

A *palette* with the different border options opens.

3 Place the pointer on the outer edge of the Borders palette, and then drag the palette away from the toolbar.

When you release the mouse button, the palette becomes a *floating palette*. The floating palette is just like a toolbar. When you are finished using the floating palette, you can click the Close button in the upper-right corner to remove it.

4 Click the third border in the third row of the Borders palette.

A thin border appears around the selected range.

Color

5 On the Formatting toolbar, click the down arrow next to the Color button.

A palette with the different color options opens. The Color palette can also be dragged away from the toolbar to float on the worksheet.

6 Click the lightest gray color.

The cells are shaded with light gray.

7 On the Tools menu, click Options and then click the View tab if it is not already in view.

8 Clear the Gridlines checkbox, and click OK.

Your worksheet should look like the following.

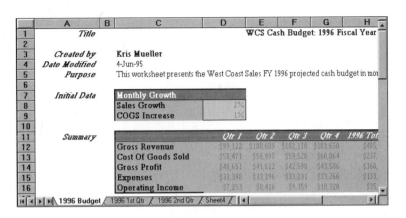

Add a double border to the bottom of the Operating Income row

To create a customized border, click Cells on the Format menu, click the Border tab, and then select individual styles and combinations.

1 Select the range Operating Income from the name box list (D45:O45).

2 The Borders palette should still be floating on the worksheet. If not, click the down arrow next to the Borders button on the toolbar.

3 Select the first border in the second row on the Borders palette.

A double border appears at the bottom of each selected cell. The underlining should look similar to the following.

Operating Income		$1,955	$2,495	$2,802

—Double-underline border

One Step Further: Changing Formats and Styles

As you saw throughout this lesson, there's more than one way to access the formatting commands. The most direct way is to use the buttons on the Formatting toolbar, but more options are available if you use the Format menu or the shortcut menu. On the Format menu, click the Cells command to open the Format Cells dialog box. On the shortcut menu, you can click Format Cells to open the Format Cells dialog box. Since the font, number, alignment, border, and pattern choices are all part of the same dialog box, you only need to use one command to change all of these aspects of a cell's format.

Format the cells on the 1996 1st Qtr sheet

In this exercise, you open the Format Cells dialog box and change the cell formats for your quarterly budgets.

1 Switch to the 1996 1st Qtr sheet.

2   Select cells C11:E20.

3   On the Format menu, click Cells.

The Format Cells dialog box opens.

4   Click the Number tab, if it is not already selected.

The number options are displayed in the dialog box.

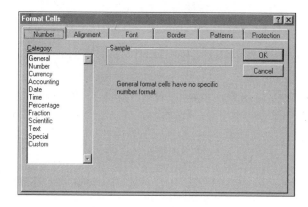

5   In the Category list, select Currency.

6   In the Decimal Places box, make sure 2 is selected, and make sure the Use $ option is checked.

7   In the Negative Numbers box, select the red format with parentheses, and click OK.

This formats your numbers to have a dollar sign and two decimal points, and negative numbers to be identified by parentheses and the color red. Widen the columns if necessary.

8   Select the entire worksheet.

9   On the Format menu, click Cells, and then click the Font tab.

The font choices are displayed.

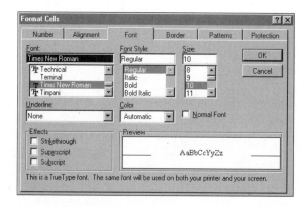

10 In the Font box, scroll downward and select Times New Roman.

11 In the Size box, select 9, and then click OK.

The dialog box closes, and the font in your worksheet changes to 9 point Times New Roman with numbers formatted as currency.

12 Press CTRL+HOME.

Cell A1 becomes the active cell. Your worksheet should look like the following.

	A	B	C	D	E	F	G
1	Title	WCS Cash Budget: 1996 1st Quarter					
2							
3	Created by	Kris Mueller					
4	Date Modified	6/4/95 8:52					
5							
6							
7							
8	Budget Model Area						
9			Jun	Jul	Aug		
10		Gross Revenue					
11		Sales	$27,000.00	$27,405.00	$27,816.08		
12		Shipping	$5,550.00	$5,633.25	$5,717.75		
13		GR Total	$32,550.00	$33,038.25	$33,533.82		
14		Cost of Goods Sold					
15		Goods	$17,710.00	$17,869.39	$18,030.21		
16		Freight	$270.00	$272.43	$274.88		
17		Markdowns	$1,240.00	$1,251.16	$1,262.42		

1996 Budget \ **1996 1st Qtr** / 1996 2nd Qtr / Sheet4

Change the font for the entire workbook

You have learned how to change the font for an entire worksheet, but the rest of your sheets are still formatted with the old font. If you want to change the font throughout the workbook, changing the Normal style is faster. Normal is the name of the default *style*, or collection of formats, that every new workbook is formatted with. In this lesson, you'll change the font portion of Normal style for this workbook.

To change the default font for all new workbooks, click Options on the Tools menu, click the General tab, and then select a font from the Standard Font box.

1 On the Format menu, click Style.

The Style Includes list displays all of the formatting included in Normal style. When you apply a style to cells, all the formatting attributes of the style are applied.

2 Click Modify, and then click the Font tab.

3 In the Font box, select Times New Roman, and in the Size box, select 9.

4 Click OK to close the Format Cells dialog box, and then click OK to close the Style dialog box.

5 Select the 1996 2nd Qtr sheet.

The font has changed throughout the workbook. If you select a blank sheet and type some text, the typing will be formatted with the new font.

NOTE If you apply a specific font to cells, as you did on the 1996 Budget sheet, the applied font format will take precedence over the Normal style font. Even though you changed the Normal style for the workbook, the 1996 Budget sheet is still formatted with the MS Serif font that you applied earlier.

If You Want to Continue to the Next Lesson

1   On the File menu, click Save.

2   On the File menu, click Close.

If You Want to Quit Microsoft Excel for Now

➤ On the File menu, click Exit.

   If you see the Save dialog box, click Yes.

Lesson Summary

To	Do this	Button
Format a range of data	Select a cell within the range. On the Format menu, click AutoFormat. Select a table format, and click OK.	
Copy a cell format	Select the cell or range to copy, click the Format Painter button on the toolbar, and select a cell or range to paste the format. *or* Select the cell or range to copy. Click the Copy button on the toolbar. Select the cell or range to paste. On the Edit menu, click Paste Special. In the Paste Special dialog box, select Formats, and then click OK.	
Change number formats	Select the cell and then click a number format button, such as the Currency Style, Percent Style, or Decrease Decimal button on the toolbar. *or* On the Format menu, click Cells and click the Number tab. Select a number format, and click OK.	

To	Do this	Button
Change fonts	Select the cell or range and then click the down arrows next to the Font box or the Font Size box to select a font name or size. Click the Bold, Italic, or Underline buttons on the toolbar. *or* On the Format menu, click Cell and click the Font tab. Select a font name, size, and other attributes, and click OK.	**B** *I* U
Change column width to best fit	Double-click the column header border to the right of the column you want to change.	
Change column width or row height	Drag the right-side column header border to the right or the lower row header border downward.	
Change alignment	Select the cell or range, and then click the Align Left, Center, Align Right, or Center Across Columns button on the toolbar. *or* On the Format menu, click Cells and click the Alignment tab. Select the alignment you want, and click OK.	
Add borders or colors	Select the cell or range, and then click the down arrows next to the Color, Borders, or Font Color buttons on the toolbar. Select a border or color style. *or* On the Format menu, click Cells, and click the Border or Patterns tab. Select the style you want, and click OK.	

For online information about	Use the Answer Wizard to search for
Automatically formatting a range	**format**
Copying cell formats	**copy format**
Changing cell formats	**format**
Using styles	**style**

Preview of the Next Lessons

In Part 2, you'll learn how to create and modify graphic representations of your data called *charts*. You'll also learn how to print both charts and worksheets. In the next lesson, "Charting Your Data," you'll learn how to use your data to create attractive charts easily with the ChartWizard.

Review & Practice

In the lessons in Part 1, you learned skills to enter and edit data, write formulas, and format your data. If you want to practice these skills and test your understanding before you proceed with the lessons in Part 2, you can work through the Review & Practice section following this lesson.

Review & Practice

You will review and practice how to:

Estimated time
10 min.

- Open a worksheet.
- Enter data.
- Fill a series of data into a range.
- Total columns of data.
- Write a formula.
- Format a table.

Before you move on to Part 2, which covers charting and printing, you can practice the skills you learned in Part 1 by working through the steps in this Review & Practice section. You will open a workbook, enter data, fill in a series, and total the data. You will also create a formula to calculate West Coast Sales' market share for each year and then format the table automatically.

Scenario

The accounting department at West Coast Sales is preparing a ten-year financial history. You've been asked to prepare a sales history for those ten years. You need to be sure that your part of the presentation looks like the other parts that are being prepared in the department.

Step 1: Open a File and Enter Data

You've received a list of the data for West Coast Sales, 10-year sales history, but you need to enter it into the worksheet, along with the year labels to identify the data. You also need to put your name on the worksheet so that the other people working on the presentation will know that you updated it last.

1 Open the file Part1 Review, and save it as Review Part1.

2 Fill the series 1985–1995 into column C under the Year label.

3 Enter the following data into the cells in columns D and E.

Company	Industry
59,774	1,210,000
66,174	1,230,000
86,814	1,260,000
113,490	1,300,000
125,280	1,350,000
145,452	1,380,000
178,922	1,370,000
200,340	1,400,000
262,850	1,500,000
299,468	1,690,000
350,200	2,000,000

4 Type your name in cell C3.

For more information on	See
Opening a file	Lesson 1
Saving a file	Lesson 1
Entering data	Lesson 1
Filling a series of data into a range	Lesson 1

Step 2: Total the Columns and Write a Formula

Now that you have entered the data, you need to total it, so that the presentation includes an overall view of the company's vs. the industry's performance over the last ten years. Then you need to add a formula to calculate what percentage of the industry sales comes from West Coast Sales.

1 Add a heading in row 20 for Total Sales.

2 Use AutoSum to total the Company and Industry sales figures.

3 Write a formula in column F that divides the West Coast Sales sales figure (in column D) by the industry sales figure (in column E) in each row.

For more information on	See
Totaling columns	Lesson 2
Writing formulas	Lesson 2

Step 3: *Format Numbers, Columns, and a Table*

Now that you have all of the data in place, a little formatting will finish off the presentation. Format the sales as currency and the sales percentage figures as percents.

1 Use the buttons on the toolbar to format column D as currency with no decimal places.

2 Use the Format Painter button to copy the currency formatting from column D to column E.

3 Use the buttons on the Formatting toolbar to format column F as a percentage with two decimal places.

4 Use the AutoFormat command to format the entire table to the List 1 format.

5 Change the column widths to fit the data.

Your finished worksheet should look similar to the following.

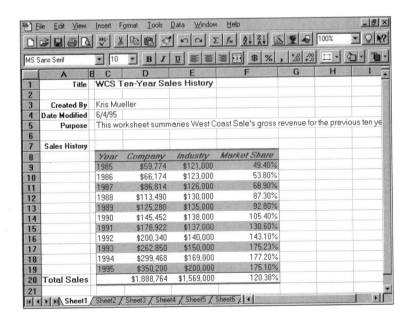

73

For more information on	See
Formatting cells	Lesson 3
Automatically formatting a table	Lesson 3
Changing column widths	Lesson 3

If You Want to Continue to the Next Lesson

1 On the File menu, click Save.
2 On the File menu, click Close.

If You Want to Quit Microsoft Excel for Now

➤ On the File menu, click Exit.
   If you see the Save dialog box, click Yes.

Part 2

Charting and Printing Your Data

Charting Your Data

Estimated time
30 min.

In this lesson you will learn how to:

- Create charts using the ChartWizard.
- Modify, add, and delete chart data.

A worksheet can calculate the relationships between numbers and the changes in numbers over time, but trends are hard to spot in a sea of numbers. Relationships between numbers are easier to grasp if they are illustrated graphically in charts. With charts, you can make your data visual. You can create a chart to show the changes in your data over time or how the parts of your data fit together as a whole. After you have charted your data, you can rearrange it or add data that was left out. With Microsoft Excel and the ChartWizard, you can easily turn your data into dynamic charts for use in your presentations or reports. Also, if you change values in the worksheet data, the chart will automatically display the new values.

Start the lesson

Follow the steps below to open the practice file called 04Lesson, and then save it with the new name Lesson04.

Open

1   On the Standard toolbar, click the Open button.
2   In the Look In box, be sure that the Excel SBS Practice folder appears.
3   In the file list box, double-click the file named 04Lesson to open it.

To select the folder containing your practice files, refer to "Open a practice file" near the start of Lesson 1.

4 On the File menu, click Save As.

The Save As dialog box opens. Be sure the Excel SBS Practice folder appears in the Save In box.

5 Double-click in the File Name box, and then type **Lesson04**

6 Click the Save button, or press ENTER.

If you share your computer with others who use Microsoft Excel, the screen display might have changed since your last lesson. If your screen does not look similar to the illustrations as you work through this lesson, see the Appendix, "Matching the Exercises."

Creating Charts

You can create charts in two ways: either on the same sheet as your data or on a separate chart sheet in the same workbook. When you create a chart on the same sheet as your data, you can view both the data and the chart at the same time. When you create a chart on a separate chart sheet in the same workbook, you still have easy access to the chart, but it doesn't hide data on the worksheet. A chart created on a worksheet is called an *embedded* chart. A separate chart is called a *chart sheet*.

 NOTE Another way to display data visually is with Data Map, a new Excel feature that provides geographic maps and corresponding demographic data. You can build a map with your data and include selected demographic data to enhance the meaning of your data. To use Data Map, click the Map button on the Standard toolbar. Data Map has its own toolbar and set of Help topics. If Data Map is not available, you will need to run Setup again and use the Custom installation to install it.

Creating Charts on a Worksheet

To create a chart on a worksheet, you select the data that you want to use in the chart, and then use the ChartWizard. The type of chart you can create depends on the data you select. Your selection might include only one *data series* (either a single row or a single column of data) or several series (multiple rows or columns). Pie charts, for example, are limited to one data series. This means that no matter how many rows and columns you select, a pie chart can only display the first row or column of data. In the following illustration, a pie chart can display one of the selected series, either Gross Revenue, Gross Profit, or Expenses, but not all three.

	Qtr 1	Qtr 2	Qtr 3	Qtr 4	1996 Totals	
Gross Revenue	99122	100609	102118	103650	424491	—Single data series
Cost of Goods Sold	58471	58997	59528	60064	243617	
Gross Profit	40651	41612	42590	43586	180874	
Expenses	33398	33196	33231	33266	133762	—Multiple data series
Operating Income	7253	8416	9359	10320	47113	

A column chart, however, can show all three selected data series, as can an area chart or a bar chart. Most chart types can display several data series, as long as the data are all of the same type, as in the previous example. All of the selected series are currency, and they are divided into the same categories. Similar data series are easier to compare to one another.

 NOTE You can also create charts with dissimilar data series. You'll learn about charts made from different types of data in the One Step Further exercise at the end of this lesson.

After you select the data that you want to chart, you need to specify a location for the chart. You can select an area as large or as small as you like. You can always change your mind and resize your chart later, as you will learn in Lesson 5, "Modifying Your Charts."

In the next exercise, you'll select data to use in a column chart, and then select an area on the worksheet where the chart will appear.

Select the data and range for a chart

ChartWizard

ChartWizard pointer

1 Switch to the sheet named Summary and select C7:G11.

2 On the Standard toolbar, click the ChartWizard button.

The pointer changes to a crosshair with a small chart symbol. You use this pointer to draw a rectangular frame on your sheet where the chart will be created.

3 Drag the crosshair over cells C14:I30 to draw a frame.

Now that you have drawn a frame for your chart, the ChartWizard appears, and displays the cell references for the range that contains your chart data. The chart frame you drew will temporarily disappear.

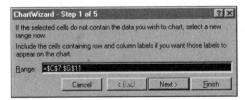

Selecting a Chart Type

Microsoft Excel's ChartWizard includes several chart types. Within each of these types or categories of charts, you can choose a variation of the basic chart type that might include gridlines, labels, or different marker variations.

Depending on the chart type that you choose, you can get different views of your data. Bar and column charts compare series of data, such as sales figures for different regions or for different years. Bar charts are better for comparisons between items, while column charts are better for showing changes over time. Pie charts show the relationship of parts

79

to a whole. Area and line charts are best for showing the amount of change in values over time. As you use different types of charts, you will get to know which chart types best suit your data. In the next exercise, you'll create a column chart.

Select a chart type and variation

1   In the ChartWizard, click the Next button.

Step 2 of the ChartWizard appears, displaying the chart types that you can choose from.

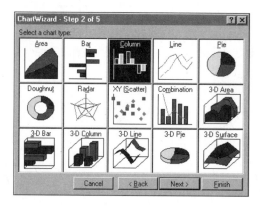

2   Be sure that the Column chart type in the first row is selected, and then click the Next button.

Step 3 of the ChartWizard appears, showing you the different variations of Column charts that you can choose from.

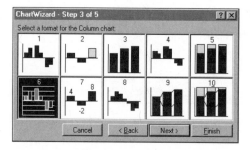

3   Be sure that the sixth format is selected, and then click the Next button.

Step 4 of the ChartWizard appears.

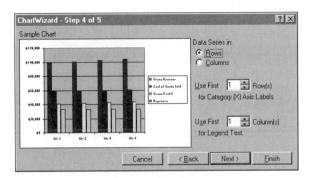

4   Under Data Series In, be sure that Rows is selected.

In a bar chart, the vertical axis is the X, or category, axis.

When you create a chart with the ChartWizard, your data is automatically classified into data series and categories. For this particular column chart, each row of data (Expenses, Gross Profit, and so on) becomes a data series, and the column labels (Qtr 1, Qtr 2, and so on) become categories. Categories are the labels that appear along the x-axis (the horizontal axis) in a column chart. Markers or columns of the same color on the chart represent a data series. If you want data in worksheet columns to become the data series and the row labels to become categories, you can specify this in the ChartWizard by selecting Data Series In Columns. The easiest way to decide which Data Series In option you want is to look at the Sample Chart in the ChartWizard dialog box while you select different options.

You can add labels, axis titles, and a chart title to further clarify your chart data. The first column and first row of data are usually assigned as the legend text and category axis labels. You can change this if you have more than one level of headings or a row or column that contains neither data nor labels. If you're not sure what to choose, look at the Sample Chart in the ChartWizard dialog while you select different options. You can choose whether to display a legend or add a chart title. For all but pie and doughnut charts, you can also use step 4 to add category and value axis titles to further explain your categories or values.

In the next exercise, you'll add labels and a chart title to your column chart.

Add a chart title and axis titles to your chart

1   Click the Next button.

Step 5 of the ChartWizard appears. The sample chart shows what the chart looks like so far.

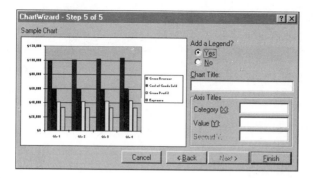

2 Click in the Chart Title text box, and type **Budget Summary Data**

3 In the Axis Titles area, click in the Category [X] box, and type **1996**

4 Click the Finish button.

The ChartWizard closes, and your completed chart appears on the worksheet.

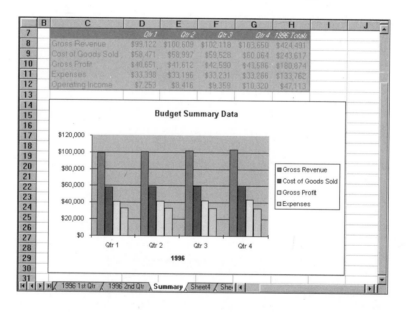

NOTE Another way to create a chart on the same sheet as your data (an embedded chart) is to point to Chart on the Insert menu and then click On This Sheet. Either way, you draw a frame on the worksheet for the chart, and then ChartWizard will start.

Creating Charts on a Chart Sheet

You've seen how you can use the ChartWizard to create an embedded chart directly on a worksheet. For reports, you probably want to keep the data and the chart together on a worksheet. But what if you are working on a presentation, with several charts that will eventually be on separate slides that you intend to print? You can create a new chart on a separate chart sheet. The As New Sheet command creates a new chart sheet to hold your chart and then starts the ChartWizard.

In the next exercise, you'll use the Chart and As New Sheet commands on the Insert menu. You'll create a pie chart to display your Cost of Goods Sold Total data for the first quarter of 1996.

Create a pie chart on a chart sheet

1   Switch to the 1996 1st Qtr sheet, and then select C9:D13.

The row labels and the June data are selected.

2   On the Insert menu, point to Chart and then click As New Sheet.

Step 1 of the ChartWizard appears and displays the range that contains your chart data.

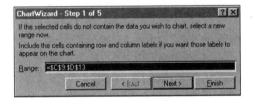

3   In the ChartWizard, click the Next button.

Step 2 of the ChartWizard appears and lists the chart types from which you can choose.

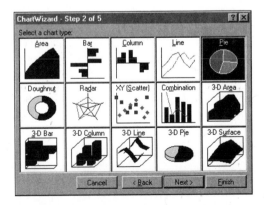

4 Under Select A Chart Type, select the Pie chart type in the top row, and then click the Next button.

Step 3 of the ChartWizard appears and shows the different variations of Pie charts to choose from.

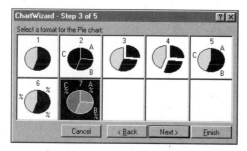

5 Be sure the seventh variation is selected, and then click the Next button.

Step 4 of the ChartWizard appears. A sample chart appears with some options you can use to alter your data series labels.

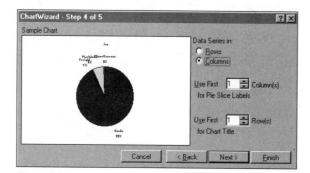

6 Be sure that the Data Series In selection is Columns and that the remaining settings are Use First **1** Column(s) For Pie Slice Labels and Use First **1** Row(s) for Chart Title. Then click the Next button.

Step 5 of the ChartWizard appears.

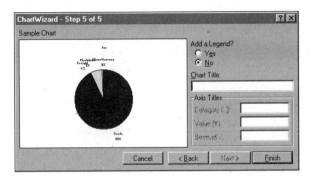

7 Under Add A Legend, be sure that No is selected.

Because the pie slices are labeled, a legend is unnecessary.

If labels in the finished chart overlap, click twice (not double-click) on a label to select it. You can then drag the label to a new position.

8 In the Chart Title text box, type **Cost of Goods Sold June 1996** and then click the Finish button.

Your chart should look similar to the following.

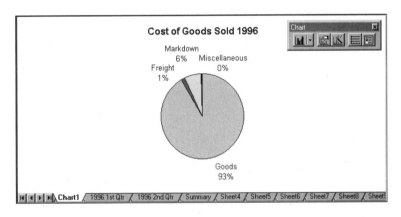

Modifying Chart Data

If you find that your chart includes too much, too little, or the wrong information, you can delete, add, or change the data. You can delete a series from the chart, add a row of data, or switch the order of the data series in your chart.

Before you can make any changes to an embedded chart, you need to *activate* the chart by double-clicking it. An activated chart is surrounded by a border, and the menu bar changes to display some menus and commands that are specifically for charts, as you will see in Lesson 5, "Modifying Your Charts." A chart sheet is automatically activated and ready for changes when you select it.

To delete a data series, select the series and press DEL. To add a data series to an embedded chart, you can simply select and drag the data onto the chart. To add a data series to a chart on a chart sheet, you use the New Data command on the Insert menu. To change the data range used in a chart, you can click ChartWizard button, then drag to select a new range while the step 1 dialog box is open, and then click Finish. To move a series to a new location in a chart, you can use the Group command on the Format menu.

In the next exercises, you'll delete a data series from your summary chart, add a new series to the chart, and then change the order of the data series for a more logical presentation.

Deleting Data

You can delete a data series directly from a chart, without affecting the worksheet data.

Activate the chart and delete a data series

1 Switch to the Summary sheet, and then double-click the column chart.

Double-clicking the chart activates it. The chart is usually surrounded by a border, or it opens in its own window and chart commands are available on the menu bar. The Chart toolbar is probably visible as well.

If you have closed the Chart toolbar in this workbook, you can display it again by clicking Chart on the toolbar shortcut menu. The Chart toolbar will once again appear whenever you activate a chart.

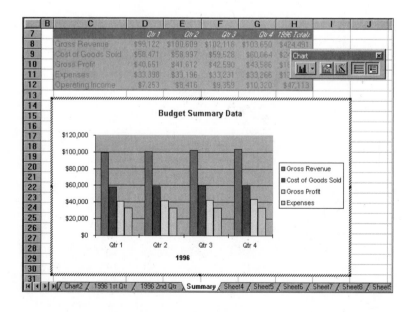

2 On the chart, click one of the column markers that represents Expenses.

Clicking one marker in a series selects the entire series. The Expenses series of data is selected.

 NOTE If you click a series and then click one marker in the series, that single marker is selected, instead of the entire series.

If you delete a chart element and then change your mind, click the Undo button on the Standard toolbar to undo the deletion.

3 Press DEL.

The entire Expenses series is deleted from your chart. Your chart should look similar to the following.

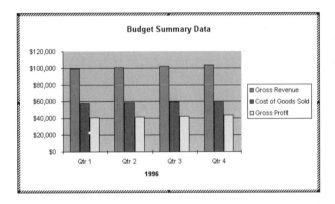

Adding Data

If you are adding data to an embedded chart, you can either drag the data to the chart or use the New Data command on the Insert menu. If you drag data to an embedded chart, you do not need to activate the chart first. If you add data to an embedded chart by using the New Data command on the Insert menu, you must activate the chart first. When you are adding data to a chart sheet, you use the New Data command on the Insert menu.

In the next exercises, you'll use both the drag and menu methods to add new data to your chart.

Add new chart data with the mouse

1 On the Summary sheet, select the range C12:G12.

This is the Operating Income data from your summary table. You will drag this data onto your chart.

To drag data in Microsoft Excel, select the range, click over the border of the range, and then drag the data to the destination.

2 Drag the data onto the chart, and release the mouse button.

The chart is updated to show the new data. Your chart should look similar to the following.

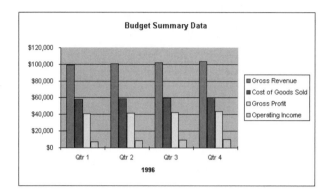

Add new chart data with the menus and the mouse

1 Double-click the chart to activate it.

2 On the Insert menu, click New Data.

The New Data dialog box appears, ready for you to enter the range where the new data is stored.

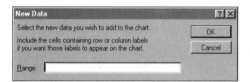

3 In the Summary sheet, click outside the chart, and then drag to select C11:G11.

You might need to drag the New Data dialog box out of the way first. Cells C11:G11 contain the Expenses data that you deleted in the previous exercise.

4 In the New Data dialog box, click OK.

The dialog box closes, and the chart is updated. Your chart should look similar to the following.

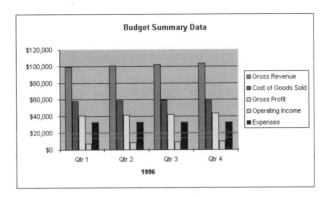

Rearranging Chart Data

If you want to emphasize the differences or similarities between data series, or show a logical progression of categories, you might want to rearrange the series in your chart. For example, if you want to contrast low and high values, you can rearrange the data so that the low and high values are next to each other. If you want to minimize the differences between values, you can rearrange the data so that it develops progressively from low to high or from high to low. You can easily rearrange the data in your chart without rearranging your worksheet data.

Change the order of data in a chart

In this exercise, you change the order of your data series to emphasize the differences between Gross Revenue and the other categories.

1 Be sure that the chart is still active and, on the Format menu, click 1 Column Group.

The Format Column Group dialog box appears, ready for you to make changes to the chart.

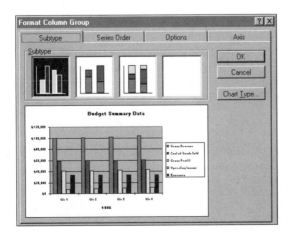

2   Click the Series Order tab.

The dialog box displays the Series Order options and a preview of the chart.

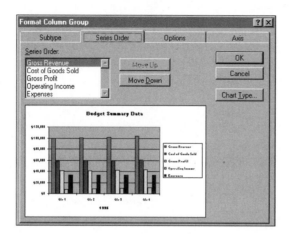

3   In the Series Order list, select Operating Income, and then click the Move Up button twice.

The Operating Income series now appears to the right of Gross Revenue in your chart.

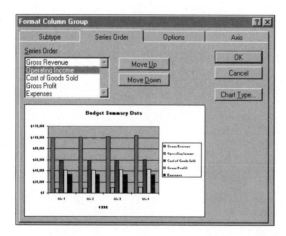

4   In the Series Order list, select Expenses, and then click the Move Up button twice.

The Expenses series moves up in the Series Order list. It now appears to the right of Operating Income in your chart.

5 In the Series Order list, select Cost of Goods Sold, and then click the Move Down button once.

The Cost of Goods Sold series moves to the bottom of the Series Order list. It will now appear at the right end of each category.

6 Click OK.

The dialog box closes, and your chart is updated with your changes. Your chart should look similar to the following.

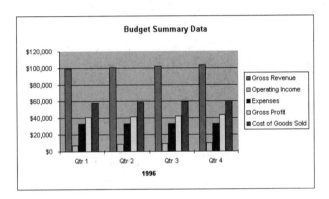

One Step Further: Combination Charts

You used column charts and pie charts throughout this lesson. Most of the other chart types work similarly to these two, with one or more series of the same type of data. When you need to chart data that is dissimilar or needs to be visually separated for better under-standing, you can create combination charts that combine, for example, column and line markers, or column and area markers. You can track two streams of data (with one or more series each) by creating a combination chart with different chart types for different series. You can also use a second value axis to display data of different magnitudes (for example, tens and thousands).

Try creating a chart with different chart types for different series to display your Gross Revenue data for second quarter 1996.

Create a combination chart

1 Switch to the sheet named 1996 2nd Qtr, and then select C9:F12.

2 On the Insert menu, point to Chart, and then click As New Sheet.

Step 1 of the ChartWizard appears.

3 In the ChartWizard, click the Next button.

Step 2 of the ChartWizard appears and displays the possible chart types.

91

4 Select the Combination chart, and then click the Next button.

Step 3 of the ChartWizard appears and displays the possible chart variations.

5 Select format #1, and then click the Next button.

Format #1 is a combination column/line chart with a single y-axis (value axis). Step 4 of the ChartWizard appears and displays the sample chart and some options about your data and data labels.

6 Be sure the Data Series In Rows option is selected, and Use First **1** Column(s) For Pie Slice Labels and Use First **1** Row(s) for Chart Title are set.

7 Click the Finish button.

The ChartWizard closes, and your completed chart appears on the new chart sheet. Your chart should look similar to the following.

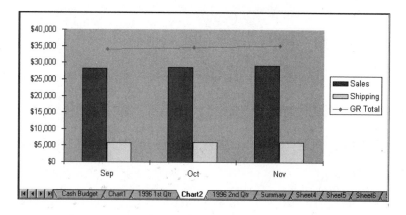

The Total data is displayed as a line series and is visually differentiated from Sales and Shipping values, which are displayed as column series. All three series values are displayed on the same y, or value, axis on the left side of the chart.

If You Want to Continue to the Next Lesson

1 On the File menu, click Save

2 On the File menu, click Close.

If You Want to Quit Microsoft Excel for Now

➤ On the File menu, click Exit.

If you see the Save dialog box, click Yes.

Lesson Summary

To	Do this	Button
Create a chart on a worksheet	Select the data that you want to chart, and then click the ChartWizard button on the toolbar. Draw a chart frame on the worksheet, and click Next. Select a chart type, and click Next. Select a chart variation, and click Next. Add a chart title and axis titles as needed, and click Finish.	
Create a chart on a chart sheet	Select a data range. On the Insert menu, point to Chart, and then click As New Sheet. Click Next. Select a chart type, and click Next. Select a chart variation, and then click Next. Add a chart title and axis titles as needed, and click Finish.	
Activate an embedded chart	Double-click the chart. (Chart sheets do not need to be activated.)	
Delete a data series	Activate the chart or select the chart sheet, then select the data series, and press DEL.	
Add data to an embedded chart on a worksheet	Select the data, drag it onto the chart, and release the mouse button.	
Add data to a chart on a chart sheet	Select the chart sheet. On the Insert menu, click New Data. Select the data range, and click OK.	
Rearrange chart data	Activate the embedded chart, or select the chart sheet. On the Format menu, click the Group command for the chart type. In the Group dialog box, click the Series Order tab. In the Series Order list, select the series that you want to move, and then click the Move Up or Move Down button. Click OK.	

For online information about	Use the Answer Wizard to search for
Creating a chart	**create a chart**
Modifying chart data	**add data to a chart**

Preview of the Next Lesson

In the next lesson, "Modifying Your Charts," you'll learn more about customizing your charts to emphasize data. You'll learn how to add lines and change colors, how to use chart AutoFormats, and how to create your own custom chart AutoFormat.

Modifying Your Charts

Estimated time

40 min.

In this lesson you will learn how to:

- Change the chart type of an existing chart.
- Add clarity and impact with arrows, color, and text.
- Skip repetitive formatting steps by using automatic formatting.

When you chart your data, you might not always end up with exactly what you envisioned when you began. Perhaps you decide that a pie chart would work better than a bar chart or that a 3-D chart would present your data with more impact. Maybe the values aren't as visible as you'd like them to be or you can't quite see the relationships between a series and the value labels.

Microsoft Excel's charting features are flexible so that you can change your chart to match your ideas. In this lesson, you'll learn how to modify your chart, switch chart types, add lines, color, and text, and use chart AutoFormats to streamline the process of creating a set of standardized charts. You'll also learn how to create your own custom chart AutoFormats so that you can apply all of your formatting choices automatically.

Start the lesson

Follow the steps in the next exercise to open the practice file called 05Lesson, and then save it with the new name Lesson05.

Open

To select the folder containing your practice files, refer to "Open a practice file" near the start of Lesson 1.

1 On the Standard toolbar, click the Open button.

2 In the Look In box, be sure that the Excel SBS Practice folder appears.

3 In the file list box, double-click the file named 05Lesson to open it.

4 On the File menu, click Save As.

The Save As dialog box opens. Be sure the Excel SBS Practice folder appears in the Save In box.

5 Double-click in the File Name box, and then type **Lesson05**

6 Click the Save button, or press ENTER.

If you share your computer with others who use Microsoft Excel, the screen display might have changed since your last lesson. If your screen does not look similar to the illustrations as you work through this lesson, see the Appendix, "Matching the Exercises."

Changing Chart Types

You might decide that a chart you already created would be better if it were a different chart type. Perhaps a column chart would look better in 3-D or you want to change the chart type for one series. The quickest way to change from one chart type to another is to use the Chart Type button on the Chart toolbar. When you select a chart type from the Chart Type button palette, your chart is automatically updated with the new chart type. You can also change the chart type easily by using the Chart Type command on the shortcut menu.

When you change chart types, depending on the chart type that you choose, the resulting chart could appear very different from your original. If you change to a similar chart type, (for example, from a column chart to a 3-D column chart) you will see little difference. But if you change to a dissimilar chart type, for example from a column chart to a pie chart, you will notice a lot of difference. If you don't like a chart type change you've made, you can instantly switch back to the original chart type by using the Undo Chart Type command on the Edit menu.

The following illustrations show the same budget summary data as a bar chart and a 3-D column chart.

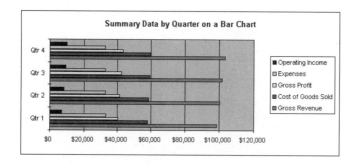

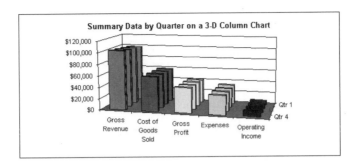

The bar chart and the column chart show the comparisons between quarters clearly, although the 3-D column chart has a bit more visual impact. Bar charts and column charts are quite similar, and switching between the two does not often change the presentation very much.

In the following illustration, you can see what happens if you show the same summary data as a pie chart.

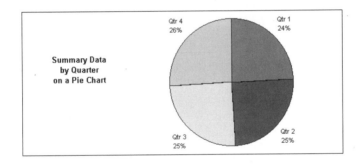

The pie chart type is not suited to the data you want to show, which consists of more than a single data series. The pie chart only displays the first series in the selected worksheet range, either Gross Revenue or Qtr 1 depending on whether you select the Rows or Columns option for Data Series In. However, the pie chart is an excellent choice for illustrating income and expenses for an individual quarter, as you can see in the following illustration.

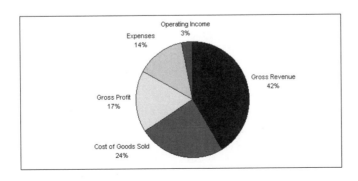

After you work with charts a little and experiment with different chart types, you might decide that the column chart that you created for the summary data in the previous lesson would have more impact on your audience in 3-D column format. You can change your summary chart from a simple column to a 3-D column chart with stacked columns to emphasize the total values, rather than the differences between items in a series. The following illustration shows how your chart will look after you have completed the next few exercises.

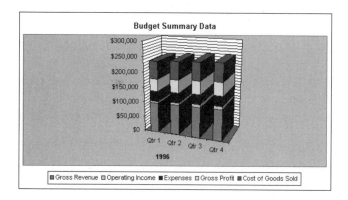

Change a column chart to a 3-D column chart

In this exercise, you change your chart to a 3-D column chart.

1 Switch to the Summary sheet, and double-click the Budget Summary Data column chart.

The column chart is activated.

2 Use the right mouse button to click an open area, and then on the chart shortcut menu, click Chart Type.

The Chart Type dialog box opens.

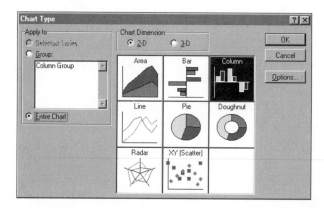

3 In the Chart Dimension area, select 3-D.

4 Be sure the 3-D Column chart type is selected, and click OK.

If the axis labels are missing or hard to read, make the chart larger by dragging a chart corner.

Your chart changes from a 2-D column chart to a 3-D column chart. The formatting options that you chose earlier, such as the legend and the legend text, remain in effect. Your chart should look similar to the following.

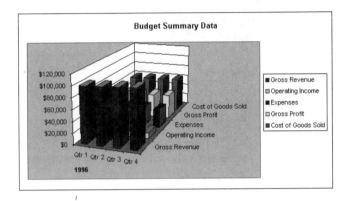

Remove the legend and make the plot area larger

A legend is redundant on a 3-D column chart, because the Z axis is labeled with the same information. To remove the legend, you can click on the legend and press DEL. Then you can select the plot area and drag to make it larger.

1 Click on the legend, and then press DEL.

The legend is removed from your chart.

2 Click in an empty space near the chart walls.

The plot area is selected. When the plot area is selected, you'll see the name Plot in the Name box on the formula bar.

3 Drag the side handles on the plot border until the plot fills the empty space in the chart.

Your chart should look similar to the following.

99

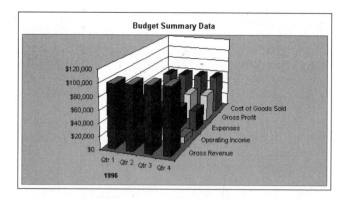

 NOTE If you cannot see all of the category and data labels, you can either make the chart larger or format the axis font smaller. To format the axis font smaller, use the right mouse button to click on the axis and then click Format Axis on the shortcut menu. Click the Font tab, then select a smaller font size, and click OK.

When you change between dissimilar chart types, you might not see all of your data, or you might find that your data does not appear the way you expected. You can change the type of chart with the Chart Type command on the Format or shortcut menus. If you need to change the order of your data series, as you did in Lesson 4, you can use the Group command at the bottom of the Format or shortcut menus. The Group command changes according to the type of chart you are using. For example, for the Summary column chart, the command would be called the Column Group command. For the 3-D version of the Summary column chart, the command would be called the 3-D Column Group command.

Change chart subtypes

In this exercise, you change the Summary chart to a stacked 3-D column chart.

1   With the 3-D column chart activated, on the Format menu, click one 3-D Column Group.

The Format 3-D Column Group dialog box opens.

2   Click the Subtype tab, if it is not already selected.

The chart subtype options appear in the dialog box.

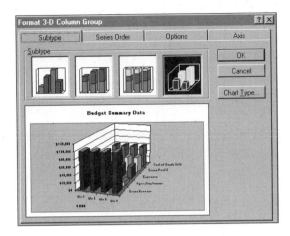

3 Click the second chart subtype, and then click OK.

The dialog box closes, and your chart is updated with your changes. The chart needs a legend again.

Legend

4 On the Chart toolbar, click the Legend button.

The legend reappears in your chart.

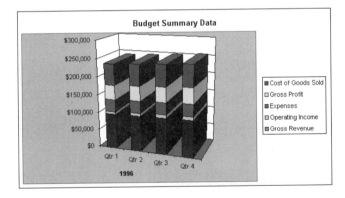

Formatting Gridlines and Legends

Some chart formats include gridlines and legends, and some do not. If you like a format that doesn't normally have gridlines or a legend, but you want these features, you can easily add them. When you add gridlines to your chart, your data values are easier to estimate. Legends help explain your data and make the chart more readable. You can also delete gridlines or a legend from a chart if you don't want them.

You can add or delete gridlines by using the Gridlines command on the Insert menu or the Gridlines button on the Chart toolbar. You can delete or add a legend by using the Legend command on the Insert menu or the Legend button on the Chart toolbar.

Add gridlines and move the legend

In this exercise, you add more gridlines to your chart, and then move the legend to the bottom of the chart.

You can also move and re-size the legend by dragging it with the mouse.

1 On the Insert menu, click Gridlines.

The Gridlines dialog box opens.

2 In the Value [Z] Axis area, be sure that Major Gridlines is selected, and then select Minor Gridlines.

3 Click OK.

The dialog box closes, and major and minor horizontal gridlines appear on your chart. Your chart should look like the following.

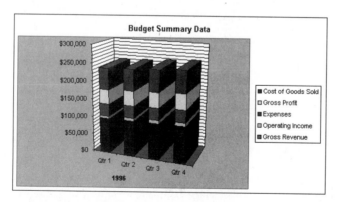

4 On the chart, double-click an empty space in the legend.

The Format Legend dialog box opens.

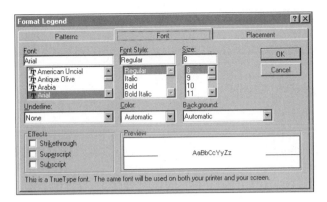

5 In the dialog box, click the Placement tab.

You can also move the legend by dragging it with the mouse.

6 In the Type box, select Bottom, and then click OK.

The dialog box closes, and the legend is moved and reshaped to fit along the bottom of the chart. Your chart should look like the following. (You can resize the plot area again if you want to center the chart.)

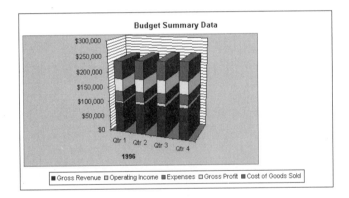

Enhancing Charts

If you want to emphasize a particular data point or create a unique look for a chart, you can add elements, such as lines, arrows, and different colors to your charts. You can emphasize a specific data marker with a line or an arrow, or change the color for an entire series or a single data marker. You can also add text boxes, or change the fonts and other attributes used in your chart text.

Suppose you want to point out the progress in the Cost of Goods Sold value with a *trendline*. Trendlines illustrate mathematical trends in your data. You can also add extra information about a specific value in your chart by pointing to it with an arrow and labeling it with a text box. After you get these elements in place, you can refine them by formatting the text box label or adjusting the lines and the colors in your data series until your chart looks similar to the following.

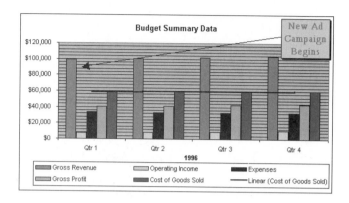

Showing Trends

In some chart types, you need to clearly emphasize relationships between points in a particular data series. For example, if you need to forecast sales for the next six months based on sales for the previous 18 months, you can add a trendline to one data series that will clearly show the trend in sales and the forecast for the next six months. Or you might want to use a trendline to smooth out the fluctuations in a stock's daily prices so that you can make better decisions based on the stock's performance. Trendlines are most often used to display trends in scientific data, such as the linear correlation between two variables, or the half-life of a radioactive compound and its value at a future time.

You can add trendlines to bar, column, area, line, and xy (scatter) charts. You cannot add trendlines to pie, doughnut, 3-D, or radar charts. Trendlines are only calculated for a specific series, not the entire chart, so you need to select the series before you can add a trendline. If you remove a series with a trendline, or change the series to a pie, doughnut, 3-D, or radar chart type, the trendline is deleted.

For more infor-
mation about
trendline types,
click the Answer
Wizard on the
Help menu,
and search for
"trendline."

You can choose from several types of trendlines, depending on the mathematical relationship of the data points in the series. For example, if you were smoothing out the fluctuations in a stock price over a period of time, you would use either a linear trendline or a moving average. If you were showing half-life data for a radioactive compound, you would use an exponential trendline.

Since your column chart is currently in 3-D, you'll need to change it back to a 2-D column chart before you can add a trendline. In the next exercises, you'll change your summary column chart back to a 2-D column chart so that you can add a trendline to it. Then, you'll add a linear trendline to the Cost of Goods Sold series.

Change your chart back to a 2-D column chart

1   Double-click the column chart to activate it, if it is not already activated.

2   On the Format menu, click Chart Type.

    The Chart Type dialog box opens.

3   In the Chart Dimension box, select 2-D.

4 Be sure the Column chart is selected, and then click OK.

Your chart changes back to a 2-D column chart. The chart is no longer stacked, and it looks similar to your original chart but with the additional gridlines.

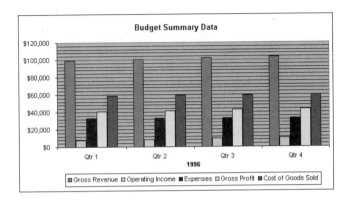

Calculate and display a trend in your chart data

1 Click a marker in the Cost of Goods Sold series once.

The Cost of Goods Sold data series is selected.

2 On the Insert menu, click Trendline.

The Trendline dialog box opens.

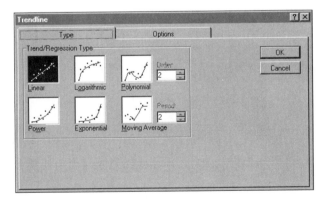

If you need to display the trendline regression equation or R-squared value on your chart, you can select them on the Options tab in the Format Trendline dialog box.

3 Click the Type tab if it is not already selected.

The Trendline dialog box shows the various types of trendlines that you can choose from.

4 Be sure that the Linear type is selected, and then click OK.

The dialog box closes, and a linear trendline is added to the Cost of Goods Sold series. Your chart should look like the following.

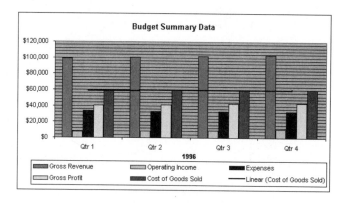

Pointing to Specific Data

If you are creating a presentation or a report and you need to emphasize or point out some specific data, you can add an arrow or a line by using the Drawing button on the Standard toolbar. Once you've placed the line where you want it, you can change the arrow type, if you like.

 NOTE When you draw an arrow, be sure that you draw from the tail to the head of the arrow. For example, if you draw an arrow to an object at the bottom of the chart, you would begin drawing the arrow at either the upper-right or upper-left corner of the chart and stop drawing when you reach the object. The arrow will automatically point to the place where you stopped drawing.

Point to a specific value

In this exercise, you create an arrow to point to a specific value on your chart.

1 Activate the 2-D Column chart on your sheet if it is not already activated.

2 On the Standard toolbar, click the Drawing button to display the Drawing toolbar.

Drawing

3 On the Drawing toolbar, click the Arrow button.

Your pointer changes to a cross hair, ready for you to draw an arrow.

Arrow

4 Click near the upper-right corner of the chart, drag to the Gross Revenue marker in the Qtr 1 category and release.

An arrow appears on your chart, pointing to the marker. Your chart should look like the following.

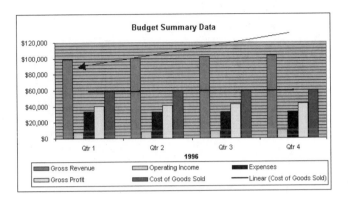

Explaining Your Chart with Text Boxes

Now that you have added an arrow, you want other people to understand to what the arrow points. You can draw a text box directly on the chart itself to explain or label any part of your chart and then resize the box as desired.

Add a text box to explain the data

In this exercise, you add an explanatory text box to your chart.

Text Box

1 On the Drawing toolbar, click the Text Box button.

Your pointer changes to a crosshair, ready for you to add a text box.

2 Drag the pointer diagonally to draw a small rectangle, about 1-inch wide by 0.5-inch tall, near the beginning of your arrow.

A text box is added to your chart. If you cannot see the text box, it will become visible when you begin to type. If your text box is not exactly in the right place, you can move it later by dragging it to the correct location.

3 Type **New Ad Campaign Begins**

4 Click outside the text box.

If you can't see the text box or all of your text, don't be concerned. You will resize the text box and make it opaque later in this lesson. Your text box should look similar to the following.

If the Drawing toolbar is docked and has no Close button, click any toolbar with the right mouse button and then click Drawing on the shortcut menu.

107

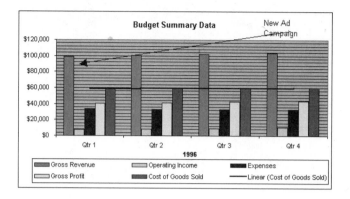

5 Click the Close button on the Drawing toolbar to close it.

Resize a text box

In this exercise, you resize the text box for optimum display.

1 Click the text box once to select it.

2 Move your pointer to the handle on the lower-right corner of the text box.

3 Drag the handle to resize the box until you can see all of your text and a little extra white space in the box.

Changing Your Text and Text Box Formats

If you don't like the font, color, alignment, or other attributes of the text in your chart or your text boxes, you can change them. You can format the text just as you would format any other text in a worksheet, by selecting it and using the appropriate toolbar buttons or the Format Object command. Suppose you want to use different fonts and colors in your New Ad Campaign Begins label.

Change fonts and colors of a text box

In this exercise, you change the text font to MS Serif bold 12-point and the text color to dark blue.

1 Use the right mouse button to click the text box.

The shortcut menu appears.

2 On the shortcut menu, click Format Object.

The Format Object dialog box appears.

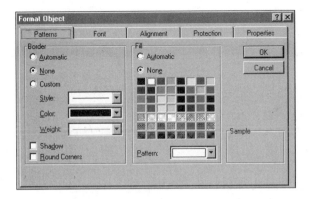

3 Click the Font tab if it is not already selected, and then in the Font list, select MS Serif.

4 In the Font Style list, select Bold.

5 In the Size list, select 12.

6 Click the down arrow next to the Color list to open the list of colors, and then select the dark blue color.

7 Click OK.

The text in your text box changes to MS Serif, bold, 12 point, dark blue. You may need to resize the text box again.

8 Click on the worksheet to view the changes.

Change colors and alignment in a text box

In this exercise, you change the background color to light gray and center the text.

1 Double-click the chart to activate it.

2 Use the right mouse button to click the text box containing "New Ad Campaign Begins."

The shortcut menu opens.

3 On the shortcut menu, click Format Object.

The Format Object dialog box opens.

4 In the dialog box, click the Patterns tab.

The Fill Color, Border, and Patterns options appear in the dialog box.

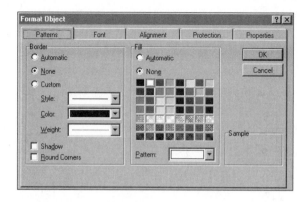

5 In the Fill area, select the lightest gray square.

6 In the Border area, select the Shadow option.

7 Click the Alignment tab.

8 In the Text Alignment area, select Center for both Horizontal and Vertical.

9 Click OK, and then click in the worksheet.

Your text box should look like the following.

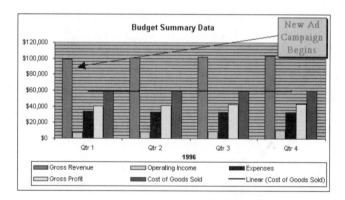

Emphasizing Data with Colors

If you don't like the colors that are used in your chart, or if you want consistency with another color scheme used in your presentation or report, you can easily change the colors. You can change the color of any object in your chart: gridlines, legend background or text, borders, data series, lines, or even text, as you saw earlier in this lesson. To change a color, select the object, and then use either the Color button on the Formatting toolbar or the Format Object command on the shortcut menu.

NOTE   The Format Object command is like the Group command—it changes depending on what you have selected. If you want to change the color of a text box or an arrow, the command is called Format Object. If you want to change the color of a data series or your gridlines, however, the commands are called Format Data Series and Format Gridlines, respectively.

Change the color of a data series

In this exercise, you change the Gross Profit data series to green.

1   Double-click the column chart if it is not activated.

2   Click on any marker in the Gross Profit data series.

3   On the Format menu, click Selected Data Series.

The Format Data Series dialog box opens.

4   Select a green square in the color area, click the Patterns tab, and then click OK.

The Gross Profit data series changes to green.

Formatting Charts Automatically

When you create a series of charts for a presentation or report, you want them to have a consistent look. Perhaps you have several charts showing similar data, such as yearly figures for different budget categories or growth figures for several offices. When you need to create several similar charts, you can use a chart AutoFormat, either built-in or one that you have custom designed.

You can use the AutoFormat command on the Format menu to create a standardized, customized chart. You can apply this custom chart format to several charts so that your series looks consistent, with the differences in the actual values emphasized by the similarities in the charts. For example, suppose you want to display a pie chart in 3-D with special focus on a single slice of the pie.

 IMPORTANT   When you apply an AutoFormat to a chart, you lose any formatting changes that you've already made.

Format a chart automatically and separate a pie slice

In this exercise, you change your pie chart to a 3-D pie chart by using an AutoFormat and then separate a single slice from the pie for emphasis.

1 Select the sheet Chart1.

This sheet contains the pie chart you created in Lesson 4.

2 With the mouse pointer over the chart, press the right mouse button.

The chart shortcut menu opens.

3 On the shortcut menu, click AutoFormat.

The AutoFormat dialog box opens.

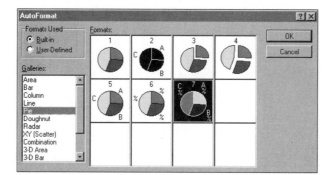

4 In the Galleries list, select 3-D Pie.

You might have to scroll through the list to find the 3-D Pie.

5 Under Formats, be sure that the number 7 chart subtype is selected.

6 Click OK.

Your chart changes to a 3-D Pie chart. You might have to select overlapping labels and drag them apart.

7 Click twice (not a double-click) on the Markdown slice to select it.

The first click selects the data series; the second click selects the Markdown slice.

8 Drag the slice away from the center of the pie.

The slice separates from the pie. You can rejoin the slice to the pie by dragging the slice back into the center of the pie. Your chart should look like the following.

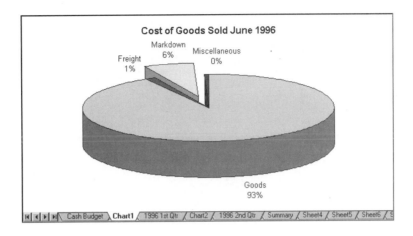

Creating Your Own Custom Chart Format

If your company or department already has a standard look for charts, or if you prefer a chart format other than those available through the AutoFormat command, you can create your own custom AutoFormat. To create a custom chart AutoFormat, you use the AutoFormat command on the Format menu. You can make changes to your sample chart and edit the AutoFormat as well, or you can delete an old AutoFormat that you no longer need.

Create a custom chart format

In this exercise, you use your 3-D column chart to create a custom AutoFormat that you can store permanently and reuse at any time with any data.

1   Switch to the Summary sheet and activate the column chart.

2   Click the text box and press DEL, click the title and press DEL, click the arrow and press DEL, and then click the trendline and press DEL.

   To save you time, only those formats and features that you will always want to apply should be included in the AutoFormat.

3   Use the Color palette from the Formatting toolbar to customize the colors of the data markers, plot area, legend, or other chart elements.

   This chart has been recolored, and a shadow was added to the legend text box by using the Format Legend dialog box.

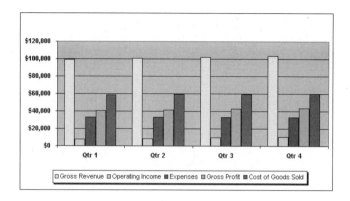

4 Use the right mouse button to click an open area.

5 On the shortcut menu, click AutoFormat.

The AutoFormat dialog box opens.

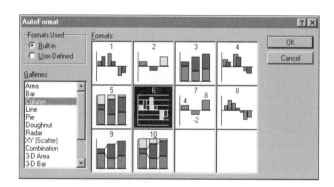

6 In the Formats Used area, select User-Defined.

The AutoFormat dialog box changes to show the Microsoft Excel 4.0 chart format and any custom AutoFormats you have already created.

7 Click the Customize button.

The User-Defined AutoFormats dialog box opens.

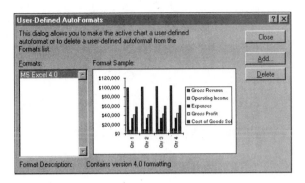

8   Click the Add button.

The Add Custom AutoFormat dialog box opens.

9   In the Format Name box, type **Budget Summary**

10   In the Description box, type **Use for quarterly report** and then click OK.

Your format is added to the gallery of user-defined formats.

11   In the User-Defined AutoFormats dialog box, click Close.

The User-Defined AutoFormats dialog box closes. Now you can apply this AutoFormat to any chart by choosing the AutoFormat command, selecting User-Defined, and then selecting the AutoFormat name from the list.

Apply a custom chart format

In this exercise, you apply your custom AutoFormat to the Chart2 chart sheet.

1   Select the Chart2 sheet.

This is the column chart you created in Lesson 4.

2   Use the right mouse button to click the chart, and then click AutoFormat on the shortcut menu.

3 Select the User Defined option.

The AutoFormat dialog box changes to show the Microsoft Excel 4.0 chart format and the Budget Summary custom AutoFormat.

4 Select the Budget Summary format, and then click OK.

The chart is formatted with all the formatting you set in your custom AutoFormat.

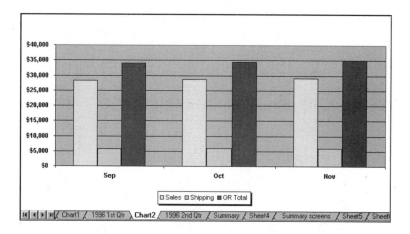

One Step Further: Changing 3-D Chart Perspective

You can modify most aspects of your charts by using the commands on the Format or shortcut menus. You've seen how to add gridlines, change chart types, and format your charts in other ways. If you are working with 3-D charts, you can change even more options than you can with 2-D charts. You can modify the 3-D view of your chart to change the perspective, elevation, or rotation of your chart. You can give your chart a sharper perspective or change the elevation to look down on the chart or up from beneath it. You can change the rotation so that the gridlines appear on one side or the other. You can even change the rotation so that you look at the back, rather than the front, of the chart.

Changing your perspective, elevation, or rotation can make 3-D markers easier to see and interpret and make the chart stand out in a presentation.

Change the perspective for a 3-D column chart

1 On the Summary sheet, select your column chart.

2 Change the chart type to 3-D column by clicking the 3-D Column Chart button on the Chart Type button palette.

The chart does not need to be activated to change chart type by using the Chart Type palette. The Chart Type palette is a drag-away floating palette, like the Color and Borders palettes.

3 Double-click the 3-D column chart to activate it.

4 Click the corner of the chart floor that is nearest the bottom of the chart.

The chart corners will be selected, and the name Corners will appear in the Name box in the formula bar. The pointer will be a crosshair when it is on any of the corners.

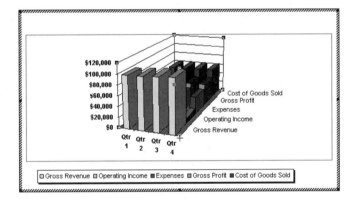

5 Drag the corner to the right.

The chart's perspective changes. You can drag more accurately if you press and hold down CTRL while you drag the corner.

 TIP If all the category labels do not appear, try deleting the legend, resizing the plot area, resizing the chart, making the axis font smaller, or adjusting the perspective by small amounts.

By using the mouse to rearrange the chart elements, you can make the chart look like the following illustration. If larger markers are hiding smaller markers, you can rearrange the series order by using the Format 3-D Column Group command on the shortcut menu.

117

*In this chart,
the legend was
deleted and
the plot border
was removed.*

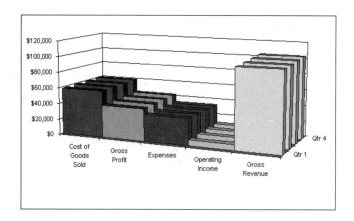

If You Want to Continue to the Next Lesson

1 Click the close button on the Drawing toolbar to close it, if it is open.

2 On the File menu, click Save.

3 On the File menu, click Close.

If You Want to Quit Microsoft Excel for Now

➤ On the File menu, click Exit.

If you see the Save dialog box, click Yes.

Lesson Summary

To	Do this	Button
Change chart types	Activate the chart, and press the right mouse button to display the shortcut menu. Click Chart Type. In the Chart Type dialog box, select the type you want and click OK.	
Add gridlines	Activate the chart. On the Insert menu, click Gridlines. Select the gridlines that you want, and then click OK. *or* Display the Chart toolbar. On the Chart toolbar, click the Gridlines button.	

To	Do this	Button
Add a legend	Activate the chart. On the Insert menu, click Legend. *or* Display the Chart toolbar. On the Chart toolbar, click the Legend button.	
Position a legend	Double-click the legend in the chart. In the Format Legend dialog box, make your selections and click OK. *or* Drag the legend using the mouse.	
Add a trendline	Click a marker in the series that you want to plot a trendline for. On the Insert menu, click Trendline. Select the trendline you want, and then click OK.	
Add an arrow	Activate the chart. Display the Drawing toolbar, and click the Arrow button. Drag toward the object to draw an arrow, and then release the mouse button.	
Add a text box	On the Drawing toolbar, click the Text Box button. Drag to create the text box, and then type your text.	
Change text formats	Select the text you want to change. On the shortcut or Format menu, click Format Object. Make your selections, and then click OK. *or* Select the text, and use the buttons on the Formatting toolbar to change the text formats.	
Change chart colors	Activate the chart, and select the object or series that you want to change. On the shortcut or Format menu, click Format Object or Format Data Series. Click the Patterns tab, and select the color you want. Click OK. *or* Activate the chart, and select the object or series that you want to change. Select a color from the Color button palette on the Formatting toolbar.	

To	Do this
Format a chart automatically	Activate the chart that you want to base your AutoFormat on. On the Format or shortcut menu, click AutoFormat. Select the chart type and format that you want, and then click OK.
Create a custom chart format	Activate the chart and, on the Format or shortcut menu, click AutoFormat. In the Formats Used area, select User-Defined. Click the Customize button, and then click Add. Type a name and a description, click OK, and then click Close.

For online information about	Use the Answer Wizard to search for
Changing chart types	**change chart type**
Enhancing charts	**draw on a chart**
Formatting charts automatically	**autoformat a chart**

Preview of the Next Lesson

In the next lesson, "Printing Worksheets and Charts," you'll preview your data before you print it. You'll learn about setting up your worksheets, reports, or presentations for printing, and you'll learn how to print chart sheets.

Printing Worksheets and Charts

Estimated time
35 min.

In this lesson you will learn how to:

- Preview your worksheets.
- Set up pages for printing.
- Print a chart sheet.

So far in this book, you've learned to enter data and create formulas, format text, and create charts. Now you want to present the data or charts to someone else. You want your report or presentation to print clearly, with page breaks in the right places. You also might want a header or a footer to show a date, a page number, or the name of the workbook. In this lesson, you'll learn how to set up your pages with print titles, margins, headers, and footers and how to preview the pages before you send them to the printer. You'll also learn how to print charts without cutting off any areas or without having them take up too much space.

Start the lesson

Follow the steps below to open the practice file called 06Lesson, and then save it with the new name Lesson06.

Open

1   On the Standard toolbar, click the Open button.
2   In the Look In box, be sure that the Excel SBS Practice folder appears.
3   In the file list box, double-click the file named 06Lesson to open it.

To select the folder containing your practice files, refer to "Open a practice file" near the start of Lesson 1.

4 On the File menu, click Save As to open the Save As dialog box.

Be sure that the Excel SBS Practice folder appears in the Save In box.

5 Double-click in the File Name box, and then type **Lesson06**

6 Click the Save button, or press ENTER.

If you share your computer with others who use Microsoft Excel, the screen display might have changed since your last lesson. If your screen does not look similar to the illustrations as you work through this lesson, see the Appendix, "Matching the Exercises."

Previewing Your Worksheet

You want your pages to print clearly, but you probably don't want to waste a lot of paper checking to see whether the necessary rows and columns appear on the sheet, whether the margins are set to the right size, or whether the data fits in the columns. Previewing your work shows you what you need to change before you print.

Preview the Cash Budget sheet

In this exercise, you preview your page layout, and then print the Cash Budget sheet.

1 Be sure that the Cash Budget is the active sheet.

2 On the toolbar, click the Print Preview button.

Print Preview

You can also use the Print Preview command on the File menu.

Your sheet appears in the Preview window. The Purpose statement does not fit on the sheet in the Preview window. You need to correct this before you print the worksheet. Your Budget sheet should look like the following.

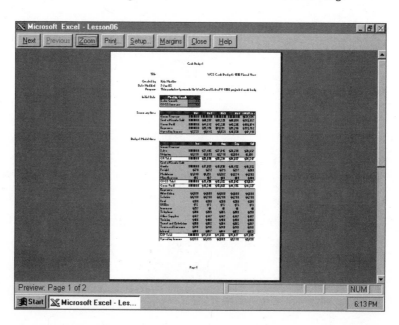

3   Move the pointer over the sheet.

The pointer changes to look like a small magnifying glass.

You can also use the Zoom button to zoom in and out in the preview window.

4   Click near the middle of the sheet.

The sheet zooms in, so you can see the budget data. Some of the cells in the budget might contain number signs rather than actual figures, indicating that you need to widen the columns before printing.

5   Click again to zoom out, and then click the Close button.

The Preview window closes.

Setting Up Pages

When you work with larger worksheets, your data may not fit on one page. In addition, you might want to add information at the top or bottom of your pages to identify the date that the sheet was printed or perhaps its filename. If your data requires more than one page, you'll need to adjust page breaks. You can modify your sheets to print the way you want them to, with page breaks in specific places, margins adjusted, titles repeated on every page, and headers and footers.

Fitting Your Data into a Limited Printing Space

Sometimes you need to print only part of a sheet. You might need only one section of a database or just part of the information in your budget. You can print as much or as little of a sheet as you need. At other times, you might have too much information for one page. With the Page Setup command on the File menu, you can adjust the area that is printed and the scale at which it is printed.

NOTE   In the remaining exercises in this lesson, your computer needs to be connected to an active printer before you can print. If a printer is not available, click Cancel instead of OK in the Print dialog box. Even if you don't have an active printer available, you will still need a printer driver installed to use many of the print setup features.

Print part of a worksheet

To print the same range repeatedly, set a print area and then select the range. On the File menu, point to Print Area and then click Set Print Area.

In this exercise, you use the Print dialog box to print only a selected part of your worksheet data.

1   In the Cash Budget sheet, select A7:H16.

This range includes the initial data on your budget, plus the budget summary table.

2   On the File menu, click Print.

The Print dialog box opens.

Print What area

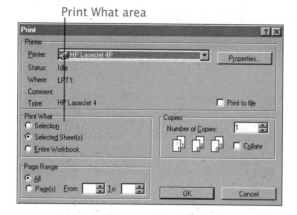

The Print button on the Standard toolbar prints your worksheet without displaying the Print dialog box (the options last set in the Print dialog box are used).

3 In the Print What area, select the Selection option, and then click OK.

A dialog box opens, telling you that your selection is being printed. Only the selected worksheet data will be printed.

Fit the cash budget worksheet onto one page

In this exercise, you use the Page Setup dialog box to fit an entire worksheet onto one printed page.

1 Click cell A1.

2 On the File menu, click Page Setup.

The Page Setup dialog box opens.

3 In the Page Setup dialog box, click the Page tab.

The Page options appear in the dialog box.

Orientation area

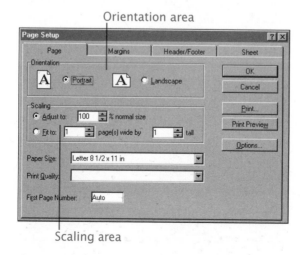

Scaling area

4   In the Orientation area, select Landscape.

Selecting Landscape changes your page from a tall to a wide orientation. Since your budget data covers several columns, you can fit more information onto a wide page than you can onto a tall page.

5   In the Scaling area, click the Fit To 1 Page(s) Wide By 1 Tall option button.

This scales your worksheet down to fit on only one page. You can change the number of pages to whatever you need.

6   Click the Print Preview button.

The Print Preview window opens and displays your entire budget on one sheet. Your budget should look like the following.

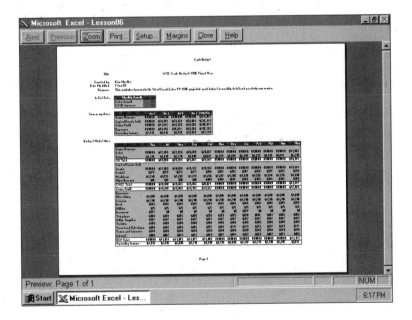

Fit the cash budget worksheet onto two pages

If the data is too small when it is reduced to fit onto one page, you can adjust the worksheet to print on two or more pages for better readability.

1   In the Print Preview window, click the Setup button.

The Page Setup dialog box opens.

2   In the dialog box, click the Page tab.

The Page options appear in the dialog box.

3 In the Orientation area, select Portrait.

Selecting Portrait changes your page from a wide to a tall orientation.

4 In the Scaling area, be sure that the Fit To 1 Page(s) Wide By 1 Tall option is selected, and change it to Fit To **2** Page(s) Wide By **1** Tall.

This scales your worksheet to fit onto two pages. You can change the number of pages to whatever you need.

5 Click OK.

The Print Preview window changes and displays the first page of your two-page budget. Your budget should look like the following.

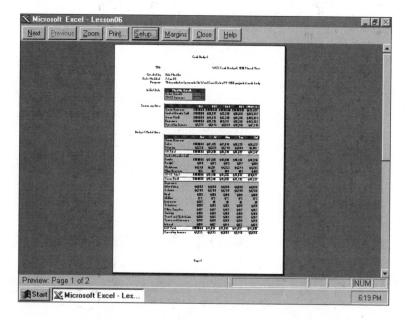

6 Click the Print button and then, in the Print dialog box, click OK.

7 When the message box closes, on the File menu, click Page Setup.

8 In the Scaling area, select Adjust To, and then click OK.

This returns scaling to the default setting in preparation for the next exercises.

Adding Print Titles

A large worksheet that is printed on several pages needs row or column labels at the left side or top of every printed page. You can add print titles to repeat the labels and clearly identify the data on each page.

Add print titles to your pages

In this exercise, you add print titles to your worksheet to list the budget categories along the left side of each printed page.

1   On the File menu, click Page Setup.

    The Page Setup dialog box opens.

2   In the dialog box, click the Sheet tab.

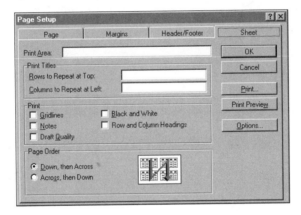

3   In the Print Titles area, click in the Columns To Repeat At Left box.

4   In your budget sheet, click the column header for column C.

    $C:$C appears in the Columns To Repeat At Left box.

5   In the dialog box, click the Print Preview button.

    The Print Preview window opens and displays your worksheet.

6   Click the Next button.

    The budget categories are repeated at the left side of each page. Page 2 of your worksheet should look similar to the following.

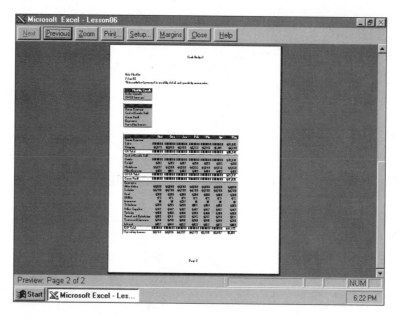

7 Click the Close button.

The Print Preview window closes.

Adjusting Margins

When you print a worksheet, your margins are automatically set at 1 inch for the top and bottom margins, and 0.75 inch for the left and right margins. You can adjust the margins with the Page Setup dialog box to any size you want. Suppose you want wider margins for your Cash Budget sheet.

Change your margins

In this exercise, you change the margins in your Cash Budget sheet to 1.25 inches for the top and bottom margins, and 1 inch for the left and right margins.

1 On the File menu, click Page Setup.

The Page Setup dialog box opens.

2 Click the Margins tab on the Page Setup dialog box.

The Margins options appear.

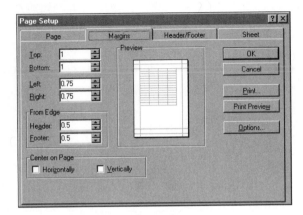

3 In the Top box, click the up arrow once.

The margin changes to 1.25 inches.

4 In the Bottom box, click the up arrow once.

The margin changes to 1.25 inches.

You can also adjust margins by dragging them. In the Print Preview window, click the Margins button and then drag margin lines with the mouse.

5 In the Left box, click the up arrow once.

The margin changes to 1 inch.

6 In the Right box, click the up arrow once.

The margin changes to 1 inch.

7 Under Center On Page, click the Horizontally check box.

The dialog box Preview changes as you select options.

8 Click the Print Preview button.

The Print Preview window opens, displaying the Cash Budget sheet with your changes.

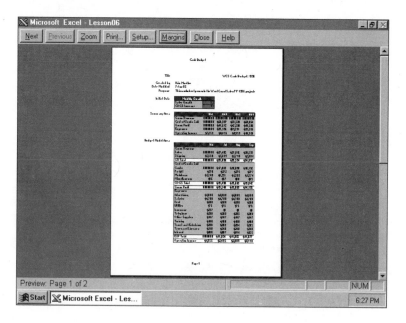

9 Click the Close button.

The Print Preview window closes.

Breaking Your Worksheet into Pages

When you print a large document, page breaks are inserted automatically at the cell nearest the margin. You might not always like where your pages break, however, since the automatic page breaks do not always follow your spreadsheet design. If you want to insert your own page breaks at specific rows, you can select a row and use the Page Break command on the Insert menu. The page break is inserted above the selected row. To remove a page break that you added manually, select the row below the page break, and use the Remove Page Break command on the Insert menu.

You might also find that your pages are not printing in the order that you want. If your document is more than one sheet wide, pages automatically print down your worksheet and then across it. You can change the printing order by using the Sheet tab in the Page Setup dialog box.

Insert a page break and change the printing order

In this exercise, you add a horizontal page break by selecting a row before inserting the break, and you alter the printing order to print across and then down.

You can also create a vertical page break by selecting a column, with the break appearing to the left of the selected column. If you select a single cell, both a horizontal and a vertical page break are inserted.

1 Click the row header for row 18 in the Cash Budget sheet.

This row contains the Budget Model Area title and is a good place for a page break if you want to keep the two tables intact.

2 On the Insert menu, click Page Break.

A dotted line appears above row 18, showing the page break you inserted.

3 On the File menu, click Page Setup.

The Page Setup dialog box opens.

4 In the dialog box, click the Sheet tab.

The Sheet tab appears.

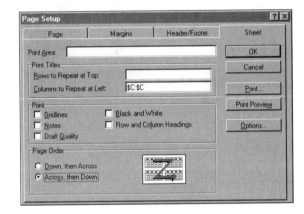

5 In the Page Order area, select Across, then Down.

This changes your page numbering to go across the pages and then down them.

6 Click the Print Preview button in the dialog box.

The Print Preview window opens, and your sheet has been divided into four pages. You can click the Next and Previous buttons to view each page. Your screen should look like the following.

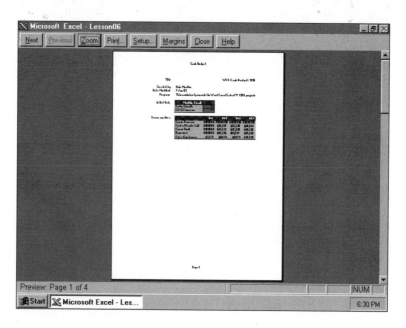

7 Click the Close button.

Adding Headers and Footers

Microsoft Excel automatically adds the name of your file to the header area and the page number to the footer area of anything that you print. If you want a title or the date to appear at the top or bottom of your pages, you can change the header or footer on your document. You can also delete the header or footer.

Using Standard Headers and Footers

Excel provides standard header and footer options that you can select in the Page Setup dialog box. With these built-in formats, you can add the company name, the filename with or without the extension, the date, the page number, or your own name. You can also mark documents as confidential, or you can add a document title.

Modify a header and a footer

In this exercise, you remove all of the information from the header and then move the page number and filename into the footer.

1 On the File menu, click Page Setup.

The Page Setup dialog box opens.

2 Click the Header/Footer tab in the dialog box.

Header list box

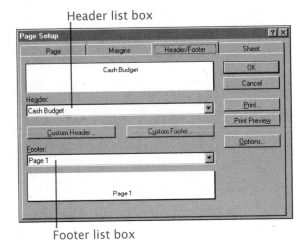

Footer list box

3 Click the down arrow next to the Header list box.

4 In the Header list, scroll upward and select (none).

Selecting (none) removes the header.

5 Click the down arrow next to the Footer list box.

6 In the Footer list, scroll and select Lesson06, Page 1.

This option places the filename and the page number at the bottom of the page. Your header and footer options should look like the following.

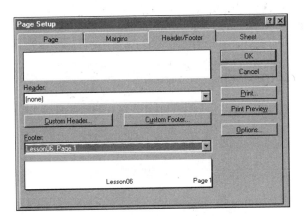

7 In the dialog box, click the Print Preview button.

The Print Preview window opens and displays your document with the new footer. Your document should look like the following.

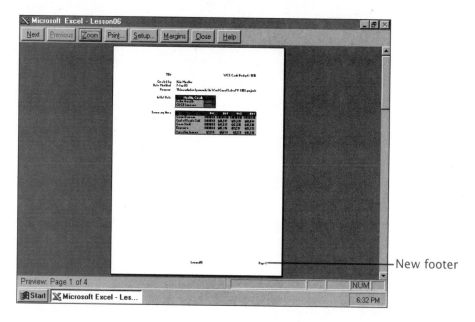
New footer

8 Click the Close button.

The Print Preview window closes.

Creating Custom Headers and Footers

You can create your own headers and footers by using the Custom Header and Custom Footer buttons in the Page Setup dialog box. You can add the page number, date, time, filename, or sheet name, and any other text that you want to include. In the next exercise, you'll add the document title, the date, and your name to the header with the Custom Header button.

Add a custom header

1 On the File menu, click Page Setup.

The Page Setup dialog box opens.

2 On the Header/Footer tab in the dialog box, click the Custom Header button.

The Header/Footer options appear.

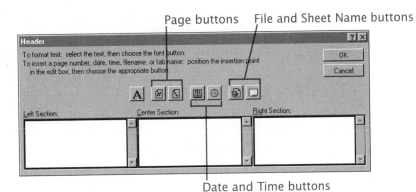

Page buttons   File and Sheet Name buttons

Date and Time buttons

3 Click in the Left Section box, and then type your name.

Whatever you place in this box appears at the left margin of the header.

4 Click in the Center Section box, and then type **1996 Cash Budget**

Whatever you place in this box appears at the center of the header.

Date

5 Click in the Right Section box, and then click the Date button.

Whatever you place in this box appears at the right margin of the header. Your dialog box should look like the following.

Font button

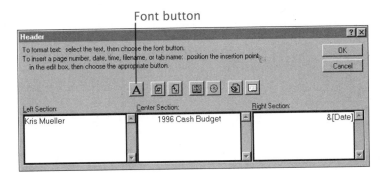

6 Select the text in the Center Section box, and then click the Font button.

The Font dialog box appears.

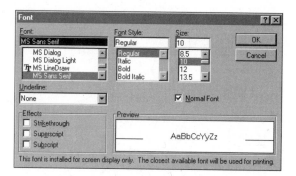

7 In the Font Style list, select Bold. In the Size list, select 12, and then click OK.

The Font dialog box closes.

8 In the Header dialog box, click OK.

The dialog box closes, and the Page Setup dialog box changes to reflect the new header. Your dialog box should look like the following.

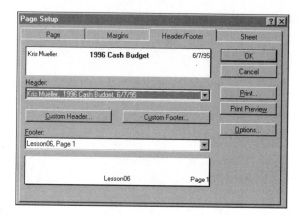

9 Click OK.

The Page Setup dialog box closes.

Printing a Worksheet

Now that you've set up your pages, you can print them. To print your worksheet, you can either use the Print button on the Standard toolbar or the Print command on the File menu. When you use the Print button, your worksheet is printed immediately to the default printer, using the last print options you selected.

When you use the Print command, you can make additional choices before you print, such as number of copies or selected pages to print. You can also use the Print buttons in the Print Preview window and the Page Setup dialog box to print your worksheet. You can print a selected range, a selected sheet, or your entire workbook. You can print multiple copies or a specific page range in your worksheet.

Print your worksheet

In this exercise, you use the Print command to print two copies of the selected sheet.

1   On the File menu, click Print.

The Print dialog box opens.

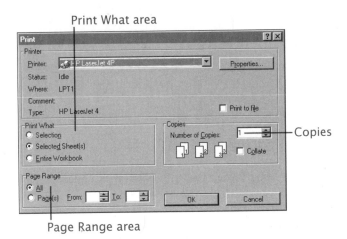

Print What area

Copies

Page Range area

2   In the Print What area, be sure that the Selected Sheet(s) option is selected.

3   In the Number Of Copies box, click the up arrow once to change the number to 2.

4   Click OK.

The dialog box closes and another opens, informing you that two copies of your worksheet are being printed on your printer.

Printing a Chart Sheet

Whether you create a chart on a separate sheet or as an embedded chart on a worksheet, you can print that chart separately and make page setup decisions for that chart page alone. You can also decide how to scale your chart when you print it and whether to print it in color or in black and white. You can reduce your chart to fit the page size or enlarge it to fill the full page. You can also resize the chart on the screen to create a custom chart size. The procedures for printing a chart are the same whether the chart is embedded or on a chart sheet. To print a chart on a chart sheet, you first select the chart sheet; to print an embedded chart, you first activate the chart.

Print a chart

In this exercise, you scale your chart to fit the page and then print it in black and white.

1 Select the Chart 1 sheet.

If you were going to print an embedded chart, you would activate the chart.

2 On the File menu, click Page Setup.

The Page Setup dialog box opens.

3 In the dialog box, click the Chart tab.

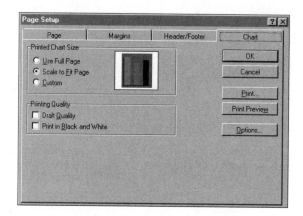

4 In the Printed Chart Size area, select Scale To Fit Page, if it is not already selected.

5 In the Printing Quality area, select Print In Black And White, and then click the Print button in the dialog box.

The Print dialog box opens.

6 Click OK.

A dialog box opens, telling you that your chart is printing.

Printing a Worksheet Without Its Embedded Chart

When you print a worksheet, any embedded charts are also printed by default. But you can print a worksheet without its embedded chart, without moving or deleting the chart, by changing the chart's properties.

Print a worksheet without its embedded chart

1 Select the Summary sheet.

2 Click the Print Preview button.

You want to print the worksheet without the chart covering the data.

3   Click Close.

4   Use the right mouse button to click the chart.

The chart object is selected, and the object shortcut menu appears.

5   Click on Format Object, and then click the Properties tab.

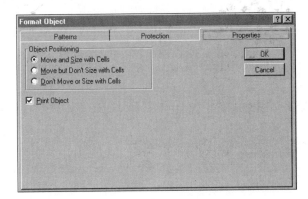

6   Select the Print Object option to clear the check box, and then click OK.

7   On the toolbar, click the Print Preview button.

Print Preview

The Print Preview window opens, and your worksheet is set up to print without its embedded chart.

8   Click the Print button.

The Print dialog box appears.

9   In the Print dialog box, click OK.

One Step Further: Printing With or Without Gridlines

Microsoft Excel does not print gridlines by default, but you can print them if you want them. Suppose you need to print an inventory form that will be carried around the warehouse and filled out by hand—you can print a worksheet full of gridlines. You can turn on the gridlines printing option in the Page Setup dialog box.

Try turning on the gridlines on your 1996 2nd Qtr sheet so that the data will appear in a grid.

Turn on gridlines

1   Switch to the 1996 2nd Qtr sheet.

2   On the File menu, click Page Setup.

The Page Setup dialog box opens.

139

3 Click the Sheet tab.

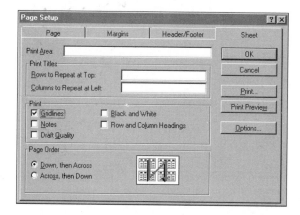

4 In the Print area, click Gridlines to place a check mark in the check box.

5 Click the Print Preview button.

The Print Preview window opens with the 1996 2nd Qtr sheet open. Your data is now in a grid.

To cover the page with gridlines, select a large area of the worksheet, then on the File menu, point to Print Area and click Set Print Area.

To remove a print area, select a cell on the worksheet, and then on the File menu, point to Print Area and click Clear Print Area.

6 Click the Print button.

The Print dialog box appears.

7 In the Print dialog box, click OK.

If You Want to Continue to the Next Lesson

1   On the File menu, click Save.
2   On the File menu, click Close.

If You Want to Quit Microsoft Excel for Now

➤   On the File menu, click Exit.
    If you see the Save dialog box, click Yes.

Lesson Summary

To	Do this	Button
Preview your worksheet	On the Standard toolbar, click the Print Preview button. *or* On the File menu, click Print Preview.	
Print part of a worksheet	Select the range you want to print. On the File menu, click Print. In the Print What area, click the Selection option, and then click OK.	
Fit your worksheet onto specified pages	On the File menu, click Page Setup. Click the Page tab and, in the Scaling area, type the number of pages wide by the number tall. Choose OK.	
Add print titles	On the File menu, click Page Setup. Click the Sheet tab. In the Print Titles area, select Columns or Rows. Select the column or row that includes the labels in the worksheet, and then click OK.	
Change margins	On the File menu, click Page Setup. Click the Margins tab. In the Top, Bottom, Left, and Right margin boxes, type or set the margins you want. Click OK.	
Add a page break	Select the row below or the column to the right of where you want the page break to occur. On the Insert menu, click Page Break.	

To	Do this	Button
Change the printing order of pages	On the File menu, click Page Setup. Click the Sheet tab and, in the Page Order box, select a printing order. Click OK.	
Add or delete a standard header or footer	On the File menu, click Page Setup. Click the Header/Footer tab. In the Header or Footer list box, select the style you want, or click (none) to remove the header or footer. Click OK.	
Add a custom header or footer	On the File menu, click Page Setup. Click the Header/Footer tab. Click the Custom Header or Custom Footer button, and type the information that you want. Click OK, and then click OK again.	
Print a worksheet	On the File menu, click Print. Select the options you want, and click OK. *or* On the Standard toolbar, click the Print button.	
Print a worksheet without its embedded chart	Select the embedded chart. On the Format menu, click Format Object, and then click the Properties tab. Clear the Print Object option, and click OK.	
Print a chart sheet	On the File menu, click Page Setup. Click the Chart tab, and change the scaling if necessary. Click the Print button in the dialog box. Click OK. *or* Click the Print button.	

For online information about	Use the Answer Wizard to search for
Printing	print
Printing a chart sheet	print a chart

Preview of the Next Lessons

In Part 3, you'll learn how to manage your data by sorting and filtering it to find specific information. You'll create reports that make your data clear to others, and you'll link data between different files to save time and effort in using the same data for different purposes. In the next lesson, "Organizing Your Workbooks," you'll learn how to copy and move sheets within and between your workbooks, add cell notes and text boxes to your sheets, add summary information to your files, and find files quickly in Microsoft Excel.

Review & Practice

In the lessons in Part 2, you learned skills to help you chart your data, modify your charts, and print your data and charts. If you want to practice these skills and test your understanding before you proceed with the lessons in Part 3, you can work through the Review & Practice section following this lesson.

Review & Practice

Estimated time
15 min.

You will review and practice how to:

- Create a chart on a separate chart sheet.
- Add gridlines and text to a chart.
- Preview the document and then add a header and footer.
- Print a worksheet and chart sheet.

Before you move on to Part 3, which covers sorting, organizing, and linking your data, and creating reports, you can practice the skills you learned in Part 2 by working through the steps in this Review & Practice section. You will create a 3-D column chart on a separate chart sheet, add gridlines and a text box to explain the data, and then print the worksheet and the chart.

Scenario

As part of the 10-year financial history for West Coast Sales (WCS), you need to create a chart showing how WCS's share of the market has increased over the decade. You've got the skills now to create a chart that can show the changes, as well as the skills to make sure that the information is clear and well presented. You need to print the data and the chart when you are finished so that two of your co-workers can review them and make suggestions.

145

Step 1: *Create a Chart on a Separate Chart Sheet*

Use the Year, Company, and Industry data on your 10-year sales history sheet to create a new 3-D column chart on a chart sheet.

1 Open the file Part2 Review, and save it as Review Part2.

2 Use the Chart command and the ChartWizard to create a 3-D column chart on a chart sheet.

Do not include the totals row or the market share column in your chart data. In Step 3 of the ChartWizard, use 3-D Column format #4.

3 Use Data Series In Columns, and use the first column of your data (the year column) for the category axis labels.

For more information on	See
Creating a chart on a separate chart sheet	Lesson 4

Step 2: *Modify Your Chart*

Modify your completed 3-D column chart by adding and rearranging some chart elements to create a cleaner look.

1 Change the chart subtype to the fourth subtype, the subtype with one series in front of another.

2 Add major gridlines to all three of the axes in your chart.

3 Move the legend to the bottom of your chart.

4 Add a text box to the top of your chart, insert the following description, and center the text.

This chart compares WCS sales growth to the industry as a whole over the last ten years.

For more information on	See
Modifying a chart	Lesson 5

Step 3: *Preview the Document and Add a Header and Footer*

Add a custom header and footer, and then select both sheets and preview them before printing.

1   Use the Page Setup dialog box and the Custom Header and Custom Footer buttons to add the following header and footer information.

Header: West Coast Sales, date, Confidential.

Footer: Page #, sheet name, filename.

2   Use the Print Preview button to preview your worksheet and then the chart sheet.

Your chart sheet should look similar to the following.

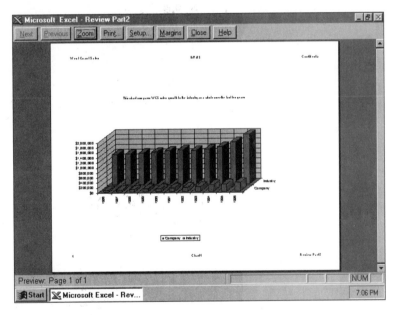

For more information on	See
Adding headers and footers	Lesson 6
Previewing your document	Lesson 6

Step 4: Print the Sheets

Print two copies of your sheets for your co-workers to review.

➤ Change the number of copies to two, and print your document.

For more information on	See
Printing a worksheet	Lesson 6

If You Want to Continue to the Next Lesson

1 On the File menu, click Save.
2 On the File menu, click Close.

If You Want to Quit Microsoft Excel for Now

➤ On the File menu, click Exit.
   If you see the Save dialog box, click Yes.

Managing Your Data

Part 3

Organizing Your Workbooks

Estimated time
35 min.

In this lesson you will learn how to:

- Copy and move sheets to make your workbooks more manageable.
- Document your work with cell notes, text boxes, and summary information.
- Find files quickly by searching for summary information.

When you organize your workbooks logically, other people are better able to understand and use them. Even if you don't share your workbooks, it makes sense to organize them well for your own convenience.

Copying or moving sheets into logical positions is one aspect of organizing your workbooks. Documenting your workbooks is another aspect of organizing them. You can add cell notes and text boxes to annotate your sheets and explain specific formulas or values. You can also fill in summary information for your files to make them easier to find and identify later.

In this lesson, you'll learn how to manage your workbooks by copying and moving sheets, document your work by adding text boxes and cell notes, and search for files.

Start the lesson

Follow the steps below to open the practice file called 07Lesson, and then save it with the new name Lesson07.

Open

1 On the Standard toolbar, click the Open button.

2 In the Look In box, be sure that the Excel SBS Practice folder appears.

To select the folder containing your practice files, refer to "Open a practice file" near the start of Lesson 1.

3   In the file list box, double-click the file named 07Lesson to open it.

4   On the File menu, click Save As.

The Save As dialog box opens. Be sure that the Excel SBS Practice folder appears in the Save In box.

5   Double-click in the File Name box, and then type **Lesson07**

6   Click the Save button, or press ENTER.

If you share your computer with others who use Microsoft Excel, the screen display might have changed since your last lesson. If your screen does not look similar to the illustrations as you work through this lesson, see the Appendix, "Matching the Exercises."

Managing Your Workbooks

When you create a workbook, you might know what information you want to include, but not the best way to organize it. For example, if you are building a workbook that contains several detail sheets and one summary sheet, you might want the summary sheet to appear first if you work mostly with the summary sheet or to appear last if you work mostly with the detail sheets. With Microsoft Excel, you can easily begin your workbook without getting the order of the sheets exactly right the first time. You can always add or remove sheets, or copy or move them around in your workbook. For example, if you have set up a sheet for each of the districts or regions in your company, you can add a sheet if a new district opens. You learned how to add and delete sheets in Lesson 1. Now you'll learn how to copy and move sheets to put them in the best possible order for your work.

Copying Sheets

Copying a sheet creates an identical copy that you can place in the same workbook or in a different workbook.

Copy a sheet to another file

In this exercise, you open the file 07LessonA and copy the Fax Inventory sheet to your Lesson07 practice file.

1   Open the file 07LessonA and save it as Lesson07A.

You now have two files open, Lesson07 and Lesson07A.

2   In Lesson07A, be sure that the Fax Inventory sheet is the active sheet.

3   On the Edit menu, click Move Or Copy Sheet.

The Move Or Copy dialog box opens.

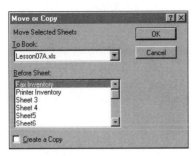

4 Click the down arrow next to the To Book box, and then select Lesson07.

5 In the Before Sheet list, select Sheet 2.

This places the copy on the left of Sheet 2 in the Lesson07 workbook.

6 Select the Create A Copy check box.

If this check box is not selected, the sheet would be moved instead of copied, which would remove it from the original workbook.

7 Click OK.

The Fax Inventory sheet is copied to your practice file, Lesson07, between the Copier Inventory sheet and Sheet 2. Microsoft Excel automatically displays the new worksheet. Your workbook should look similar to the following.

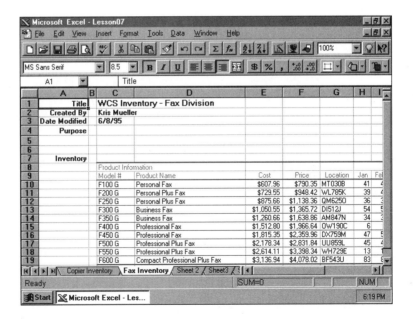

If you need to build another sheet that is similar or identical to an existing sheet, you don't need to copy the individual items from the existing sheet and paste them onto a new sheet. Instead, you can copy the entire existing sheet. To copy a sheet within a workbook, you can either use the same command that you used to copy a sheet between workbooks or use your mouse. In the next exercises, you'll copy the Fax Inventory sheet and then rename and modify the copy to be a totals sheet for your inventories.

Copy a sheet within a workbook

You can also copy sheets between workbooks by dragging a sheet from one workbook window to another workbook window. You'll learn more about using multiple windows in Lesson 14.

1   Point to the Fax Inventory sheet tab, and press and hold down CTRL while you press the mouse button.

Your mouse pointer changes to look like a small sheet with a plus sign on it, as shown in the following.

2   Drag the pointer until it appears immediately to the left of the Copier Inventory sheet.

A small triangle appears between the sheet tabs to show where the copied sheet will be placed. Your pointer should be immediately to the left of the Copier Inventory sheet, as shown in the following.

3   Release the mouse button, and then release the CTRL key.

The Fax Inventory sheet is copied and then dropped into place immediately left of the Copier Inventory sheet. It is automatically renamed Fax Inventory (2), as shown in the following.

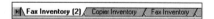

Rename and modify a sheet

1   Double-click the Fax Inventory(2) sheet tab.

The Rename Sheet dialog box opens with the Name box highlighted.

2   Type **Inventory Totals**, and then click OK.

The dialog box closes, and your sheet is renamed.

3   In cell C1, select the words Fax Division, type **Totals**, and then press ENTER.

4 Select the range C10:U19, and then press DEL.

All of the contents for cells C10:U19 are removed from the cells, leaving only the categories and headings for your inventory data.

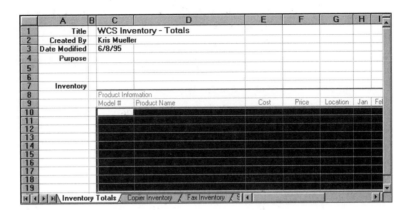

Moving Sheets

Just as you can copy sheets within and between workbooks, you can also move them without creating copies. You can move a sheet to a new position within the same workbook as you did in Lesson 1, or you can move a sheet to a different workbook.

Move a sheet between files and close a file

In this exercise, you move an inventory sheet from the Lesson07A file to your Lesson07 file.

You can also move sheets between workbooks by dragging a sheet from one workbook window to another workbook window. You'll learn more about using multiple windows in Lesson 14.

1 On the Window menu, click Lesson07A.

The Lesson07A workbook becomes active.

2 Click the Printer Inventory sheet tab.

3 On the Edit menu, click Move Or Copy Sheet.

The Move Or Copy dialog box opens.

4 Click the down arrow next to the To Book box, and then select Lesson07.

5 In the Before Sheet list, select Copier Inventory.

This places the Printer Inventory sheet to the left of the Copier Inventory sheet in the Lesson07 workbook.

6 Be sure that the Create A Copy check box is not checked. If it is checked, click the check box to clear it.

7 Click OK.

The Printer Inventory sheet is moved to Lesson07, immediately left of the Copier Inventory sheet. Your workbook will look similar to the following.

	A	B	C	D	E	F	G	
1	Title		WCS Inventory - Printer Division					
2	Created By		Kris Mueller					
3	Date Modified		6/8/95					
4	Purpose							
5								
6								
7	Inventory							
8			Product Information					
9			Model #	Product Name	Cost	Price	Location	J
10			P100 G	Personal Printer - Dot Matrix	$307.95	$400.34	OP731E	
11			P100 L	Personal Printer - Dot Matrix	$323.36	$420.37	WN767Q	
12			P100 S	Personal Printer - Dot Matrix	$339.52	$441.38	LB200Z	
13			P310 G	Personal Plus Printer - Bubble Jet	$708.32	$920.82	LZ712M	
14			P310 L	Personal Plus Printer - Bubble Jet	$743.73	$966.85	WD104D	
15			P310 S	Personal Plus Printer - Bubble Jet	$780.91	$1,015.18	YY998C	
16			P500 G	Business Printer - Laser	$1,770.78	$2,302.01	LH428J	
17			P500 L	Business Printer - Laser	$1,859.32	$2,417.12	JG0923Q	
18			P500 S	Business Printer - Laser	$1,952.28	$2,537.96	DX759M	
19			P1000 G	Professional Printer - Laser PostScript	$3,451.56	$4,487.03	UU859L	
20			P1000 L	Professional Printer - Laser PostScript	$3,718.64	$4,834.23	WH729E	

Inventory Totals \ **Printer Inventory** / Copier Inventory

8 On the Window menu, click Lesson07A.

9 On the File menu, click Close.

10 In the Save Changes dialog box, click Yes.

If you only need to move sheets within a workbook, you can simply drag them with the mouse. When you do this, your pointer displays a small sheet symbol next to it. This pointer is similar to the one you saw when you copied a sheet. As you saw in the last section, a plus sign in the sheet symbol indicates that you are creating a copy. The pointer without the plus sign indicates that you are moving the sheet without creating a copy.

Move sheets within a workbook

In this exercise, you arrange the inventory sheets in alphabetical order by moving the Printer Inventory sheet so that it appears on the right of the Fax Inventory sheet.

1 Point to the sheet tab for the Printer Inventory sheet, and then press and hold down the mouse button.

Your pointer should look similar to the following.

2 Drag the sheet to the right of the Fax Inventory sheet until the small triangle points to where the sheet will be inserted, as shown in the following.

3 Release the mouse button.

The Printer Inventory sheet appears to the right of the Fax Inventory sheet.

Documenting Workbooks

It's important to be able to identify and understand the sources of the information on a sheet. You've already seen how to use names to clarify formulas, and to add titles and text to explain charts, but what about the data in your worksheets? You need to be sure that whoever uses your workbooks will be able to understand how you put your formulas together and what data you used to generate a chart or report. With *cell notes* and *text boxes*, you can leave a trail of information for other people to use. With the File Properties dialog box, you can identify and find the files you want before you open them.

Adding Cell Notes

Sometimes a cell contains a reference to another sheet or contains a formula that points to data in another location. Or perhaps a particular value is used throughout a sheet. For example, on the Budget sheet you created earlier, the Sales Growth and Cost of Goods Sold Increase figures are values that the rest of the sheet depends on. The values in the Sales and Expenses budget items increase over the year according to the Sales Growth and Cost of Goods Sold Increase percentages. If you leave such values undocumented, another user might be confused or might even delete them by mistake. If you want to be sure that another user knows what the source or use of a particular value or formula is, you can add a note to the appropriate cell, explaining what the data is for or what data the formula refers to.

Document the price, totals, and values formulas

You add cell notes with the Note command on the Insert menu. In this exercise, you add cell notes to the Price, Totals, and Values headings on the Inventory Totals sheet to explain how these formulas were constructed.

1 Click the Inventory Totals sheet tab.

If you don't see the tab, you can either scroll through the tabs or use the right mouse button to click a tab scrolling button with the right mouse button and then select the sheet name.

2 Select cell F9, the cell that contains the label Price.

3 On the Insert menu, click Note.

The Cell Note dialog box opens.

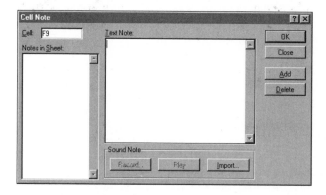

4 In the Text Note box, type **Price equals Cost * 130%** and then click the Add button.

5 Click cell T9 in the sheet.

This cell holds the Totals label.

6 Select the text in the Text Note box, and then type **This number represents the entire inventory over the whole year, including projections for September through December.**

7 Click the Add button.

8 Click cell U9 in the sheet.

This cell holds the Values label.

9 In the Text Note box, select the text. Type **Value equals Price * Totals** and then click the Add button.

10 Click OK.

The Cell Note dialog box closes, and note indicators (red dots in the upper-right corner of each cell) are added to cells F9, T9, and U9.

11 Move the mouse pointer over cell F9, T9, or U9.

The cell note appears. Your sheet should look like the following.

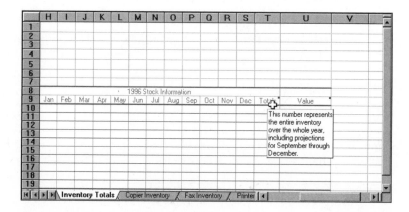

NOTE If you do not see cell note indicators (red dots in the upper-right corners of the cells), you can turn them on by using the Options command on the Tools menu. Click the View tab, and then in the Show area, select Note Indicator and click OK.

If you have several sheets in a series with the same data and you want to be sure that the cell notes you added to one sheet appear on the others, you can simply copy the cells containing the notes to the other sheets.

Copy the cell notes to the other sheets

In this exercise, you copy the entire heading row from the Inventory Totals sheet to the Copier, Fax, and Printer Inventory sheets.

1 On the Inventory Totals sheet, select C9:U9.

2 Use the right mouse button to click your selected range, and then click Copy on the shortcut menu.

3 Click the Copier Inventory sheet tab.

4 Use the right mouse button to click cell C9, and then click Paste Special on the shortcut menu.

The Paste Special dialog box opens.

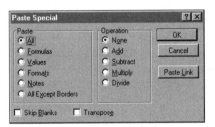

5 In the Paste Special dialog box under Paste, select Notes, and then click OK.

The dialog box closes, and the notes are added to cells C9:U9.

6 Repeat steps 3 through 5 for both the Fax Inventory and Printer Inventory sheets.

The cell notes from the Inventory Totals sheet are copied to the Fax Inventory and Printer Inventory sheets.

Adding Notes with Text Boxes

Text boxes are another good way to add explanations or extra information to a worksheet. A text box "floats" on top of a worksheet. With a text box, you can type as much text as you need and manipulate the size and formatting of the text box without affecting the structure of the worksheet.

In the next exercises, you'll add a text box to explain the product codes on the Copier Inventory sheet, and then you'll copy the text box and paste and modify it on the other inventory sheets.

Explain the inventory product codes

Drawing

Text Box

1   Click the Copier Inventory sheet tab, and then display the Drawing toolbar by clicking the Drawing tool on the Standard toolbar.

2   On the Drawing toolbar, click the Text Box button.

When your pointer is over the worksheet, it changes to a thin plus sign.

3   Drag to create a box that approximately covers cells D27:I31.

A text box appears, ready for you to enter text.

4   In the text box, type the following (use the SPACEBAR and the ENTER key where indicated):

X00 SPACEBAR SPACEBAR **Basic copier** ENTER

X10 SPACEBAR SPACEBAR **Basic copier plus extra trays** ENTER

X20 SPACEBAR SPACEBAR **Basic copier plus extra trays, AutoFeed, AutoSort**

5   Click anywhere outside of the text box.

Copy the text box to the other inventory sheets

Copy

Paste

1   Click the text box once to select it, and then click the Copy button on the toolbar.

2   Click the Fax Inventory sheet tab, and then click the Paste button on the toolbar.

The text box is pasted onto the Fax Inventory sheet. Placement is not important at this point; you'll move it into position and modify the text later.

3   Click the Printer Inventory sheet tab, and then click the Paste button on the toolbar again.

The text box is pasted onto the Printer Inventory sheet as well.

Move and modify the text boxes

In this exercise, you adjust the positions of the text boxes and update their text to match the printer and fax codes.

1   On the Printer Inventory sheet, drag the text box by its border to cover the range D27:G31.

2   Select all of the text in the text box, and type the following (use the SPACEBAR and the ENTER key where indicated):

G SPACEBAR SPACEBAR **Basic printer model** ENTER

L SPACEBAR SPACEBAR **Basic printer model plus extra trays** ENTER

S SPACEBAR SPACEBAR **Basic printer model plus extra trays and extended service contract**

Your worksheet should look similar to the following.

	A	B	C	D	E	F	G	
17			P500 L	Business Printer - Laser	$1,859.32	$2,417.12	JG0923Q	
18			P500 S	Business Printer - Laser	$1,952.28	$2,537.96	DX759M	
19			P1000 G	Professional Printer - Laser PostScript	$3,451.56	$4,487.03	UU859L	
20			P1000 L	Professional Printer - Laser PostScript	$3,718.64	$4,834.23	WH729E	
21			P1000 S	Professional Printer - Laser PostScript	$3,904.57	$5,075.94	BF543U	
22								
23								
24								
25								
26								
27				G Basic printer model				
28				L Basic printer model plus extra trays				
29				S Basic printer model plus extra trays and extended service contract				
30								
31								
32								
33								
34								
35								
36								

Copier Inventory / Fax Inventory \ Printer Inventory / Sheet

3 Click the Fax Inventory sheet tab.

4 Drag the text box by its border to cover the range D27:H31.

5 Select all of the text in the text box, and type the following:

X00 SPACEBAR SPACEBAR **Basic fax** ENTER

X50 SPACEBAR SPACEBAR **Basic fax plus automatic redial, memory feed**

Your worksheet should look similar to the following.

	A	B	C	D	E	F	G	H	
15			F400 G	Professional Fax	$1,512.80	$1,966.64	OW190C	6	
16			F450 G	Professional Fax	$1,815.35	$2,359.96	DX759M	47	
17			F500 G	Professional Plus Fax	$2,178.34	$2,831.84	UU859L	45	
18			F550 G	Professional Plus Fax	$2,614.11	$3,398.34	WH729E	13	
19			F600 G	Compact Professional Plus Fax	$3,136.94	$4,078.02	BF543U	83	
20									
21									
22									
23									
24									
25									
26									
27				X00 Basic fax					
28				X50 Basic fax plus automatice redial, memory feed					
29									
30									
31									
32									
33									
34									

Copier Inventory \ Fax Inventory / Printer Inventory / Sheet

6 Click outside the text box to prepare for the next exercise.

Updating File Properties

Now that you've placed your pages in the correct order and you've documented your information for future users (or to prompt your own memory at a later date), how can you make the file itself identifiable? If you have files with similar names or similar data on the sheets, it's often difficult to determine which file you need. By taking the time to fill in and update the file properties for a file, you'll make the file easier to find.

You can update the file properties when you save a file or by using the Properties command on the File menu. In the Properties dialog box, you can specify a title for your worksheet, a subject, an author, keywords, and comments about the file. In the Comments section, you can add information such as the last person who updated the file.

Add a description and keywords to your file

In this exercise, you update the file properties for a file to add a more detailed description and other information.

1   On the File menu, click Properties.

The Lesson07 Properties dialog box opens.

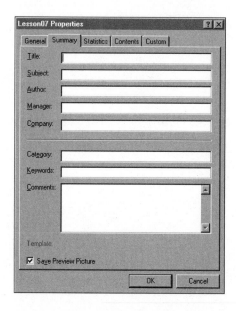

You can use the TAB key to move from one box to the next in a dialog box.

2   In the Title box, type **WCS Inventory for 1996 - All Divisions**

3   In the Subject box, type **Copier, Fax, and Printer inventories**

4   In the Author box, type your name.

5   In the Keywords box, type **Inventory**

6   In the Comments box, type **Includes projections for September thru December 1996.**

7   Be sure that there's a check mark in the Save Preview Picture box, and then click OK.

The Properties dialog box closes and saves your new file properties information.

Save

8   On the toolbar, click the Save button.

Finding Files

By organizing your files, you'll be able to locate a specific file when you need it. You can look through lists of filenames, but you might have trouble identifying the file you want. Not every workbook will have a long filename, and even some long filenames can seem cryptic. But with the file-finding features in the Open dialog box, you can find a file by searching for a title, a subject, an author name, keywords, or other information.

Find files with a common name

In this exercise, you use the file-finding features to locate an Excel inventory file and then preview it.

1   On the File menu, click Open.

The dialog box opens.

2   Be sure that the folder where your practice files are stored is selected in the Look In box.

3   Click the List button, if it's not already selected.

The names of the files in the Look In folder are displayed as a list.

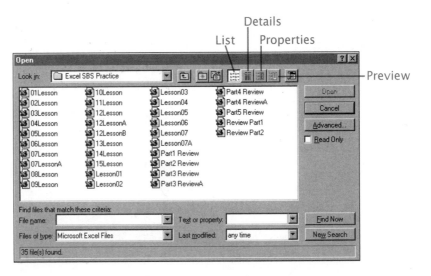

4 In the File Name box, type ***Lesson**

This narrows the search to any files with names that end in "Lesson."

5 In the File Of Type box, click the down arrow, and select Microsoft Excel Files from the list (if it's not already selected).

6 Click Find Now.

The results of the search are listed, as in the illustration below.

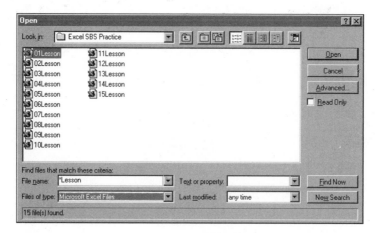

7 Select file 06Lesson, and then click the Properties button.

File properties are displayed for the selected file.

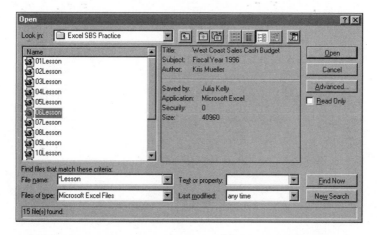

8 Click the Preview button.

A preview of the upper-left corner of the first sheet in the selected workbook appears.

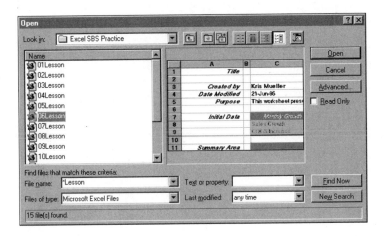

9 Click the List button.

The files appear in a list again.

Search for a file using a keyword

1 In the Open dialog box, click the New Search button.

The search criteria you set are cleared, and the complete list of practice files reappears in the dialog box.

2 Click the Advanced button.

The Advanced Find dialog box opens.

3 Under Define More Criteria, click the Property down arrow, and then select Keywords.

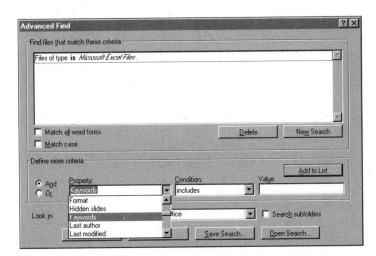

4 In the Value box, type **inventory**

5 Click the Add To List button.

The keyword "inventory" is added to the list in the Find Files That Match These Criteria box.

6 Click Find Now.

The Open dialog box opens again and displays the results of your search. Files currently saved with "Inventory" as a keyword appear, including files Lesson07 and 09Lesson.

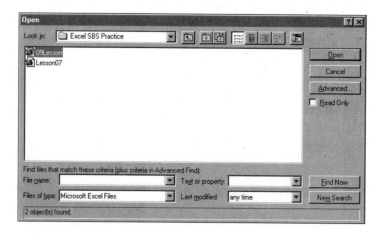

7 Click New Search.

The search criteria are removed, and all Microsoft Excel files in the Practice folder are listed.

8 Click Cancel to close the dialog box.

One Step Further: Printing Cell Notes

If you decide that you don't need a particular cell note, you can delete it easily, leaving the others intact. If you want to keep a paper record of your cell notes, you need to print them separately. Cell notes do not automatically print when you print the rest of your worksheet.

Try deleting a note and then printing all of your cell notes for the worksheet.

Delete a cell note and print the rest

1 Switch to the Copier Inventory sheet, and on the Insert menu, click Note.

The Cell Note dialog box opens. If your text box is still selected, the Note command will be unavailable—click any cell to deselect the text box.

2 In the Notes In Sheet list, select F9, and then click the Delete button. Click OK to confirm the deletion.

The note is removed from the list.

3 Click OK to close the dialog box.

The note marker in cell F9 is removed from your sheet.

4 On the File menu, click Page Setup.

The Page Setup dialog box opens.

5 Click the Sheet tab.

The Sheet tab opens. The dialog box should look similar to the following.

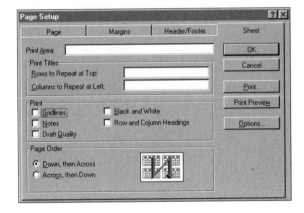

6 In the Print area, select the Notes and the Row And Column Headings options.

Selecting Row And Column Headings allows cell addresses to be printed with each cell note (without that information, you won't know to which cells the notes belong).

7 Click Print, and then click OK in the Print dialog box.

The Page Setup and Print dialog boxes close, and your worksheet and cell notes are printed.

If You Want to Continue to the Next Lesson

1 On the File menu, click Save.

2 Hold down SHIFT, and then on the File menu, click Close All.

If You Want to Quit Microsoft Excel for Now

➤ On the File menu, click Exit.

If you see the Save dialog box, click Yes.

Lesson Summary

To	Do this	Button
Copy a sheet to another file	Select the sheet to copy. On the Edit menu, click Move Or Copy Sheet. In the Move Or Copy dialog box, select a destination filename, and select where to place the new sheet in the workbook. Select the Create A Copy option, and then click OK.	
Copy a sheet within a workbook	Hold down CTRL, and drag the sheet tab to another location in your workbook.	
Rename a sheet	Double-click the sheet tab. In the Name box, type the new name and click OK.	
Move a sheet to or from another workbook	Select the sheet to move. On the Edit menu, click Move Or Copy Sheet. In the Move Or Copy dialog box, select a destination filename, and select where to add the new sheet. Clear the Create A Copy check box, and click OK.	
Move a sheet within a workbook	Drag the sheet tab to another location in your workbook.	
Add a cell note	Select a cell, and then on the Insert menu, click Note. Type your note in the Text Note box, and then click Add. Click OK.	
Add a text box	Click the Text Box button on the Standard toolbar, and then drag to draw the text box. Type your text, and then click outside the text box.	
Update file properties	On the File menu, click Properties. Type the information you want, and then click OK.	
Find a file	On the File menu, click Open. In the dialog box, enter a filename and select a file type. Click Advanced. In the Find Files dialog box, select a property and type the value that you want to search for, and then click Find Now.	

For online information about	Use the Answer Wizard to search for
Copying and moving sheets	**copy sheet**
Adding cell notes	**cell note**
Adding text boxes	**text box**
Updating summary information	**file properties**
Finding a file	**find file**

Preview of the Next Lesson

In the next lesson, "Sorting and Managing Lists," you'll learn how to sort your data by different criteria and how to filter your data to show only the information you need. Then you'll create subtotals in a few quick steps.

Sorting and Managing Lists

Estimated time
20 min.

In this lesson you will learn how to:

- Use automatic filtering to view only the data that you need.
- Enter data in a list rapidly with the new AutoComplete and Pick From List features.
- Sort data by specific criteria.

One of the things you'll probably do often in Microsoft Excel is sort and manage lists of data. The data in the following illustration is organized into a list, with column headings that define *fields* and rows that contain *records*. A field is a specific category of information in your list of data, such as Employee ID, Last Name, First Name, and Position. A record contains all of the categories of information about a specific item in your list. In the illustration, each record contains all of the personnel information for one person, including the employee ID number, last name, first name, position, department, division, salary, start date, and birth date. An entire set of data organized into fields and records, such as the employee list in the illustration, is referred to as a *list* or a *database* (in general, the terms *list* and *database* are interchangeable in Microsoft Excel).

Fields

	Emp ID	Last Name	First Name	Position	Department	Division	Salary	Start Date	Birth
1975	Franklin	Larry	Accounting Assist.	Accounting	Copier	$21,888	5/7/91	9
1976	Petry	Robin	Group Admin. Assist.	Engineering	Printer	$23,036	4/29/91	1
1168	Asonte	Toni	Group Admin. Assist.	Engineering	Fax	$23,036	4/10/91	
1169	Dorfberg	Jeremy	Software Engineer	Engineering	Copier	$34,002	10/13/92	7
1167	Berwick	Sam	Sales Rep.	Marketing	Copier	$31,914	4/18/91	8
1931	Mueller	Ursula	Accountant	Accounting	Copier	$26,101	6/20/89	5
1967	Aruda	Felice	Admin. Assist.	Admin.	Copier	$23,212	11/9/91	5
1676	Wells	Jason	Admin. Assist.	Admin.	Copier	$23,212	10/18/81	9
1075	Kane	Sheryl	Design Assist.	Art	Printer	$23,239	8/7/92	8
1966	Corwick	Rob	Design Assist.	Art	Fax	$23,239	11/17/91	
1816	Lin	Michael	Software Engineer	Engineering	Fax	$35,480	7/8/90	
1814	Al-Sabah	Daoud	Technician Assist.	Engineering	Fax	$21,304	3/4/89	8
1968	Martinez	Sara	Product Marketer	Marketing	Copier	$35,989	1/1/93	5
1675	Miller	Janet	Sales Rep.	Marketing	Copier	$33,301	10/26/81	
1677	Levine	Eric	Research Scientist	R and D	Fax	$37,896	11/6/87	9
1793	Able	Aaron	Admin. Assist.	Admin.	Fax	$24,180	12/16/90	10
1792	Barton	Eileen	Design Specialist	Art	Copier	$28,859	12/24/90	1
1794	Goldberg	Malcolm	Product Marketer	Marketing	Fax	$37,489	12/18/84	10
1426	Lampstone	Pete	Sales Rep.	Marketing	Fax	$34,689	9/8/77	
1530	Stewart	Iain	Admin. Assist.	Admin.	Printer	$25,147	1/20/91	1

Records

Personnel List / Sheet2 / Sheet3 / Sheet4 / Sheet5 / S

Whenever you have a list (or database) of people, places, or products, you need a way to filter out everything except the specific information that you need at the moment. You also need to be able to sort the data by specific criteria. If you were preparing a report on how many employees are in the administration department, for example, you would need to be able to display only the administration department in your list. Microsoft Excel provides two useful tools for locating and displaying specific information in a list: filtering and sorting. With these tools, you can easily sort and filter the data in your worksheet.

In this lesson, you'll learn how to use AutoFilter to filter out only the data that you need. You'll also learn to sort your data easily with multiple sorting criteria, called *keys*.

Start the lesson

Follow the steps below to open the practice file called 08Lesson, and then save it with the new name Lesson08.

Open

To select the folder containing your practice files, refer to "Open a practice file" near the start of Lesson 1.

1 On the Standard toolbar, click the Open button.

2 In the Look In box, be sure that the Excel SBS Practice folder appears.

3 In the file list box, double-click the file named 08Lesson to open it.

4 On the File menu, click Save As.

The Save As dialog box opens. Be sure that the Excel SBS Practice folder appears in the Save In box.

5 Double-click in the File Name box, and then type **Lesson08**

6 Click the Save button, or press ENTER.

If you share your computer with others who use Microsoft Excel, the screen display might have changed since your last lesson. If your screen does not look similar to the illustrations as you work through this lesson, see the Appendix, "Matching the Exercises."

Filtering Lists to Show Only the Data You Need

When you work with a database, you need to be able to find information quickly. Perhaps you have a list of client phone numbers or a list of product codes and descriptions. If you need to find all of the phone numbers in one area code or all of the product codes for printers, you probably don't want to look through the whole list and pick out the numbers or codes manually. You can use the field names in your database to filter your data automatically and show only the records you need.

To do this, you can select any cell in your list and use the AutoFilter command to turn on automatic filtering. When you select a single cell within a list, Excel selects the entire list around the cell. Then you select criteria, using field names, to show only the records you need. When you have finished filtering data, you can turn off automatic filtering with a single command.

In the next exercises, you'll use the AutoFilter command to prepare your data for filtering, and then you'll select criteria and filter your data. You'll also use one of Excel's new features, the AutoFilter with Top 10, to filter the ten highest salaries in a division.

Prepare your data for filtering

1 Select cell C10.

You could select any cell within your list; Excel will then select the entire range.

2 On the Data menu, point to Filter, and then click AutoFilter.

Filtering arrow buttons appear next to your column labels, similar to the following illustration.

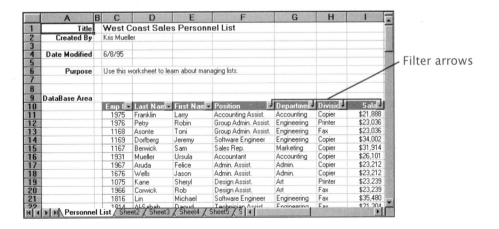

Filter arrows

NOTE In some databases, you might see a dialog box asking whether you want to use the top row as your header row. Click OK to proceed.

3   Click the filter down arrow in cell H10, the Division column header or field name.

A list of all criteria in the Division field appears so that you can choose a criteria, or key, to filter on.

All of the criteria present in the field, or column, will be listed in alphabetical order. In addition to specific field criteria, there are five choices that always appear in the list. The All, Top 10, Custom, Blanks, and NonBlanks options let you show all of the records, the records with the highest or lowest numbers in that field, only records that meet custom criteria, all records that are blank in that field, and all records that contain information in that field. You can select any choice in the data list as the criterion for filtering your data.

When you select an item in the criteria list, any records that don't match the filter criteria are hidden. In the next exercises, you'll filter out all of the employees except those in the Copier division and then filter out all but the accounting employees in the Copier division.

Filter out everything but the Copier division

   Select Copier from the filter list in the Division field (cell H10).

Every record in the Copier division appears. The other records still exist, but they are hidden for the moment. The visible row numbers from 11 to 124 are no longer continuous; the filter arrow for the Division column appears blue on your worksheet, while the others are still black. Your worksheet should look like the following.

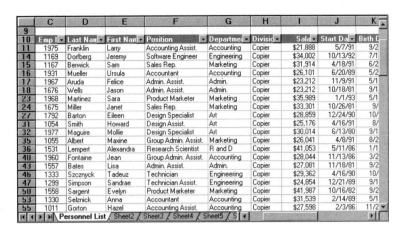

Filter out all but the accounting department in the Copier division

▶ Click the filter down arrow for the Department field (cell G10), and then select Accounting from the list.

The Accounting personnel in the Copier division appear in your worksheet.

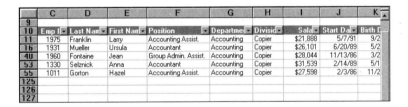

You can redisplay the entire database by selecting All in any column where you filtered criteria. Or, you can use the Filter command on the Data menu and then click Show All.

Restore your data

In the next exercise, you restore your data to include all departments and all divisions, and then you extract the ten records with the highest salaries in the Copier division.

▶ On the Data menu, point to Filter, and then click Show All.

All departments and divisions appear in the worksheet again.

Display the Top 10 salaries in the Copier division

1 Click the filter down arrow for the Division field (cell H10), and then select Copier from the list.

2 Click the filter down arrow in the Salaries field (cell I10), and then select Top 10 from the list.

The Top 10 AutoFilter dialog appears.

3 Be sure that the dialog options are "Top," "10," and "Items," and then click OK.

The records for personnel with the 10 highest salaries in the Copier division appear. The Top 10 filter option only works for numeric data, such as salaries and dates. Your worksheet should look like the following.

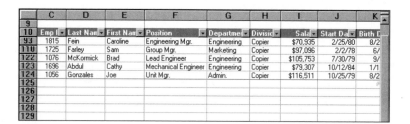

4 On the Data menu, point to Filter, and then click Show All.

Finding Data Using Custom Filters

Although you can usually find the information you need by selecting a single item from a filter list, sometimes you need to find records that match a custom set of criteria. If you need to find every person in your list who started on or before November 9, 1991, for example, you can select Custom from the Start Date filter list and then place "<= 11/9/91" in the Custom AutoFilter dialog box (this custom criteria means "start date less than or equal to 11/9/91"). You use *operators* such as an equal sign (=), greater-than sign (>), or less-than sign (<) to define your custom criteria. In the next exercise, you find all employees who have the title "Admin. Assist." or "Group Admin. Assist." in your data.

Find all administration assistants and group administration assistants

1 Click the filter down arrow in the Position field (cell F10), and then select Custom.

The Custom AutoFilter dialog box opens.

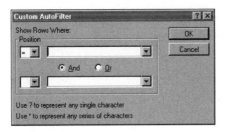

2 In the Position area, be sure that "=" is selected in the top operator box.

3 Click the down arrow next to the criteria list box, and then select Admin. Assist.

4 Click the Or option button.

The Or option means "all records where Position is Admin. Assist. *or* Group Admin. Assist."

5 Click the down arrow next to the lower operator box, and then select "=".

6 Click the down arrow next to the lower criteria list box, and then select Group Admin. Assist.

The Custom AutoFilter dialog box should look similar to the following.

7 Click OK.

Your data is filtered to show only administration assistants and group administration assistants.

	C	D	E	F	G	H	I	J	K
10	Emp I	Last Nam	First Nam	Position	Departme	Divisio	Sala	Start Da	Birth D
12	1976	Petry	Robin	Group Admin. Assist.	Engineering	Printer	$23,036	4/29/91	10/
13	1168	Asonte	Toni	Group Admin. Assist.	Engineering	Fax	$23,036	4/10/91	7/
17	1967	Aruda	Felice	Admin. Assist.	Admin.	Copier	$23,212	11/9/91	5/1
18	1676	Wells	Jason	Admin. Assist.	Admin.	Copier	$23,212	10/18/81	9/1
26	1793	Able	Aaron	Admin. Assist.	Admin.	Fax	$24,180	12/16/90	10/1
30	1530	Stewart	Iain	Admin. Assist.	Admin.	Printer	$25,147	1/20/91	1/1
33	1529	Kellerman	Tommie	Admin. Assist.	Engineering	Printer	$25,147	1/28/87	1/
35	1055	Albert	Maxine	Group Admin. Assist.	Marketing	Copier	$26,041	4/8/91	8/2
37	1290	Cooper	Linda	Admin. Assist.	Admin.	Fax	$26,114	1/3/85	4/
40	1960	Fontaine	Jean	Group Admin. Assist.	Accounting	Copier	$28,044	11/13/86	3/2
41	1153	Plant	Allen	Group Admin. Assist.	Accounting	Printer	$28,044	1/13/90	11/
42	1961	Mueller	Kris	Admin. Assist.	Admin.	Fax	$27,081	11/5/86	4/
43	1557	Bates	Lisa	Admin. Assist.	Admin.	Copier	$27,081	11/18/81	9/2
48	1301	Sindole	Randy	Admin. Assist.	Marketing	Fax	$27,081	8/6/84	6/2
49	1724	Chu	Steven	Group Admin. Assist.	Marketing	Printer	$28,044	7/29/90	5/2
51	1041	Tercan	Robert	Group Admin. Assist.	R and D	Printer	$28,044	4/16/92	1/2
52	1334	Kaneko	Midori	Group Admin. Assist.	R and D	Fax	$28,044	4/8/90	10/1
55	1675	Melendez	Jaime	Group Admin. Assist.	Accounting	Fax	$29,045	3/17/92	1/2
67	1656	Kourios	Theo	Admin. Assist.	Marketing	Copier	$29,015	12/14/87	9/2
68	1079	Price	Ellen	Admin. Assist.	Admin.	Printer	$29,983	3/24/86	12/

Personnel List / Sheet2 / Sheet3 / Sheet4 / Sheet5 / S

Turn off the filter

➤ On the Data menu, point to Filter, and then click AutoFilter.

The filter arrows on the column labels disappear, and all the records are displayed.

Using AutoComplete to Add Data

AutoComplete is a new feature that speeds the typing of repeated entries in a list by completing the entries for you. In your personnel list, the Position, Department, and Division fields contain repeated entries. Suppose you need to add a new record to the list, for a new accountant in the accounting department of the copier division. Instead of typing out Accountant, Accounting, and Copier, you can use AutoComplete or Pick From List to complete the entry for you. As you type, the AutoComplete feature will attempt to complete your entry using previous entries in the column. You can also click an empty cell by using the right mouse button, click Pick From List, and then select from a list of all existing entries in the column (a great way to avoid misspellings).

Add a new record to the personnel list

To get to the bottom of a long list quickly, click a cell in the column you want, and then double-click the bottom border of the cell.

1. In cell C125, enter **1979** and then enter your name in cells D125:E125.

2. Use the right mouse button to click cell F125, and then click Pick From List.

3. In the list box that appears, click Accountant.

   Accountant is entered in cell F125.

4. In the Department field (cell G125), begin typing **Accounting**

   As soon as you type the second letter, the entire entry appears in the cell. If you wanted to type a different word, such as Access, you would just keep typing.

5. Enter **Copier** in the Division field (H125) with the method of your choice.

NOTE To turn AutoComplete off, click Options on the Tools menu, click the Edit tab, and then click the Enable AutoComplete For Cell Values check box to clear it.

Sorting Data

When you want to display or print your list of records in a particular order, you need to sort your data. Sorting works somewhat like filtering—you select the range that you want to sort and then use field names to define how you want to sort your data. You can sort your data by any field name in the database. The field name that you sort by is referred to as a *sort key*. To sort a range, you can select any cell within the range and then use the Sort command on the Data menu. When you choose the Sort command, the range around the active cell is automatically selected for sorting.

Sort the personnel list by division

In this exercise, you sort your personnel list by division so that you first see all of the employees in the Copier division, then the Fax division, and then the Printer division.

1 Select cell C10.

You can select any cell in the database to select the entire database for sorting.

2 On the Data menu, click Sort to open the Sort dialog box.

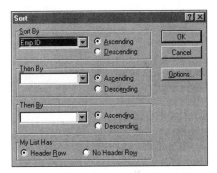

3 Under Sort By, click the down arrow, and then select Division from the list.

The database will be sorted by Division, and the Divisions will be in alphabetical order.

4 Be sure that the two Then By boxes are blank, and then click OK.

 NOTE Unlike filtering, sorting your database moves the rows to new positions. If you do not want to rearrange your data, use the Undo Sort command on the Edit menu to restore the database to its original order.

Sometimes you might want to use more than one sorting criteria, or sort key. Your data is sorted by division, but what order is it in within each division? You can use multiple sort keys to sort your data further. You can also change the sort order to *descending*, from Z to A, instead of *ascending*, from A to Z. In the next exercise, you'll sort your data again, but this time in ascending order by division, and then you'll sort each division in descending order by salary.

Sort the personnel list by division and then by salary

1 On the Data menu, click Sort.

The Sort dialog box opens.

2 Be sure that Division is still in the Sort By box, and the Ascending option is selected.

3 Click the down arrow next to the first Then By box, select Salary, and then select the Descending option.

4 Click OK.

Your data is sorted first by divisions alphabetically and then by salaries from highest to lowest salary within each division. Your worksheet should look like the following.

	C	D	E	F	G	H	I	J	K
10	Emp ID	Last Name	First Name	Position	Department	Division	Salary	Start Date	Birth D
11	1056	Gonzales	Joe	Unit Mgr.	Admin.	Copier	$116,511	10/25/79	8/2
12	1076	McKormick	Brad	Lead Engineer	Engineering	Copier	$105,753	7/30/79	9/
13	1725	Farley	Sam	Group Mgr.	Marketing	Copier	$97,096	2/2/78	6/
14	1696	Abdul	Cathy	Mechanical Engineer	Engineering	Copier	$79,307	10/12/84	1/1
15	1815	Fein	Caroline	Engineering Mgr.	Engineering	Copier	$70,935	2/25/80	8/2
16	1354	Beech	Susan	Senior Engineer	Engineering	Copier	$69,070	5/6/86	8/
17	1949	Sampson	Carla	Product Marketer	Marketing	Copier	$62,981	10/12/81	2/2
18	1427	Price	David	Chief Scientist	R and D	Copier	$59,455	8/31/77	3/1
19	1967	Cortlandt	Charles	Sales Rep.	Marketing	Copier	$58,278	4/13/82	9/1
20	1154	Solomon	Ari	Software Engineer	Engineering	Copier	$56,177	7/7/87	11/
21	1510	White	Jessica	Mechanical Engineer	Engineering	Copier	$46,387	6/11/85	11/
22	1658	Coyne	Dennis	Software Engineer	Engineering	Copier	$44,351	6/6/88	10/1
23	1558	Sargent	Evelyn	Product Marketer	Marketing	Copier	$41,987	10/16/82	9/2
24	1531	Lempert	Alexandra	Research Scientist	R and D	Copier	$41,053	5/11/86	1/1
25	1968	Martinez	Sara	Product Marketer	Marketing	Copier	$35,989	1/1/93	5/1
26	1169	Dorfberg	Jeremy	Software Engineer	Engineering	Copier	$34,002	10/13/92	7/1
27	1675	Miller	Janet	Sales Rep.	Marketing	Copier	$33,301	10/26/81	9/
28	1360	Raye	Alice	Group Admin. Assist.	Engineering	Copier	$33,051	8/1/88	6/1
29	1167	Berwick	Sam	Sales Rep.	Marketing	Copier	$31,914	4/18/91	6/2
30	1330	Selznick	Anna	Accountant	Accounting	Copier	$31,539	2/14/89	5/1
31	1674	Cummins	Dave	Group Admin. Assist.	R and D	Copier	$31,048	4/8/90	9/1

Personnel List / Sheet2 / Sheet3 / Sheet4 / Sheet5 / S

Sharing Lists with Other Users

If you are using Microsoft Excel on a network, you might have workbooks that are shared and modified by different people. A new feature in Microsoft Excel is the capability to share lists (workbooks) between multiple network users simultaneously.

Allow workbook editing simultaneously by multiple users

1 Open the workbook you want to share.

2 On the File menu, click Shared Lists, and then click the Editing tab.

3 Click Allow Multi-User Editing, and then click OK.

4 To see a list of users who currently have the workbook open, click the Status tab in the Shared Lists dialog box.

One Step Further: Sorting by Four Keys

Although the Sort dialog box allows you to sort on only three keys, you might want to sort a long or complex list by more than three sort keys. If you need more sort keys to sort your list adequately, you can sort your data more than once. To make a sort with more than three keys successful, you need to sort by the minor categories first and then by the major categories.

In the personnel list you've been working with in this lesson, you have columns for Last Name, Position, Division, and Department. To sort the records in the order of Division, Department, Position, and Last Name, you would need to perform two sorts. For the first sort, you would use the minor categories: Department, Position, and Last Name. Then, for the second sort, you would use the major category, Division.

By performing two sorts, you can sort by all four criteria, as long as you perform the sorts in the correct order. In other words, if you want your information to be sorted by department within each division, by position within each department, and by last name within each position, you would perform the first sort by Department in the Sort By box, by Position in the first Then By box, and by Last Name in the second Then By box. For the second sort, select Division in the Sort By box. Whatever you sort by in the second sort will take precedence over what you sorted by in the first sort.

Sort by Division, Department, Position, and Last Name

This exercise will demonstrate the multiple sorting concept by sorting the personnel list by Division, Department, Position, and Last Name.

1 Select cell C10, and on the Data menu, click Sort.

The Sort dialog box opens.

2 In the Sort By area, select Department.

Department is the first minor sort key in your four keys.

3 In the first Then By box, select Position, and select the Ascending option button.

4 In the second Then By box, select Last Name.

5   Click OK.

Your data is sorted alphabetically by the three minor sort keys: Department, then Position, and then Last Name. Your list should look similar to the following.

	C	D	E	F	G	H	I	J	K
10	Emp ID	Last Name	First Name	Position	Department	Division	Salary	Start Date	Birth [
11	1932	McGuire	Ellen	Accountant	Accounting	Fax	$47,853	6/12/89	6/
12	1931	Mueller	Ursula	Accountant	Accounting	Copier	$26,101	6/20/89	5/2
13	1979	Mueller	Kris	Accountant	Accounting	Copier			
14	1300	Richards	Phillip	Accountant	Accounting	Printer	$30,452	12/13/89	6/
15	1573	Robbins	Bob	Accountant	Accounting	Fax	$35,889	7/7/88	5/3
16	1330	Selznick	Anna	Accountant	Accounting	Copier	$31,539	2/14/89	5/1
17	1657	Wells	Rose	Accountant	Accounting	Printer	$32,627	12/6/87	10/1
18	1516	Bell	Tom	Accounting Assist.	Accounting	Printer	$28,550	3/6/85	6/2
19	1674	Boughton	Frank	Accounting Assist.	Accounting	Fax	$27,598	3/25/92	1/1
20	1975	Franklin	Larry	Accounting Assist.	Accounting	Copier	$21,888	5/7/91	9/2
21	1011	Gorton	Hazel	Accounting Assist.	Accounting	Copier	$27,598	2/3/86	11/2
22	1152	Henders	Mark	Accounting Assist.	Accounting	Printer	$26,646	1/21/90	10/2
23	1960	Fontaine	Jean	Group Admin. Assist.	Accounting	Copier	$28,044	11/13/86	3/2
24	1675	Melendez	Jaime	Group Admin. Assist.	Accounting	Fax	$29,045	3/17/92	1/2
25	1153	Plant	Allen	Group Admin. Assist.	Accounting	Printer	$28,044	1/13/90	11/
26	1793	Able	Aaron	Admin. Assist.	Admin.	Fax	$24,180	12/16/90	10/1
27	1967	Aruda	Felice	Admin. Assist.	Admin.	Copier	$23,212	11/9/91	5/1
28	1557	Bates	Lisa	Admin. Assist.	Admin.	Copier	$27,081	11/18/81	9/2
29	1291	Constance	Burt	Admin. Assist.	Admin.	Printer	$35,786	12/26/84	4/1
30	1290	Cooper	Linda	Admin. Assist.	Admin.	Fax	$26,114	1/3/85	4/
31	1961	Mueller	Kris	Admin. Assist.	Admin.	Fax	$27,081	11/5/86	4/

Personnel List / Sheet2 / Sheet3 / Sheet4 / Sheet5 / S

6   On the Data menu, click Sort again.

The Sort dialog box opens.

7   In the Sort By area, select Division.

Division is your major sort key.

8   In the first Then By box, select (none).

9   In the second Then By box, select (none), and then click OK.

Your data is sorted by Division, and within each division the previously sorted Department, Position, and Last Name categories are still in order. Your list should look similar to the following.

	C	D	E	F	G	H	I	J	K
10	Emp ID	Last Name	First Name	Position	Department	Division	Salary	Start Date	Birth [
11	1931	Mueller	Ursula	Accountant	Accounting	Copier	$26,101	6/20/89	5/2
12	1979	Mueller	Kris	Accountant	Accounting	Copier			
13	1330	Selznick	Anna	Accountant	Accounting	Copier	$31,539	2/14/89	5/1
14	1975	Franklin	Larry	Accounting Assist.	Accounting	Copier	$21,888	5/7/91	9/2
15	1011	Gorton	Hazel	Accounting Assist.	Accounting	Copier	$27,598	2/3/86	11/2
16	1960	Fontaine	Jean	Group Admin. Assist.	Accounting	Copier	$28,044	11/13/86	3/2
17	1967	Aruda	Felice	Admin. Assist.	Admin.	Copier	$23,212	11/9/91	5/1
18	1557	Bates	Lisa	Admin. Assist.	Admin.	Copier	$27,081	11/18/81	9/2
19	1676	Wells	Jason	Admin. Assist.	Admin.	Copier	$23,212	10/18/81	9/1
20	1056	Gonzales	Joe	Unit Mgr.	Admin.	Copier	$116,511	10/25/79	8/2
21	1054	Smith	Howard	Design Specialist	Art	Copier	$25,176	4/16/91	8/
22	1792	Barton	Eileen	Design Specialist	Art	Copier	$28,859	12/24/90	10/
23	1977	Maguire	Mollie	Design Specialist	Art	Copier	$30,014	6/13/80	9/1
24	1673	Dixon-Waite	Sherrie	Admin. Assist.	Engineering	Copier	$29,983	4/16/90	9/
25	1815	Fein	Caroline	Engineering Mgr.	Engineering	Copier	$70,935	2/25/80	8/2
26	1360	Raye	Alice	Group Admin. Assist.	Engineering	Copier	$33,051	8/1/88	6/1
27	1076	McKormick	Brad	Lead Engineer	Engineering	Copier	$105,753	7/30/79	9/
28	1696	Abdul	Cathy	Mechanical Engineer	Engineering	Copier	$79,307	10/12/84	1/1
29	1510	White	Jessica	Mechanical Engineer	Engineering	Copier	$46,387	6/11/85	11/
30	1354	Beech	Susan	Senior Engineer	Engineering	Copier	$69,070	5/6/86	8/
31	1658	Coyne	Dennis	Software Engineer	Engineering	Copier	$44,351	6/6/88	10/1

Personnel List / Sheet2 / Sheet3 / Sheet4 / Sheet5 / S

If You Want to Continue to the Next Lesson

1 On the File menu, click Save.

2 On the File menu, click Close.

If You Want to Quit Microsoft Excel for Now

➤ On the File menu, click Exit.

If you see the Save dialog box, click Yes.

Lesson Summary

To	Do this
Filter data	Select any cell in your database. On the Data menu, point to Filter, and then click AutoFilter. Use the filter arrows to select your filtering criteria.
Filter data using multiple criteria	On the Data menu, point to Filter, and then click AutoFilter. Click the filter arrow and select Custom. In the Custom AutoFilter dialog box, select the operators and criteria that you want, and then click OK.
Show all data	On the Data menu, point to Filter, and then click Show All.
Turn off AutoFilter	On the Data menu, point to Filter, and then click AutoFilter.
Sort data	Select any cell in your database, and then on the Data menu, click Sort. In the Sort dialog box, select the criteria you want, and then click OK.
AutoComplete a list entry	Begin typing the entry.
Pick From List a list entry	Click a cell by using the right mouse button. On the shortcut menu, click Pick From List, and then click the entry you want in the list box that appears.
Enable multi-user workbook editing	Open a workbook. On the File menu, click Shared Lists, and then click the Editing tab. Click Allow Multi-User Editing, and then click OK.

To	Do this
See a list of users currently sharing a workbook	On the File menu, click Shared Lists, then click the Status tab.

For online information about	Use the Answer Wizard to search for
Filtering lists	**filter**
Sort data	**sort**

Preview of the Next Lesson

In the next lesson, "Creating Reports," you'll learn how to outline your worksheet to see different levels of detail and how to consolidate your data to present an overview, rather than the detail information, for a report.

Creating Reports

Estimated time

25 min.

In this lesson you will learn how to:

- Subtotal an entire table of data at one time.
- Outline your data to show only the level of detail that you need.
- Consolidate several worksheets with similar data into a summary report.

If you use Microsoft Excel in a business or organizational setting, you will need to share the information in your workbooks with other people. Presenting your data to others usually involves summarizing the data in a logical way. Microsoft Excel makes it easy to produce clear and logical reports by providing several ways for you to summarize or consolidate your data. Reports rarely consist of every detail; rather, reports show an overview, a trend, or a synopsis, with supporting data in the background. In this lesson, you'll learn how to quickly add subtotals and a grand total to the data in a table, modify worksheet outlines to summarize information the way you want, and consolidate your data to produce a concise and accurate summary of it.

Start the lesson

Follow the steps below to open the practice file called 09Lesson, and then save it with the new name Lesson09.

Open

1   On the Standard toolbar, click the Open button.

2   In the Look In box, be sure that the Excel SBS Practice folder appears.

3   In the file list box, double-click the file named 09Lesson to open it.

To select the folder containing your practice files, refer to "Open a practice file" near the start of Lesson 1.

4   On the File menu, click Save As.

The Save As dialog box opens. Be sure that the Excel SBS Practice folder appears in the Save In box.

5   Double-click in the File Name box, and then type **Lesson09**

6   Click the Save button, or press ENTER.

If you share your computer with others who use Microsoft Excel, the screen display might have changed since your last lesson. If your screen does not look similar to the illustrations as you work through this lesson, see the Appendix, "Matching the Exercises."

Creating Summary Reports

When you're preparing a report or organizing your data, you often need to summarize information. Whether it's a question of how many copiers were sold, how much the sales totaled, or how many products are made in a particular division, you need to add space in your worksheet for the totals and then design a formula to summarize your information. With Microsoft Excel, you can add subtotals automatically, without manually adding space for them or entering formulas.

You also need a way to show only as much information as is necessary in your report. Rather than showing all of the detail in your worksheet, you can determine the level of detail that will appear in your report when you use subtotals and worksheet outlining. You can show all of the information, show only subtotals and grand totals, or show only grand totals, depending on the purpose of your report.

Inserting Subtotals in a List of Data

With Microsoft Excel, you can create subtotals for your data automatically. Instead of manually inserting rows and formulas, you can use the Subtotals command to insert the rows and formulas for you.

You can create several types of subtotals. You can count the number of items in a list, add up the amounts, average the amounts or number of items, find the maximum or minimum numbers in your list, or perform more complex statistical functions, such as standard deviation. In your inventory list, for example, you could find out the average cost of a copier, or how many different copier units the Copier division has in its inventory.

Before you use the Subtotals command, you will usually need to sort the data to be sure that you are adding the subtotals at logical points in your worksheet. However, because your inventory list is already sorted by product name, you won't need to sort your data in the next exercise.

Show the total inventory value for each type of copier

In this exercise, you create subtotals on the Copier Inventory sheet to see the total cost for each type of copier.

1 Click the Copier Inventory sheet tab, and then select cell C9.

2 On the Data menu, click Subtotals.

The Subtotal dialog box opens.

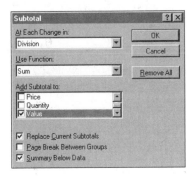

3 Click the down arrow on the At Each Change In box, and select Product Name.

This provides a subtotal for each product name.

4 In the Use Function box, be sure that Sum is selected.

5 In the Add Subtotal To box, be sure that only the Value category is checked.

You'll need to scroll through the list to see every item.

6 Make sure there are check marks in Replace Current Subtotals and Summary Below Data, and then click OK.

Subtotals are added to your worksheet in the Value field in column I, showing the total inventory value for each category of copier. Your worksheet should look similar to the following.

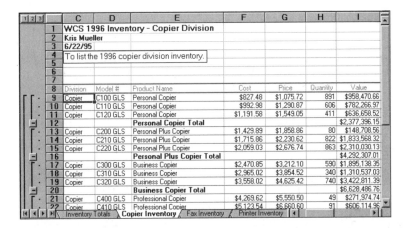

187

If you've used the subtotal command to create a set of subtotals and decide that you don't need them after all, you can use the Remove All button in the Subtotal dialog box to remove them.

Remove the subtotals you just created

In this exercise, you use the Remove All button to remove the subtotals you just created in the copier inventory.

1   Be sure that a cell within the subtotaled data is selected.

2   On the Data menu, click Subtotals.

The Subtotal dialog box opens.

3   In the Subtotal dialog box, click the Remove All button.

The subtotals are removed. Your worksheet should look like it did before you added subtotals.

Creating Nested Subtotals

If you are creating a more complex report that uses a lot of information from your inventory list, you can create multiple, or *nested*, subtotals to supply that information. As long as you turn off the Replace Current Subtotals check box in the Subtotal dialog box, you can create as many nested subtotals as you need.

In the following exercises, you'll sort the Inventory Totals database by division and by product name, and then you'll use nested subtotals to find out the average cost and price for each product in each division.

Sort by division and then by product name

1   Click the Inventory Totals sheet tab, and then select cell C9.

2   On the Data menu, click Sort.

The Sort dialog box opens.

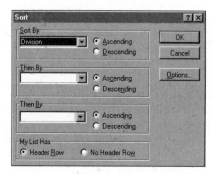

3 In the Sort By area, be sure that Division and Ascending are selected.

4 In the first Then By area, select Product Name, and be sure that Ascending is selected.

5 Click OK.

The Sort dialog box closes, and your data is sorted by Division and then by Product Name.

Average the cost and price of each product

1 On the Data menu, click Subtotals.

The Subtotal dialog box opens.

2 In the At Each Change In box, select Product Name.

3 In the Use Function box, select Average.

4 In the Add Subtotal To box, be sure that only the Cost and Price check boxes are selected.

5 Click OK.

Subtotals are added to average the cost and price for each product. Your worksheet should look similar to the following.

	B	C	D	E	F	G	H	I
7								
8		Division	Model #	Product Name	Cost	Price	Quantity	Valu
9		Copier	C300 GLS	Business Copier	$2,470.85	$3,212.10	590	$1,895,1
10		Copier	C310 GLS	Business Copier	$2,965.02	$3,854.52	340	$1,310,5
11		Copier	C320 GLS	Business Copier	$3,558.02	$4,625.42	740	$3,422,8
12				**Business Copier Average**	$2,997.96	$3,897.35		
13		Copier	C100 GLS	Personal Copier	$827.48	$1,075.72	891	$958,4
14		Copier	C110 GLS	Personal Copier	$992.98	$1,290.87	606	$782,2
15		Copier	C120 GLS	Personal Copier	$1,191.58	$1,549.05	411	$636,8
16				**Personal Copier Average**	$1,004.01	$1,305.21		
17		Copier	C200 GLS	Personal Plus Copier	$1,429.89	$1,858.86	80	$148,7
18		Copier	C210 GLS	Personal Plus Copier	$1,715.86	$2,230.62	822	$1,833,5
19		Copier	C220 GLS	Personal Plus Copier	$2,059.03	$2,676.74	863	$2,310,0
20				**Personal Plus Copier Average**	$1,734.93	$2,255.41		
21		Copier	C400 GLS	Professional Copier	$4,269.62	$5,550.50	49	$271,9
22		Copier	C410 GLS	Professional Copier	$5,123.54	$6,660.60	91	$606,1
23		Copier	C420 GLS	Professional Copier	$6,148.25	$7,992.72	199	$1,590,5
24				**Professional Copier Average**	$5,180.47	$6,734.61		
25		Copier	C500 GLS	Professional Plus Copier	$7,377.90	$9,591.27	759	$7,279,7
26		Copier	C510 GLS	Professional Plus Copier	$8,853.48	$11,509.52	580	$6,675,5
27		Copier	C520 GLS	Professional Plus Copier	$10,624.18	$13,811.43	665	$9,184,5
28				**Professional Plus Copier Averag**	$8,951.85	$11,637.41		
29		Fax	F300 G	Business Fax	$1,050.55	$1,365.72	653	$891,8
30		Fax	F350 G	Business Fax	$1,260.66	$1,638.86	404	$662,0

Inventory Totals / Copier Inventory / Fax Inventory / Printer Inventory

The subtotals appear in the columns you selected in the Add Subtotal To box. When you select one or more items in this box, you are telling Microsoft Excel to subtotal the information in those columns and to place the results in the columns as well.

Average the cost and price of all products per division

1 Select cell C9, and then on the Data menu, click Subtotals.

The Subtotal dialog box opens.

2 In the At Each Change In box, select Division.

3 In the Use Function box, be sure that Average is selected.

4 In the Add Subtotal To box, be sure that only the Cost and Price check boxes are selected.

5 Clear the Replace Current Subtotals check box, and then click OK.

Subtotals are added to average the cost and price of products for each division. Your worksheet should look similar to the following, with subtotals for each division as well as for each product within the division. You may have to scroll down the worksheet to see the division subtotals.

	Division	Model #	Product Name	Cost	Price	Quantity	V
7							
8	Division	Model #	Product Name	Cost	Price	Quantity	V
9	Copier	C300 GLS	Business Copier	$2,470.85	$3,212.10	590	$1,89
10	Copier	C310 GLS	Business Copier	$2,965.02	$3,854.52	340	$1,31
11	Copier	C320 GLS	Business Copier	$3,558.02	$4,625.42	740	$3,42
12			**Business Copier Average**	$2,997.96	$3,897.35		
13	Copier	C100 GLS	Personal Copier	$827.48	$1,075.72	891	$95
14	Copier	C110 GLS	Personal Copier	$992.98	$1,290.87	606	$78
15	Copier	C120 GLS	Personal Copier	$1,191.58	$1,549.05	411	$63
16			**Personal Copier Average**	$1,004.01	$1,305.21		
17	Copier	C200 GLS	Personal Plus Copier	$1,429.89	$1,858.86	80	$14
18	Copier	C210 GLS	Personal Plus Copier	$1,715.86	$2,230.62	822	$1,83
19	Copier	C220 GLS	Personal Plus Copier	$2,059.03	$2,676.74	863	$2,31
20			**Personal Plus Copier Average**	$1,734.93	$2,255.41		
21	Copier	C400 GLS	Professional Copier	$4,269.62	$5,550.50	49	$27
22	Copier	C410 GLS	Professional Copier	$5,123.54	$6,660.60	91	$60
23	Copier	C420 GLS	Professional Copier	$6,148.25	$7,992.72	199	$1,59
24			**Professional Copier Average**	$5,180.47	$6,734.61		
25	Copier	C500 GLS	Professional Plus Copier	$7,377.90	$9,591.27	759	$7,27
26	Copier	C510 GLS	Professional Plus Copier	$8,853.48	$11,509.52	580	$6,67
27	Copier	C520 GLS	Professional Plus Copier	$10,624.18	$13,811.43	665	$9,18
28			**Professional Plus Copier Averag**	$8,951.85	$11,637.41		
29	**Copier Average**			$3,973.84	$5,166.00		
30	Fax	F300 G	Business Fax	$1,050.55	$1,365.72	653	$89
31	Fax	F350 G	Business Fax	$1,260.66	$1,638.86	404	$66
32			**Business Fax Average**	$1,155.61	$1,502.29		
33	Fax	F600 G	Compact Professional Plus Fax	$3,136.94	$4,078.02	992	$4,04
34			**Compact Professional Plus Fax**	$3,136.94	$4,078.02		
35	Fax	F100 G	Personal Fax	$607.96	$790.35	495	$39
36			**Personal Fax Average**	$607.96	$790.35		

Inventory Totals / Copier Inventory / Fax Inventory / Printer Inventory

Working with Summary Report Outlining

When you create a report, you might not need to show every detail that's recorded in your worksheet, or even in your subtotals. Often, you need more of an overall or summary view of your data. You can display a wide scope of information, without minor details, by creating an outline of the worksheet.

When you created your subtotals, Microsoft Excel automatically outlined your worksheet. Each division and its products were grouped together, and each product name and its cost and price were grouped together, as in the preceding illustration.

The vertical lines that you see in the margin to the left of the worksheet and the number buttons above the lines are outlining buttons that allow you to control how much detail is displayed in your report. In the Inventory Totals sheet, you now have four levels of outlining. You can create up to eight vertical and eight horizontal levels of outlining on a worksheet. Level 1 is the highest level, consisting of only the grand average of cost and price for all products in the inventory. Level 2 breaks it down a little more, into product averages for each division. Level 3 adds the subtotals by product name, and level 4 shows all of the details in your worksheet.

You can hide the details of the outline by clicking the outline level buttons, the numbered buttons at the top of the outlining area. The outline level buttons are numbered 1, 2, 3, and 4 to correspond with the levels of detail in your worksheet. If you want to see only the grand totals, click the first outline level button. If you want to see all details, you can click the fourth outline level button.

In the next exercise, you'll hide details of your outline to show only the Cost and Price averages for each Division and then show details of the Cost and Price averages for each product, but not the details for each individual product.

Hide and then show some details in the outline

1   Click the level 2 outline button.

Your worksheet changes to show only the Cost and Price averages for each Division.

Outline level buttons

	B	C	D	E	F	G	H
7							
8		Division	Model #	Product Name	Cost	Price	Quantity
29		Copier Average			$3,973.84	$5,166.00	
46		Fax Average			$1,578.19	$2,051.65	
63		Printer Average			$1,655.08	$2,151.60	
64				Grand Average	$2,574.34	$3,346.64	
65							
66							
67							

2   Click the level 3 outline button.

Your worksheet changes to show the Cost and Price averages for each Product Name. Your worksheet should look similar to the following.

1 2 3 4	B	C	D	E	F	G	H	
7								
8		Division	Model #	Product Name	Cost	Price	Quantity	
12				Business Copier Average	$2,997.96	$3,897.35		
16				Personal Copier Average	$1,004.01	$1,305.21		
20				Personal Plus Copier Average	$1,734.93	$2,255.41		
24				Professional Copier Average	$5,180.47	$6,734.61		
28				Professional Plus Copier Averag	$8,951.85	$11,637.41		
29		Copier Average			$3,973.84	$5,166.00		
32				Business Fax Average	$1,155.61	$1,502.29		
34				Compact Professional Plus Fax ,	$3,136.94	$4,078.02		
36				Personal Fax Average	$607.96	$790.35		
39				Personal Plus Fax Average	$802.61	$1,043.39		
42				Professional Fax Average	$1,664.08	$2,163.30		
45				Professional Plus Fax Average	$2,396.23	$3,115.09		
46		Fax Average			$1,578.19	$2,051.65		
50				Business Printer - Laser Averag	$1,860.79	$2,419.03		
54				Personal Plus Printer - Bubble J	$744.32	$967.62		
58				Personal Printer - Dot Matrix Av	$323.61	$420.69		
62				Professional Printer - Laser Pos	$3,691.59	$4,799.07		
63		Printer Average			$1,655.08	$2,151.60		
64				Grand Average	$2,574.34	$3,346.64		
65								
66								
67								

In the previous exercise, you worked with whole levels of your outline. You can also show or hide portions of a level. For example, under the Copier division, you have five copier subtotals. You can show all details for any one of these subtotals, or for all of them, by using the show detail buttons.

Show and then hide all details for the Personal Plus Copier

In this exercise, you show and then hide all of the details for the Personal Plus Copier.

1   Locate and then click the show detail button for the Personal Plus Copier on your worksheet (the plus sign in the outlining area to the left of the Personal Plus Copier Average).

The details for only the Personal Plus Copier appear. The other copiers are still only shown as subtotals. Your worksheet should look like the following.

Show detail button

Hide detail button

1 2 3 4	B	C	D	E	F	G	H	
7								
8		Division	Model #	Product Name	Cost	Price	Quantity	
12				Business Copier Average	$2,997.96	$3,897.35		
16				Personal Copier Average	$1,004.01	$1,305.21		
17		Copier	C200 GLS	Personal Plus Copier	$1,429.89	$1,858.86	80	$14
18		Copier	C210 GLS	Personal Plus Copier	$1,715.86	$2,230.62	822	$1,83
19		Copier	C220 GLS	Personal Plus Copier	$2,059.03	$2,676.74	863	$2,31
20				Personal Plus Copier Average	$1,734.93	$2,255.41		
24				Professional Copier Average	$5,180.47	$6,734.61		
28				Professional Plus Copier Averag	$8,951.85	$11,637.41		
29		Copier Average			$3,973.84	$5,166.00		
32				Business Fax Average	$1,155.61	$1,502.29		
34				Compact Professional Plus Fax ,	$3,136.94	$4,078.02		
36				Personal Fax Average	$607.96	$790.35		
39				Personal Plus Fax Average	$802.61	$1,043.39		
42				Professional Fax Average	$1,664.08	$2,163.30		
45				Professional Plus Fax Average	$2,396.23	$3,115.09		
46		Fax Average			$1,578.19	$2,051.65		
50				Business Printer - Laser Averag	$1,860.79	$2,419.03		
54				Personal Plus Printer - Bubble J	$744.32	$967.62		
58				Personal Printer - Dot Matrix Av	$323.61	$420.69		
62				Professional Printer - Laser Pos	$3,691.59	$4,799.07		
63		Printer Average			$1,655.08	$2,151.60		
64				Grand Average	$2,574.34	$3,346.64		
65								

2 Click the hide detail button for the Personal Plus Copier Average.

The Personal Plus Copier details are hidden again. Your worksheet should now show only the subtotals, with no detail information.

Outlining a Sheet Without Subtotals

If you need to create a report that shows summary information without the details, even though your worksheet was already subtotaled manually, you can still outline the data with the Auto Outline command. To outline your data, you must have formulas to total your data, either below or to the right of your data. These formulas determine how many levels your automatic outline will have and where the divisions will be. The formulas can also deter-mine the orientation of your outline. When you created subtotals before, they were below your data; your outline was vertically oriented and the outline buttons were on the left side of your worksheet. If the formulas in your data are to the right of your data, the out-line will be horizontal instead, and the outline buttons will be along the top of your work-sheet. In the next exercises, you'll use automatic outlining to turn your Fax Inventory sheet into a summary report, and then you'll hide some of the data.

Change your fax inventory data into a summary report

1 Switch to the Fax Inventory sheet.

The Fax Inventory sheet has been subtotaled manually by entering SUM formulas in the Quantity and Value columns.

2 Select cells C9:I21.

3 On the Data menu, point to Group And Outline, and then click Auto Outline.

Your data is outlined in three levels. You can manipulate this worksheet to show as much or as little data as you need to, just like on the Inventory Totals worksheet. Your worksheet should look similar to the following.

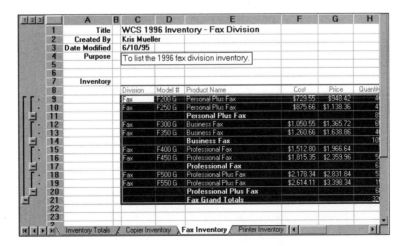

193

Hide data in the Fax Inventory outline

1 Click the hide detail button to the left of the Fax Grand Totals row.

All of the individual product data is hidden. Only the Fax Grand Totals are visible, as in the following illustration.

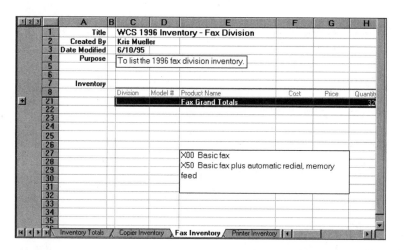

2 Click the show detail button next to the Fax Grand Totals row.

Microsoft Excel displays all of the detail data again.

NOTE In the previous exercises, you applied automatic outlining to a worksheet that contained SUM formulas, and the SUM formulas determined the structure of the outline. You can also apply an outline to data that has no summary formulas by manually grouping the data. To apply a manual outline to data in rows, separate the groups of data by inserting rows, and then select the data in one of the groups. On the Data menu, point to Group And Outline, and then click Group. Click Rows, and then click OK.

Removing Worksheet Outlining

If you decide that you do not want to use the outlining that has been applied to an existing worksheet or that you changed your mind about the outlining that you created, you can remove the outlining. To do so, select a cell within the range that was outlined, and then use the Clear Outline command on the Data menu to remove the outlining. You can also use this command to remove the outlining from a subtotaled list. When you clear the out-line in a subtotaled list, only the outlining buttons are removed; the subtotals remain.

Remove the outlining from the fax inventory sheet

In this exercise, you use the Clear Outline command to remove your outlining from the Fax Inventory sheet.

1 Select cell G9.

You can select any cell within the outlined range to remove the outlining.

2 On the Data menu, point to Group And Outline, and then click Clear Outline.

The outline and all of the outlining buttons are removed. Your Fax Inventory sheet should look like it did before you outlined it.

Creating Consolidated Reports

Suppose you have three sheets of unsummarized inventory data and you need to produce a report that summarizes all of the data on those sheets. You already saw how you can place all of the data in one sheet and then use subtotals and outlining to create a report in which you can show or hide levels of detail. Another way to create a report is to consolidate all of the data onto one sheet, summarizing as you go. Consolidating pulls all of the detail data together from separate sheets or separate ranges, summarizes the information, and then places the summary onto a sheet that you specify.

When you consolidate data, you need to select a destination for the summary, a function (such as SUM) to use in consolidating the data, and the detail data that you want to consolidate. The destination can be another sheet or another workbook. The function you use depends on the type of data and the type of report that you are creating. For the inventory data, you would want to use SUM to summarize the inventory totals. You can consolidate data from other sheets in the same workbook or from several different workbooks. When you consolidate data, however, you need to be sure that the data on each sheet has the same column and/or row headings. Otherwise, you will end up with a list of details, rather than the summary you want. In this case, you'll consolidate the data from the three division sheets in the inventory workbook.

In the next four exercises, you'll prepare the data, select a destination for your consolidated inventory and a function for your consolidation, select the data that you want to consolidate, and then add labels and finish consolidating all of your inventory data onto one sheet.

Prepare the data for consolidation

1 Be sure the Fax Inventory sheet is active.

To clear a row, select the row header, and then press the DEL key.

2 Clear the contents of rows 11, 14, 17, 20, and 21, since they contain subtotals or grand totals.

The Consolidate command will treat all rows containing data as if they were line items; therefore, the rows that contain summary formulas must be cleared before the data can be properly consolidated.

Select a destination and a consolidating function

1 Switch to the Inventory Report sheet.

This sheet is mostly blank, ready for you to add the consolidated data from the Printer Inventory sheet.

2 Select cell C8, and then on the Data menu, click Consolidate.

The Consolidate dialog box opens.

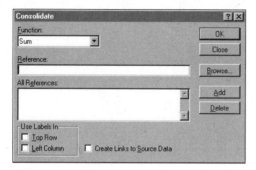

3 In the Function box, be sure that Sum is selected.

Select the data to consolidate

1 Click in the Reference text box, and then click the Printer Inventory sheet tab.

2 Drag the Consolidate dialog box out of the way, and then drag to select cells E8:I20.

The sheet name and range references appear in the Reference box. Cells E8:I20 contain all of the printer inventory data and the row of headings.

3 Click the Add button.

The range selected in the Reference box is added to the All References box.

4 Click the Fax Inventory sheet tab.

5 On the Fax Inventory sheet, drag to select cells E8:I19.

6 Click the Add button.

The range selected in the Reference box is added to the All References box.

7 Click the Copier Inventory sheet tab.

8 On the Copier Inventory sheet, drag to select cells E8:I23.

9 Click the Add button.

The three consolidation ranges have been added to the All References box. Your dialog box should look similar to the following.

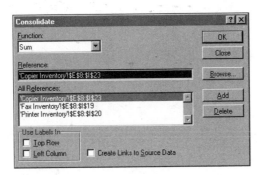

Add labels and finish consolidating the inventory data

1 In the Use Labels In area, select both the Top Row and Left Column check boxes.

You want to use the labels in both the top row and left column of your data.

2 Click OK.

The Consolidate dialog box closes, and your printer, copier, and fax data is consolidated on your worksheet. You might need to adjust the column widths before you can see all of your data. Your Inventory Report sheet should look similar to the following.

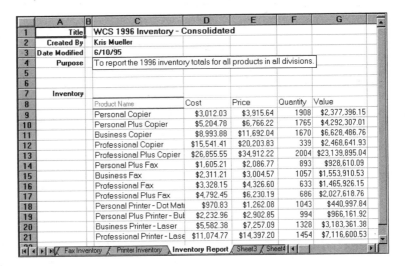

197

One Step Further: Sorting a Subtotaled List

If you find that you would prefer to show the items in a subtotaled list in a different order, for example, ascending instead of descending order, you can sort your list. To sort a subtotaled list, you just hide the detail rows and then sort the subtotal rows. When you sort a subtotaled list, the hidden detail rows are automatically moved with the subtotal rows.

 IMPORTANT   If you do not hide the detail rows before sorting a subtotaled list, your subtotals will be removed and all of the rows in your list will be reordered.

Try sorting the subtotaled data in your Inventory Totals sheet by Division in descending order.

Sort a subtotaled list

1   Switch to the Inventory Totals sheet, and then select cell C8.

2   Click the level 2 outline button in the outlining area to hide all but the Division subtotal rows.

3   On the Data menu, click Sort.

The Sort dialog box opens.

4   In the Sort By box, be sure that Division is selected, and then select Descending. Be sure that next two Then By boxes are blank (select None to make the Then By boxes blank).

5   Click OK.

The new list is sorted in descending alphabetical order by division.

If You Want to Continue to the Next Lesson

1   On the File menu, click Save.

2   On the File menu, click Close.

If You Want to Quit Microsoft Excel for Now

➤   On the File menu, click Exit.

If you see the Save dialog box, click Yes.

Lesson Summary

To	Do this
Add subtotals	Click any cell in your list or database. On the Data menu, click Subtotals. In the At Each Change In box, select which category you want to subtotal. In the Use Function box, select a formula. In the Add Subtotal To box, select the column in which you want the subtotals to appear, and then click OK.
Remove all subtotals	On the Data menu, click Subtotals. In the Subtotal dialog box, click the Remove All button.
Add a nested subtotal	Click any cell in your list or database. On the Data menu, click Subtotals. In the At Each Change In box, select which category you want to subtotal. In the Use Function box, select a formula. In the Add Subtotal To box, select the column in which you want the sub-totals to appear. Be sure that there is no check mark in the Replace Current Subtotals box, and then click OK.
Hide details in an outline	Click the hide detail button for the level that you want to collapse.
Show details in an outline	Click the show detail button for the level that you want to expand.
Outline a worksheet that contains formulas	Select the range that you want to outline. On the Data menu, point to Group And Outline, and then click Auto Outline.
Remove an outline	Select any cell in the range that is outlined. On the Data menu, point to Group And Outline, and then click Clear Outline.

To	Do this
Consolidate data from several sheets	Select a destination sheet. On the Data menu, click Consolidate. In the Function box, select a function. Click in the Reference text box, and then drag to select the first range that you want to consolidate. Click the Add button and continue selecting and adding ranges until you have selected all of the ranges. Click OK.

For online information about	Use the Answer Wizard to search for
Creating subtotals	**subtotal**
Outlining a worksheet	**outline**
Consolidating data	**consolidate**

Preview of the Next Lesson

In the next lesson, "Creating Customized Reports," you'll learn how to modify a special kind of summary table, called a pivot table, to create a detailed analytical report.

Creating Customized Reports

Lesson

10

Estimated time

55 min.

In this lesson you will learn how to:

- Summarize your data with a pivot table.
- Change your data's organization without restructuring the worksheet.
- Format your data to present a professional look.

When you create a report, you often need to view your data in different ways. Perhaps you have a list of sales by person, but you need to list sales by region. Or maybe you have a simple personnel list and you need to see totals by department or division. Instead of creating a report with subtotals, you can use a *pivot table* to assemble the data in your list and show only the categories you choose. Then you can decide which categories to show summaries for and which functions to use in the summaries. Instead of the list, you can create a report in which you can add, remove, or substitute fields easily, without affecting your original data.

In this lesson, you'll create a simple pivot table and adjust the data that appears in the table. Then you'll change how your data is summarized. You'll also learn how to format cells in a table and how to format the entire table automatically.

Start the lesson

Follow the steps below to open the practice file called 10Lesson, and then save it with the new name Lesson10.

1   On the Standard toolbar, click the Open button.

201

To select the folder containing your practice files, refer to "Open a practice file" near the start of Lesson 1.

2 In the Look In box, be sure that the Excel SBS Practice folder appears.

3 In the file list box, double-click the file named 10Lesson to open it.

4 On the File menu, click Save As.

The Save As dialog box opens. Be sure that the Excel SBS Practice folder appears in the Save In box.

5 Double-click in the File Name box, and then type **Lesson10**

6 Click the Save button, or press ENTER.

If you share your computer with others who use Microsoft Excel, the screen display might have changed since your last lesson. If your screen does not look similar to the illustrations as you work through this lesson, see the Appendix, "Matching the Exercises."

Creating a Pivot Table

Your personnel list has eight database fields, or columns, with field names across the top of the list (Last Name, Position, and so on), and it contains several records. If you want to report subtotals only, you can use the subtotals or outlining commands to create a summary report. But, if you want to create a report that combines all of the data and shows a summary of only certain subsets of the data, it would be much easier to use a pivot table.

With a pivot table, you can take an entire list of data and show summaries for parts of the data, in any orientation that you like. With your personnel list, you could create a pivot table that shows all departments in each division and that averages the number of employees. Or your pivot table could show the maximum or minimum salaries in each division, department, and position. Pivot tables are very flexible—possibilities are limited only by the type of data you are working with. You can also easily rearrange the layout of your data and hide or show specific fields and categories, without having to recreate the pivot table.

With a pivot table you can present the same set of data in both these ways.

Field buttons

Division	Fax	▼

Sum of Salary	
Department	Total
Accounting	$140,385
Admin.	$183,078
Art	$98,273
Engineering	$526,064
Marketing	$298,296
R and D	$123,696
Grand Total	$1,369,792

Sum of Salary	Division			
Department	Copier	Fax	Printer	Grand Total
Accounting	$142,082	$140,385	$146,318	$428,785
Admin.	$190,017	$183,078	$235,798	$608,893
Art	$84,049	$98,273	$59,025	$241,347
Engineering	$623,232	$526,064	$714,100	$1,863,396
Marketing	$416,603	$298,296	$527,849	$1,242,747
R and D	$131,557	$123,696	$240,528	$495,781
Grand Total	$1,587,540	$1,369,792	$1,923,617	$4,880,949

The layout can be rearranged simply by dragging field buttons to new positions on the worksheet, and detail data can be shown or hidden easily be double-clicking cells.

To create a pivot table, you select a cell within the database you want to use and then use the PivotTable command on the Data menu. After you've decided which fields to include, you can decide where the pivot table will be placed in your workbook. Usually, it's best to create your pivot tables on a separate sheet in your workbook. You will then have enough space to work with your table without overlapping or accidentally deleting other information on a sheet.

Create a pivot table from your personnel list

In this exercise, you use the data in your personnel list to create a pivot table that shows the totals for salaries by position in each department.

1 Be sure the Personnel List sheet is the active sheet, and then select cell C10.

   You can select any cell in your database—Excel will use the entire database in your pivot table.

2 On the Data menu, click PivotTable.

   The PivotTable Wizard opens. Since you are creating your pivot table from an Excel list, leave the first option selected.

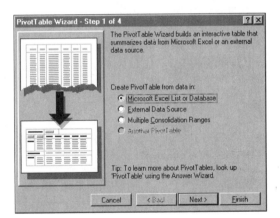

3 Click the Next button.

   Step 2 of the PivotTable Wizard appears, with your database area already entered in the Range box.

4 Choose the Next button.

   Step 3 of the PivotTable Wizard appears, ready for you to design your table.

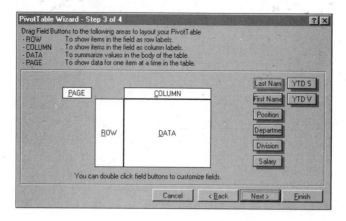

5 Drag the Position field button from the right side of the dialog box into the Row area.

On the right side of the dialog box, you'll see one field button for each field in your database. Moving the Position field button into the Row area means that each position will be listed in a separate row in your pivot table.

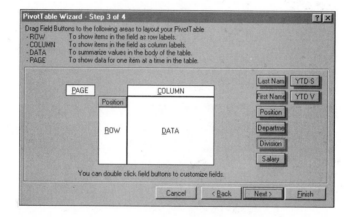

6 Drag the Division button from the right side of the dialog box into the Column area.

Each division will appear in a separate column in your pivot table.

7 Drag the Salary button from the right side of the dialog box into the Data area.

The Salary button changes to read "Sum Of Salary." The salaries for each position in each department will be summarized, using the SUM function, in the data area of your pivot table. The PivotTable Wizard dialog box should look like the following.

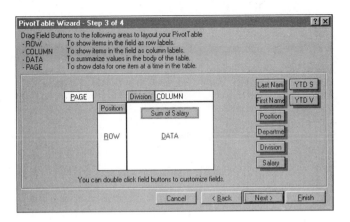

8   Click the Next button.

Step 4 of the PivotTable Wizard appears.

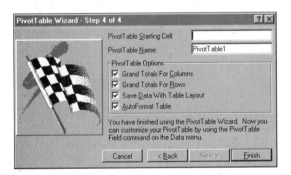

9   Click in the PivotTable Starting Cell box, and then click the Personnel Report sheet tab, and select cell C8.

You might need to move the dialog box out of the way to select cell C8. If you leave the Pivot Table Starting Cell box blank, Microsoft Excel will insert a new worksheet and place the pivot table in cell A1 of the new worksheet.

10 In the PivotTable Options area, be sure that all four options are selected, and then click the Finish button.

The pivot table appears on your Personnel Report sheet, starting in cell C8. The Query And Pivot toolbar opens so that you can make changes to your table. Your worksheet should look similar to the following.

Row area   Column area

	A	B	C	D	E	F	G	H
1	Title		West Coast Sales Personnel Report					
2	Created By		Kris Mueller					
3	Date Modified		6/10/95					
4								
5	Purpose		Use this worksheet to learn about pivot table reports					
6								
7	Report Area							
8			Sum of Salary	Division				
9			Position	Copier	Fax	Printer	Grand Total	
10			Accountant	57640.68	83742.12	63078.48	204461.28	
11			Admin. Assist.	181989.46	194919.99	233156.82	610066.27	
12			Chief Scientist	59455.2	57756.48	59455.2	176666.88	
13			Design Specialist	84048.93	98273.49	59024.91	241347.33	
14			Engineer	547034.68	429864.65	589592.91	1566492.24	
15			Group Admin. Assist.	118184.08	80124.8	140218.4	338527.28	
16			Group Mgr.	97096.35	104565.3	77179.15	278840.8	
17			Office Manager	0	0	65821.56	65821.56	
18			Product Marketer	264450.54	166649.4	327674.67	758774.61	
19			Technician	54216.4	81076.65	229353.85	364646.9	
20			Unit Mgr.	116511.36	72819.6	79061.28	268392.24	
21			Grand Total	1580627.68	1369792.48	1923617.23	4874037.39	

Personnel List **Personnel Report** Sheet3 Sheet4

The pivot table is linked to its source data. If the source data changes, the pivot table can be updated using the Refresh Data command on the Data menu. You'll practice refreshing your pivot table in a later exercise.

Modifying a Pivot Table

The first time you create a pivot table for a report, you might not always be certain which data you will need. Pivot tables make it easy to modify the data you've included. If you were creating a worksheet by hand, you would have to do a lot more restructuring and probably a lot of data entry to rearrange, add, or remove data. The Query And Pivot toolbar includes tools that you can use to modify your pivot table without using any menu commands.

With the PivotTable Wizard and the shortcut menu, you can quickly add or remove data from your table. Any data that appears in your original worksheet is available to use in your pivot table, even if it does not currently appear in the pivot table itself.

With the PivotTable Wizard and field buttons, you can modify either your entire table or only a specific field. By dragging a field button to the Page area, you can separate your data onto different 'pages' according to the categories in the field. You can use the Refresh Data button to update your pivot table if the source data in your original database

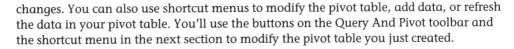

changes. You can also use shortcut menus to modify the pivot table, add data, or refresh the data in your pivot table. You'll use the buttons on the Query And Pivot toolbar and the shortcut menu in the next section to modify the pivot table you just created.

Adding Data

The pivot table in the Lesson10 file already has one column header (Division), one row header (Position), and one formula (Sum of Salary) to total the salaries for each position in each division. In the next exercise, you'll add another data field to your pivot table to summarize how much sick leave is available to all of the people in each position in each division.

Add sick leave summaries to your pivot table

1   Use the right mouse button to click cell D10.

Since you want to add a new data field to your pivot table, you need to click a cell in the data area. The shortcut menu appears.

2   In the shortcut menu, point to Add Data Field, and then click YTD S.

YTD S stands for year-to-date sick leave. The Sum Of YTD S data field is added to your pivot table.

3   Be sure that cell D10 (the first Sum of YTD S label) is still selected, and then type **YTD Sick Leave** ENTER.

All of the Sum Of YTD S labels change after you press ENTER, and the pivot table data is easier to understand. The labels and buttons in the pivot table can be edited just like any other cell. If the column is too narrow to read the labels, double-click the border between column headers D and E.

	A	B	C	D	E	F	G	
7	**Report Area**							
8					Division			
9			Position	Data	Copier	Fax	Printer	Gr
10			Accountant	YTD Sick Leave	13	8	5	
11				Sum of Salary	57640.68	83742.12	63078.48	
12			Admin. Assist.	YTD Sick Leave	24.25	44.5	36	
13				Sum of Salary	181989.46	194919.99	233156.82	
14			Chief Scientist	YTD Sick Leave	2.5	2	5	
15				Sum of Salary	59455.2	57756.48	59455.2	
16			Design Specialist	YTD Sick Leave	52.75	26	5	
17				Sum of Salary	84048.93	98273.49	59024.91	
18			Engineer	YTD Sick Leave	37.25	61.5	109.25	
19				Sum of Salary	547034.68	429864.65	589592.91	1
20			Group Admin. Assist.	YTD Sick Leave	16.75	39.5	27.5	
21				Sum of Salary	118184.08	80124.8	140218.4	
22			Group Mgr.	YTD Sick Leave	10	15	3	
23				Sum of Salary	97096.35	104565.3	77179.15	
24			Office Manager	YTD Sick Leave	0	0	7.5	
25				Sum of Salary	0	0	65821.56	
26			Product Marketer	YTD Sick Leave	32	19.5	44.75	
27				Sum of Salary	264450.54	166649.4	327674.67	
28			Technician	YTD Sick Leave	8.5	10.75	66	

Personnel List / **Personnel Report** / Sheet3 / Sheet4

You can easily add data to or rearrange your table. You can drag header buttons to different positions on your worksheet to rearrange the pivot table layout. If you have a large table and you need to divide it into segments, you can use the PivotTable Wizard to add a Page area. When you drag a field button to the Page area, you separate each item in that field onto a different 'page' in your report. These pages are not separate sheets in your workbook, but separate views of your pivot table. In the next exercises, you'll add the Department field to the Page area of your table. You'll view the different departments, and then you'll move the Department field to the row area.

Place departments on separate pages

PivotTable Wizard

You can display the Query and Pivot toolbar by clicking Toolbars on the View menu. Click Query and Pivot, and click OK.

1   Select cell C8, and then click the PivotTable Wizard button on the Query And Pivot toolbar.

You could also use the PivotTable command on the shortcut menu. The PivotTable Wizard opens, ready for you to make changes to the organization of your table.

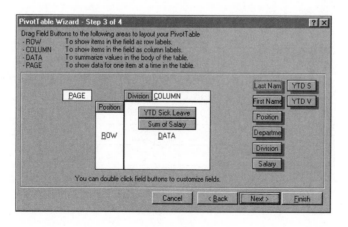

2 Drag the Department field button into the Page area in the PivotTable Wizard.

The Department field button appears in the Page area. When you drag a field to the Page area, the pivot table displays only one category from that field in your pivot table at a time. You can view the other categories, or 'pages,' in the field by selecting them from the Page area list box. The dialog box should look similar to the following illustration.

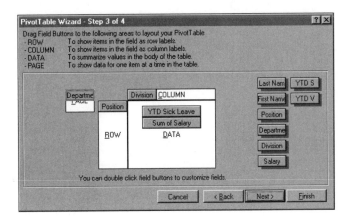

3 In the PivotTable Wizard, click the Finish button.

The PivotTable Wizard closes and the Department field appears in the Page area in your table. Initially, the summary data for all departments is displayed in the pivot table.

Page area

	A	B	C	D	E	F	G	
1	Title		West Coast Sales Personnel Rep					
2	Created By		Kris Mueller					
3	Date Modified		6/10/95					
4								
5	Purpose		Use this worksheet to learn about pivot table reports					
6			Department	(All)				
7	Report Area							
8					Division			
9			Position	Data	Copier	Fax	Printer	Gre
10			Accountant	YTD Sick Leave	13	8	5	
11				Sum of Salary	57640.68	83742.12	63078.48	2
12			Admin. Assist.	YTD Sick Leave	24.25	44.5	36	
13				Sum of Salary	181989.46	194919.99	233156.82	6
14			Chief Scientist	YTD Sick Leave	2.5	2	5	
15				Sum of Salary	59455.2	57756.48	59455.2	
16			Design Specialist	YTD Sick Leave	52.75	26	5	
17				Sum of Salary	84048.93	98273.49	59024.91	2
18			Engineer	YTD Sick Leave	37.25	61.5	109.25	
19				Sum of Salary	547034.68	429864.65	589592.91	19
20			Group Admin. Assist.	YTD Sick Leave	16.75	39.5	27.5	
21				Sum of Salary	118184.08	80124.8	140218.4	3
22			Group Mgr.	YTD Sick Leave	10	15	3	

Personnel List / **Personnel Report** / Sheet3 / Sheet4

209

View different departments

1 Click the down arrow next to the Department list box.

The Department list opens.

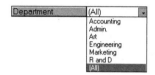

2 In the list, select Engineering.

The pivot table changes to show the YTD Sick Leave and Sum Of Salary for the Engineering department by position in each division.

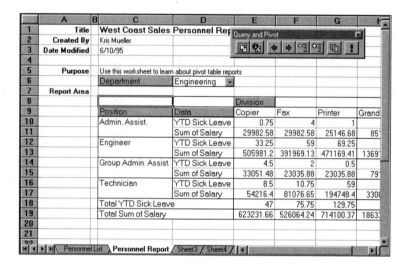

3 Click the down arrow next to the Department name.

The Department list opens again.

4 In the Department list, select (All).

The pivot table changes to show the summary data for all departments by position in each division, just as it did in the beginning of this exercise. Your worksheet should look similar to the following.

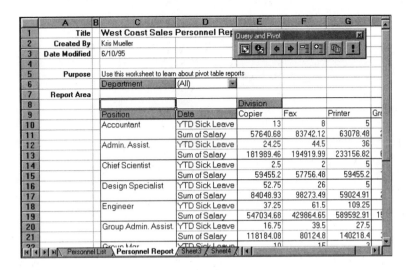

Change the department field to a row header

1 On the Personnel Report sheet, drag the Department button (cell C6) downward so that it is just above the Position button.

When you drag the field button in the Page area, the pointer changes to look like it is dragging three pages.

When you drag a field button into the Row area, the pointer changes to look like it is dragging two row headers with details to the right of them.

2 Release the mouse button.

The Department field button moves from the Page area to the Row area. It now appears in the column next to the Position field button. Each department is listed in a row with subtotals for the departments listed below each department. Your pivot table should look similar to the following.

	A	B	C	D	E	F	G
1		Title	West Coast Sales Personnel Report				
2		Created By	Kris Mueller				
3		Date Modified	6/10/95				
4							
5		Purpose	Use this worksheet to learn about pivot table reports				
6							
7		Report Area					
8						Division	
9			Department	Position	Data	Copier	Fax
10			Accounting	Accountant	YTD Sick Leave	13	
11					Sum of Salary	57640.68	83742.1
12				Admin. Assist.	YTD Sick Leave	12.25	1
13					Sum of Salary	49485.8	27597.8
14				Group Admin. As	YTD Sick Leave	3.75	3
15					Sum of Salary	28043.68	29045.2
16			Accounting YTD Sick Leave			29	4
17			Accounting Sum of Salary			135170.16	140385.2
18			Admin.	Admin. Assist.	YTD Sick Leave	10.25	18.
19					Sum of Salary	73505.68	110258.5
20				Office Manager	YTD Sick Leave	0	
21					Sum of Salary	0	
22				Unit Mgr	YTD Sick Leave	0.5	3.7

Personnel List **Personnel Report** Sheet3 Sheet4

Hiding, Showing, and Removing Data

Removing data from your pivot table is even easier than adding data. Don't worry about removing data from your table permanently; you can always add it back. You will not lose information if you remove a field from your pivot table. If you want the data to remain available in your table but you don't want it to be visible, you can hide it. You can also hide details under a particular row or column heading. You can hide or show data with the PivotTable Field dialog box.

Hide and show the Accounting department details

In this exercise, you hide the details under the Accounting department so that instead of seeing each position, you'll see a summary of all of the positions in that department.

1   Double-click cell C10—you can't see the gridlines for C10:C15, but the cells are there.

Cell C10 contains the Accounting label. Double-clicking the cell condenses the Accounting department so that it is summarized as an entire department, rather than by position within the department. The positions in the Accounting department disappear and are replaced by a summary total, as in the following illustration.

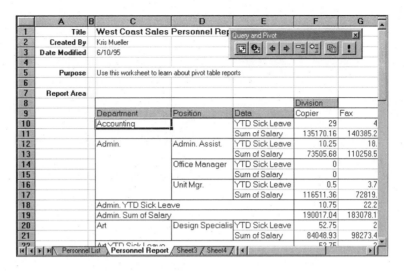

The table shown in the image contains:

	A	B	C	D	E	F	G
1	Title		West Coast Sales Personnel Rep				
2	Created By		Kris Mueller				
3	Date Modified		6/10/95				
4							
5	Purpose		Use this worksheet to learn about pivot table reports				
6							
7	Report Area						
8						Division	
9			Department	Position	Data	Copier	Fax
10			Accounting		YTD Sick Leave	29	4
11					Sum of Salary	135170.16	140385.2
12			Admin.	Admin. Assist.	YTD Sick Leave	10.25	18.
13					Sum of Salary	73505.68	110258.5
14				Office Manager	YTD Sick Leave	0	
15					Sum of Salary	0	
16				Unit Mgr.	YTD Sick Leave	0.5	3.7
17					Sum of Salary	116511.36	72819.
18			Admin. YTD Sick Leave			10.75	22.2
19			Admin. Sum of Salary			190017.04	183078.1
20			Art	Design Specialis	YTD Sick Leave	52.75	2
21					Sum of Salary	84048.93	98273.4
22			Art YTD Sick Leave			52.75	2

Query and Pivot toolbar

Tabs: Personnel List, **Personnel Report**, Sheet3, Sheet4

2 Double-click cell C10 again.

The department is expanded to show data by position again.

If you are working with sensitive data, such as a personnel list, you might want to hide certain information in your table without actually deleting it from your worksheet. In the next exercise, you'll move the Department button back to a Page orientation and then hide all but the Engineering and R and D department information.

Hide the accounting, admin., art, and marketing data

1 Drag the Department button back to cell C6—where the Page area was.

The Department field is moved from the Row area back to the Page area.

2 Click the down arrow next to the Department list box, and select (All) from the list if it is not already selected.

The summary data for all departments appears.

3 Double-click the Department button itself.

The PivotTable Field dialog box opens.

213

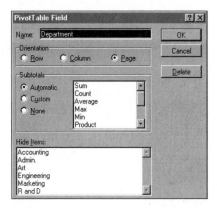

4 In the Hide Items list, select Accounting, Admin., Art, and Marketing, and then click OK.

5 Click the down arrow next to the Department button.

The list of departments now shows only Engineering and R and D.

Show all departments again

1 Double-click the Department button.

The PivotTable Field dialog box opens.

2 In the Hide Items box, click Accounting, Admin., Art, and Marketing to de-select them.

3 Click OK.

All departments are available in the department list again.

Suppose you want to know what data was used to calculate the Copier division Engineers' Sum of Salary value (in cell E19). If you want to see the source data details that were used to calculate a specific value, you double-click the data cell that contains the value, and a new sheet containing the source detail data will be added to your workbook. The source detail data will be a copy of the original database information, but this copy will include only the details underlying the cell you double-clicked. In the next exercise, you'll view the source detail information that Excel used to calculate the total of the salaries for all engineers in the Copier division.

Show all source details for the total of engineers' salaries in your table

> Double-click cell E19.

This cell contains the sum of salaries for engineers in the Copier division. A new sheet that contains the Copier engineers' salary source details from your database is inserted into the workbook.

	A	B	C	D	E	F	G	H
1	Last Name	First Name	Position	Department	Division	Salary	YTD S	YTD V
2	Lempert	Alexandra	Engineer	R and D	Copier	41053.48	4	42
3	Coyne	Dennis	Engineer	Engineering	Copier	44350.5	12	12.5
4	Dorfberg	Jeremy	Engineer	Engineering	Copier	34002.05	0.75	7.875
5	White	Jessica	Engineer	Engineering	Copier	46386.85	3	31.5
6	Fein	Caroline	Engineer	Engineering	Copier	70934.88	1.5	15.75
7	Solomon	Ari	Engineer	Engineering	Copier	56177.3	6	6.5
8	Beech	Susan	Engineer	Engineering	Copier	69070.05	3	31.5
9	McKormick	Brad	Engineer	Engineering	Copier	105753.02	6	7.75
10	Abdul	Cathy	Engineer	Engineering	Copier	79306.55	1	10.5
11								
12								
13								
14								
15								
16								
17								
18								
19								
20								
21								

Personnel List \ Sheet1 / Personnel Report / Sheet3

One of the advantages of working with pivot tables is that you can add or remove data from the pivot table without affecting the original database information. If you decide that you don't need to see a particular data field, you can simply remove it from your pivot table. You can always add the information back later if you decide that it's necessary after all.

Remove sick leave data from your pivot table

In this exercise, you remove the year-to-date sick leave data from your pivot table.

1 Switch to the Personnel Report sheet.

2 Use the right mouse button to click cell D10.

The shortcut menu appears.

3 On the shortcut menu, click PivotTable.

The PivotTable Wizard opens to Step 3 so that you can modify your pivot table.

4 Drag the YTD Sick Leave button out of the pivot table area.

The YTD Sick Leave field is removed from the Data area.

5 In the PivotTable Wizard, click the Finish button.

The PivotTable Wizard closes, and the YTD Sick Leave data is removed from the table. Your table should look similar to the following.

	A	B	C	D	E	F	G	H
1	Title		West Coast Sales Personnel Rep					
2	Created By		Kris Mueller					
3	Date Modified		6/10/95					
4								
5	Purpose		Use this worksheet to learn about pivot table reports					
6			Department	(All)				
7	Report Area							
8			Sum of Salary	Division				
9			Position	Copier	Fax	Printer	Grand Total	
10			Accountant	57640.68	83742.12	63078.48	204461.28	
11			Admin. Assist.	181989.46	194919.99	233156.82	610066.27	
12			Chief Scientist	59455.2	57756.48	59455.2	176666.88	
13			Design Specialist	84048.93	98273.49	59024.91	241347.33	
14			Engineer	547034.68	429864.65	589592.91	1566492.24	
15			Group Admin. Assist.	118184.08	80124.8	140218.4	338527.28	
16			Group Mgr.	97096.35	104565.3	77179.15	278840.8	
17			Office Manager	0	0	65821.56	65821.56	
18			Product Marketer	264450.54	166649.4	327674.67	758774.61	
19			Technician	54216.4	81076.65	229353.85	364646.9	
20			Unit Mgr.	116511.36	72819.6	79061.28	268392.24	
21			Grand Total	1580627.68	1369792.48	1923617.23	4874037.39	

Personnel List / Sheet1 \ Personnel Report / Sheet3

Changing Summary Functions

So far you've seen only one function used in your pivot table, the SUM function. You can use several other functions depending on the type of data you are using. For numeric data, the default function is Sum, but you can also use Average, Max, Min, and other functions that apply to your data. For text data, the default function is Count, but again, you can change the function as necessary.

Change summary functions

In this exercise, you add year-to-date vacation time summaries to the Data area and then change the summary functions from Sum to Max and Min to see the maximum and minimum amounts of vacation time for each position in each division.

1 Use the right mouse button to click cell D10.

2 On the shortcut menu, point to Add Data Field, and then YTD V.

The Sum Of YTD V data field appears in your pivot table.

3 Use the right mouse button to click cell D10, the Sum Of YTD V field.

4 On the shortcut menu, click PivotTable Field.

The PivotTable Field dialog box opens.

5   Edit the Name box to read Sum of YTD Vacation.

This changes the label in the pivot table, just as when you edited the YTD S label earlier.

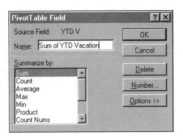

6   In the Summarize By list, select Max, and then click OK.

The PivotTable Field dialog box closes, and the YTD V description changes to "Max Of YTD Vacation."

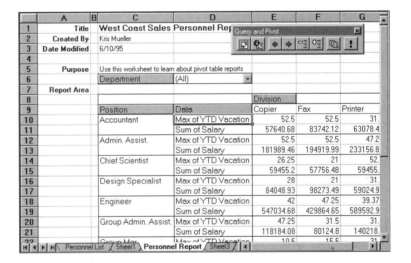

Show the minimum values for year-to-date vacation time

1   Use the right mouse button to click cell D10.

2   On the shortcut menu, point to Add Data Field, and then choose YTD V.

The Sum Of YTD V data field appears in your pivot table, just below the Max Of YTD Vacation.

3   Use the right mouse button to click cell D11.

217

4   On the shortcut menu, click PivotTable Field.

The PivotTable Field dialog box opens.

5   Edit the Name box to read Sum of YTD Vacation.

6   In the Summarize By list, select Min, and then click OK.

The Sum Of YTD Vacation field is replaced by the Min Of YTD Vacation field. Now both the minimum and maximum values for year-to-date vacation time appear in your pivot table. Your table should look similar to the following.

	A	B	C	D	E	F	G
1	Title		West Coast Sales Personnel Rep				
2	Created By		Kris Mueller				
3	Date Modified		6/10/95				
4							
5	Purpose		Use this worksheet to learn about pivot table reports				
6			Department	(All)			
7	Report Area						
8					Division		
9			Position	Data	Copier	Fax	Printer
10			Accountant	Max of YTD Vacation	52.5	52.5	31.
11				Min of YTD Vacation	8.5	31.5	2
12				Sum of Salary	57640.68	83742.12	63078.4
13			Admin. Assist.	Max of YTD Vacation	52.5	52.5	47.2
14				Min of YTD Vacation	7.875	8.5	5.2
15				Sum of Salary	181989.46	194919.99	233156.8
16			Chief Scientist	Max of YTD Vacation	26.25	21	52.
17				Min of YTD Vacation	26.25	21	52.
18				Sum of Salary	59455.2	57756.48	59455.
19			Design Specialist	Max of YTD Vacation	28	21	31.
20				Min of YTD Vacation	7.75	7	2
21				Sum of Salary	84048.93	98273.49	59024.9
22			Engineer	Max of YTD Vacation	42	47.25	39.37

Personnel List / Sheet1 \ Personnel Report / Sheet3

Removing Grand Totals

When you created your pivot table, you added grand totals to both the rows and columns in your pivot table. These grand totals make it easy to see the summaries for your data. But if you need to see only the row totals or the column totals, or perhaps you don't need to see the totals at all, you can easily remove the totals with the PivotTable Wizard.

Remove the grand totals from your pivot table

In this exercise, you use the PivotTable Wizard to remove the grand totals from both the rows and the columns of your pivot table.

1   Use the right mouse button to click cell D8.

2   On the shortcut menu, click PivotTable.

Step 3 of the PivotTable Wizard appears.

3   Click the Next button.

Step 4 of the PivotTable Wizard appears.

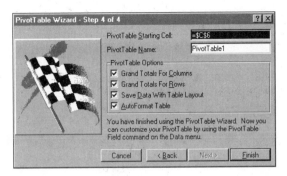

4 In the PivotTable Options area, clear the Grand Totals For Columns and Grand Totals For Rows options.

5 Click the Finish button.

The grand totals are removed from your pivot table. Your table should look similar to the following.

			Division			
	West Coast Sales Personnel Report					
	Kris Mueller					
	6/10/95					
	Use this worksheet to learn about pivot table reports					
	Department	(All)				
			Division			
Position		Data	Copier	Fax	Printer	
Accountant		Max of YTD Vacation	52.5	52.5	31.5	
		Min of YTD Vacation	8.5	31.5	21	
		Sum of Salary	57640.68	83742.12	63078.48	
Admin. Assist.		Max of YTD Vacation	52.5	52.5	47.25	
		Min of YTD Vacation	7.875	8.5	5.25	
		Sum of Salary	181989.46	194919.99	233156.82	
Chief Scientist		Max of YTD Vacation	26.25	21	52.5	
		Min of YTD Vacation	26.25	21	52.5	
		Sum of Salary	59455.2	57756.48	59455.2	
Design Specialist		Max of YTD Vacation	28	21	31.5	
		Min of YTD Vacation	7.75	7	21	
		Sum of Salary	84048.93	98273.49	59024.91	
Engineer		Max of YTD Vacation	42	47.25	39.375	

Formatting Your Pivot Table Report

When you finish setting up your pivot table and are ready to include it in a report, you might want to add number formatting, color, or other formatting. You can format your tables automatically, just as you can any other data in a worksheet, with the AutoFormat command. You can also apply number formats to make currency figures look like currency or percentage figures look like percentages. You can format your data fields with the PivotTable Field command. In the next exercises, you format your entire table automatically and then format your data fields individually.

Format your pivot tables

1 Select cell C10.

2 On the Format menu, click AutoFormat.

The AutoFormat dialog box opens.

3 In the Table Format list, select Classic 2, and then click OK.

Your pivot table is formatted with purple column headers and gray row headers. It should look similar to the following.

	C	D	E	F	G	H
1	West Coast Sales Personnel Report					
2	Kris Mueller					
3	6/10/95					
4						
5	Use this worksheet to learn about pivot table reports					
6	Department	(All)				
7						
8			Division			
9	Position	Data	Copier	Fax	Printer	
10	Accountant	Max of YTD Vacation	52.5	52.5	31.5	
11		Min of YTD Vacation	8.5	31.5	21	
12		Sum of Salary	57640.68	83742.12	63078.48	
13	Admin. Assist.	Max of YTD Vacation	52.5	52.5	47.25	
14		Min of YTD Vacation	7.875	8.5	5.25	
15		Sum of Salary	181989.46	194919.99	233156.82	
16	Chief Scientist	Max of YTD Vacation	26.25	21	52.5	
17		Min of YTD Vacation	26.25	21	52.5	
18		Sum of Salary	59455.2	57756.48	59455.2	
19	Design Specialist	Max of YTD Vacation	28	21	31.5	
20		Min of YTD Vacation	7.75	7	21	
21		Sum of Salary	84048.93	98273.49	59024.91	

Personnel List / Sheet1 \ **Personnel Report** / Sheet3 /

Format the numbers

1 Use the right mouse button to click cell E12.

You will format only the Sum Of Salary numbers for now, so you have selected a Sum of Salary data cell.

2 On the shortcut menu, click PivotTable Field.

The PivotTable Field dialog box opens.

3 In the PivotTable Field dialog box, click the Number button.

The Format Cells dialog box opens.

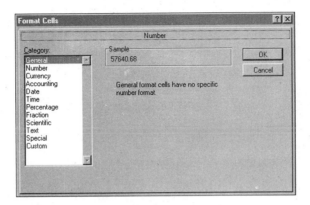

4   In the Category list, select Currency, and be sure that Decimal Places is set to 2, Use $ is checked, and Negative Numbers is the example with a minus sign.

5   Click OK, and then click OK again.

All of the Sum Of Salary cells change to the currency format you selected.

If you change some of the data on the source worksheet after you've created your pivot table, you can easily update, or *refresh*, the data in your table.

Refresh your data

In this exercise, you change some data on your personnel list and then refresh your pivot table.

1   Switch to the Personnel List sheet.

2   Select cell E11, the cell that contains Larry Franklin's position.

3   In cell E11, type **Accountant** and press ENTER.

4   In cell H11, the cell that contains Larry Franklin's salary, type **28800** and press ENTER.

5   Switch to the Personnel Report sheet, and select a cell in the pivot table.

6   On the Query And Pivot toolbar, click the Refresh Data button.

Your data is refreshed. Your table should look similar to the following.

Refresh Data

One Step Further: Charting a Pivot Table

Just as you can chart data on any worksheet, you can chart the data in your pivot tables to enhance your reports. When you work with charts and pivot tables, however, you need to be careful about how much information you put into the table. You should probably limit your pivot table to no more than two rows and two columns of fields for a successful chart. If you have more than that, your chart might become crowded and difficult to read. You also need to remove any grand totals from your pivot table before charting the data. If you include the grand totals in your chart, the chart will be hard to read because the individual data markers will be dwarfed by the total data markers.

Remove the YTD Vacation fields

You've already removed the grand totals from your pivot table, but you need to remove the year-to-date vacation summaries before you are ready to chart the remaining data. In this exercise, you remove the two YTD fields from the pivot table and then create a 3-D bar chart to show the total salaries for each position by division on a separate sheet.

1   Use the right mouse button to click cell D12.

2   On the shortcut menu, click PivotTable.

Step 3 of the PivotTable Wizard appears.

3   Drag Max Of YTD Vacation and Min Of YTD Vacation out of the pivot table area.

4   Click Finish.

The pivot table now displays only the Sum Of Salary data.

Chart a pivot table

1   Be sure a cell within the pivot table is selected.

2   On the Edit menu, click Go To, and then click the Special button.

3   Select Current Region, and then click OK.

The entire pivot table is selected, except for the Page area.

4   On the Standard toolbar, click the ChartWizard button, and then draw a chart frame near the pivot table.

The ChartWizard opens.

5   Click the Next button.

6   In Step 2, select the 3-D Bar chart type, and then click the Next button.

7   In Step 3, be sure that format #4 is selected, and then click the Next button.

8   Click the Finish button.

A new 3-D bar chart is created that shows the total salaries for each position in each division for each department. If you cannot see all of the position labels on the vertical axis, drag a chart handle to make the chart larger. Your chart should look similar to the following.

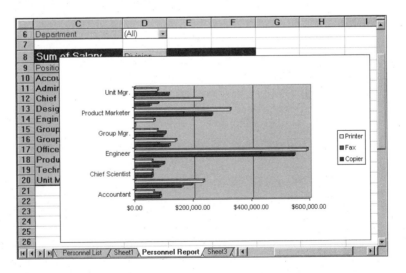

Switch departments in the chart

➤ On the pivot table Department list, select R and D.

The chart changes automatically to display the data that is displayed in the pivot table. You can print a chart for each department by changing the Department page and then printing the chart.

If You Want to Continue to the Next Lesson

1 On the File menu, click Save.

2 On the File menu, click Close.

If You Want to Quit Microsoft Excel for Now

➤ On the File menu, click Exit.

If you see the Save dialog box, click Yes.

Lesson Summary

To	Do this
Create a pivot table	Select a cell in the database you want to use for your pivot table. On the Data menu, click PivotTable. In the Pivot-Table Wizard, click the Next button. Check that the database range is correct, and then click the Next button. Drag the fields you want to the Row, Page, Column, and Data areas of the table. Click the Next button. Check the Grand Totals For Rows and Grand Totals For Columns checkboxes if you want to include the grand totals. Click the Finish button.
Add a data field to a pivot table	Click a cell in the data area of the pivot table with the right mouse button. On the shortcut menu, point to Add Data Field. Choose the data field that you want to add.
Hide or show data in a pivot table	Double-click the PivotTable field that you want to change. In the PivotTable Field dialog box, select the items that you want to hide, or select hidden items to show again, and then click OK.
Remove data from a pivot table	Drag the field button away from the pivot table area on the worksheet. *or* Drag the field button away from the pivot table area in the PivotTable Wizard dialog box.

To	Do this	Button
Move data around in a pivot table	Click the PivotTable Wizard button on the Query And Pivot toolbar, or click PivotTable on the shortcut menu. Drag the fields you want into the positions you want in the PivotTable Wizard. Click the Finish button. *or* Drag field buttons to new locations on the pivot table on the worksheet.	
Change summary functions	Use the right mouse button to click the field button for the field that you want to change. On the shortcut menu, click PivotTable Field. In the PivotTable Field dialog box, select the summary function that you want, and click OK.	
Remove grand totals	Use the right mouse button to click a cell in the pivot table, and on the shortcut menu, click PivotTable. Click the Next button to get step 4 of the PivotTable Wizard. In the PivotTable Options box, clear the Grand Totals For Columns and Grand Totals For Rows options. Click the Finish button.	
Format a pivot table automatically	Select a cell in the pivot table, and then on the Format menu, click AutoFormat. Select a format, and then click OK.	
Change a label to make it more understandable	Select a cell containing the label, and then enter new text.	
Display source details for a specific data cell	Double-click the cell.	
Format numbers in a pivot table	Use the right mouse button to click a data cell that contains the numbers that you want to format. On the shortcut menu, click PivotTable Field. In the PivotTable Field dialog box, click the Number button. In the Format Cells dialog box, select the number format that you want, and then click OK. Choose OK again to close the Pivot-Table Field dialog box.	

For online information about	Use the Answer Wizard to search for
Creating a pivot table	**create pivot**
Modifying a pivot table	**change pivot**
Formatting a pivot table	**format pivot**

Preview of the Next Lessons

In Part 4, you'll learn how to analyze data by looking at alternative outcomes and how to link data both within workbooks and between different programs. In the next lesson, "Comparing Alternatives," you'll learn how to process your data with analytical functions. You'll also learn how to do some forecasting with your data, find a specific value with the Goal Seek command, and look at various alternatives.

Review & Practice

In the lessons in Part 3, "Managing Your Data," you learned skills to help you sort and manage lists of data; organize your workbooks; and create reports with worksheet outlining, consolidation, and pivot tables. If you want to practice these skills and test your understanding before you proceed with the lessons in Part 4, you can work through the Review & Practice section following this lesson.

Review & Practice

Estimated time
20 min.

You will review and practice how to:

- Copy and move sheets to organize your workbooks.
- Add cell notes and AutoFormatting to your work.
- View only the data that you need with AutoFilter.
- Sort data by specific criteria.
- Create quick summary reports with subtotals.
- Change your data's organization without restructuring the worksheet.

Before you move on to Part 4, which covers analyzing and sharing your data, you can practice the skills you learned in Part 3 by working through the steps in this Review & Practice section. You will organize your workbook, sort and filter the data, add subtotals, and modify a pivot table.

Scenario

The Copier division keeps a sales journal that lists each product marketer and how many sales he or she has made during the last week. You need to create a report that shows the total amount and total quantities that each product marketer sold. Different members of the department have already worked on the files, but you've been assigned to the sales report as part of your regular duties. First, you'll organize the workbooks that are used in generating the report so that all of the information is in one place. Then you'll create two versions of the report so that you can offer more than one format to the product managers.

Step 1:   *Open Files and Organize Your Workbook*

Open the two workbooks that contain your copier sales journal data, and then copy the totals sheet into the main file. Also, add a note to explain the C/N code, which could be confusing to other users.

1   Open the file Part3 Review, and save it as Review Part3.

2   Open the file Part3 ReviewA, and save it as Review Part3A.

3   Use the Move Or Copy Sheet command on the Edit menu to copy the Copier Sales Total sheet from Review Part3A to Review Part3. Make the Copier Sales Total sheet the first sheet in the Review Part3 workbook.

4   On the Copier Data sheet, use the Note command on the Insert menu to add a note in the C/N column heading cell that reads The C/N code stands for Client/ New Contact.

For more information on	See
Moving and copying sheets	Lesson 7
Adding notes to explain data	Lesson 7

Step 2:   *Filter and Sort the Data on Your Data Sheet*

You need to tell someone how many Air orders there are, so you'll first filter the data to do a quick check. Then, you'll remove the filters so that you can continue to create your report. The data needs to be sorted by last name to keep each product marketer's orders separate, and you need to track whether the order is for a current or new client.

1   Use the AutoFilter command to filter out all of the data except the orders to be shipped by Air.

2   Use the AutoFilter command again to turn off the filters.

3   Use the Sort command to sort the data first by the product marketer's name and then by C/N.

For more information on	See
Filtering your data	Lesson 8
Sorting your data	Lesson 8

Step 3:   *Summarize Your Data with Subtotals*

Your report needs to include the quantity of products each product marketer sold and the amount he or she sold them for. You'll use subtotals to show the total amount and total number of products sold by each product marketer.

1. Use the Subtotal command to add Sum subtotals to the Quantity and Amount columns.

2. Adjust the column widths as necessary to show all of your data.

3. Format the list using the AutoFormat List 3 format.

Your sheet should look similar to the following.

	C	D	E	F	G	H	I	J
6								
7	Product Marke	Company	C/N	Product #	Quantity	Price	Amount	Ship B
8	Cane, Nate	261	C		1	$4,620.80	$4,620.80	Air
9	Cane, Nate	341	C		1	$5,544.96	$5,544.96	Ground
10	Cane, Nate	195	C		2	$1,289.58	$2,579.16	Air
11	Cane, Nate	362	N		1	$13,797.63	$13,797.63	Ground
12	*Cane, Nate Total*				5		$26,542.55	
13	Morton, Sara	341	C	C320 GLS	1	$4,620.80	$4,620.80	Ground
14	Morton, Sara	195	C	C100 GLS	2	$1,074.65	$2,149.30	Air
15	Morton, Sara	362	C	C210 GLS	1	$1,289.58	$1,289.58	Ground
16	Morton, Sara	261	N	C300 GLS	1	$3,208.89	$3,208.89	Air
17	Morton, Sara	261	N	C300 GLS	1	$3,208.89	$3,208.89	Air
18	Morton, Sara	341	N	C500 GLS	1	$9,581.69	$9,581.69	Air
19	*Morton, Sara Total*				7		$24,059.15	
20	Sammler, Mark	362	C	C310 GLS	1	$3,850.67	$3,850.67	Ground
21	Sammler, Mark	261	C	C400 GLS	1	$5,544.96	$5,544.96	Air
22	Sammler, Mark	341	C	C100 GLS	1	$1,074.65	$1,074.65	Air
23	Sammler, Mark	195	N	C120 GLS	3	$1,547.50	$4,642.50	Ground
24	Sammler, Mark	362	N	C520 GLS	1	$13,797.63	$13,797.63	Ground
25	*Sammler, Mark Total*				7		$28,910.41	
26	Seidel, Matt	195	C	C510 GLS	2	$11,498.02	$22,996.04	Air
27	Seidel, Matt	362	C	C300 GLS	1	$3,208.89	$3,208.89	Ground
28	Seidel, Matt	261	C	C120 GLS	3	$1,547.50	$4,642.50	Air
29	Seidel, Matt	341	N	C200 GLS	1	$1,857.00	$1,857.00	Air

Note: The C/N code stands for Client/New Contact

Tabs: Copier Sales Total / **Copier Data** / Copier Pivot

For more information on	See
Creating reports with subtotals	Lesson 9

Step 4: *Modify Your Pivot Table Report*

The report includes too much information in the pivot table. You need to switch to the Copier Pivot sheet and remove the Sum Of Price and Count Of Product # fields from the Pivot table so that only the Sum Of Quantity and Sum Of Amount fields show, echoing the data in the previous sheet. Then you need to format the entire table and the Sum Of Amount field so that they look more like the rest of the report.

1. On the Copier Pivot sheet, use the PivotTable command on the shortcut menu to modify the pivot table.

2. Remove the Sum Of Price and Count Of Product # fields.

3. Format the entire pivot table in the List 3 format with the AutoFormat command.

4. Format the numbers in the Sum Of Amount field to show as currency.

Your sheet should look similar to the following.

B	C	D	E	F	G	H	
7							
8							
9			Company #				
10	Product Marketer	Data	195	261	341	362	Gra
11	Cane, Nate	Sum of Quantity	2	1	1	1	
12		Sum of Amount	$2,579.16	$4,620.80	$5,544.96	$13,797.63	$
13	Morton, Sara	Sum of Quantity	2	2	2	1	
14		Sum of Amount	$2,149.30	$6,417.78	$14,202.49	$1,289.58	$
15	Sammler, Mark	Sum of Quantity	3	1	1	2	
16		Sum of Amount	$4,642.50	$5,544.96	$1,074.65	$17,648.30	$
17	Seidel, Matt	Sum of Quantity	3	3	1	1	
18		Sum of Amount	$25,670.71	$4,642.50	$1,857.00	$3,208.89	$
19	West, Cara	Sum of Quantity	1	2	1	2	
20		Sum of Amount	$1,857.00	$12,790.58	$6,653.95	$11,089.92	$
21	Wolf, Hilda	Sum of Quantity	1	2	2	3	
22		Sum of Amount	$11,498.02	$5,348.14	$13,726.41	$16,634.88	$
23	Total Sum of Quantity		12	11	8	10	
24	Total Sum of Amount		$48,396.69	$39,364.76	$43,059.46	$63,669.20	$1
25							
26							
27							

Copier Sales Total / Copier Data \ **Copier Pivot** /

For more information on	See
Modifying pivot tables	Lesson 10

If You Want to Continue to the Next Lesson

1 On the File menu, click Save.

2 Hold down SHIFT, and then on the File menu, click Close All.

If you see the Save dialog box, click Yes.

If You Want to Quit Microsoft Excel for Now

➤ On the File menu, click Exit.

If you see the Save dialog box, click Yes.

Analyzing and Sharing Your Data

Comparing Alternatives

Estimated time
35 min.

In this lesson you will learn how to:

- Find a value using goal seeking.
- Compare different solutions to an equation using a data table.
- Save different groups of values using Scenario Manager.

As you work with your data, you might find yourself wondering "What if that payment were $50.00 less?" or "What if the interest rate changes?" or "What if the payment period is only one year instead of three?" Doing such analyses manually can be difficult and time consuming. You can carry out these "what-if" explorations easily, however, with Microsoft Excel. Using the program's what-if analysis tools, you can try out different input data in your worksheet formulas and compare the results. To find out how much a value must change to produce a specific result, you can use goal seeking. You can use a data table to see a list of possible values that depend on one or two changing factors. If you need to test and save all of the possible scenarios for your data, you can use Scenario Manager. In this lesson, you'll learn how to use these tools to help you find out "what happens if..."

Start the lesson

Follow the steps below to open the practice file called 11Lesson, and then save it with the new name Lesson11.

Open

1   On the Standard toolbar, click the Open button.

2   In the Look In box, be sure that the Excel SBS Practice folder appears.

To select the folder containing your practice files, refer to "Open a practice file" near the start of Lesson 1.

3   In the file list box, double-click the file named 11Lesson to open it.

4   On the File menu, click Save As.

The Save As dialog box opens. Be sure that the Excel SBS Practice folder appears in the Save In box.

5   Double-click in the File Name box, and then type **Lesson11**

6   Click the Save button, or press ENTER.

If you share your computer with others who use Microsoft Excel, the screen display might have changed since your last lesson. If your screen does not look similar to the illustrations as you work through this lesson, see the Appendix, "Matching the Exercises."

Seeking a Specific Goal

If you need to find a 'best fit' solution to a problem that has multiple variables, try using Solver. To install the Solver add-in, click Add-ins on the Tools menu, then select Solver Add-in, and click OK.

When you are looking for answers to what-if questions, you might want to find out what the result of a formula would be if only one variable changed. For example, you might need to find out how much sales would have to increase to reach a specific operating income goal or how much of a down payment you would have to make to purchase a house. When you need to determine how much a variable must change to give a specific answer to a formula, you can use *goal seeking*. With goal seeking, you can work equations or formulas in reverse. You enter your goal value, select the variable that you want to change, and then let the program find the variable value that will give the desired goal.

For example, suppose you want to buy a house. In the Lesson11 file, the Down Payment sheet has information about a specific house price, closing costs, a down payment, and a loan amount. The house price is set, the down payment is 10 percent of the house price, and the closing costs are 3 percent of the loan amount. The loan amount depends on the price of the home and how much the bank is willing to lend. If your loan amount is fixed, you can use goal seeking to determine the exact closing costs, down payment, and house price you can afford.

Seek a down payment amount

In this exercise, you use goal seeking to find out how much the down payment, closing costs, and house price would be for a $110,000 loan.

1   Be sure the Down Payment sheet is the active sheet.

2   Select cell D15, and on the Tools menu, click Goal Seek.

The Goal Seek dialog box opens. The Set Cell box is set to $D$15. Cell D15 contains the formula that calculates the loan amount, =D9-D12. You'll choose a value that you want the loan amount formula to equal and find what the house price in cell D9 has to be for the formula to produce that loan amount value.

3   Click the To Value text box, and type **110000**

4   Tab to or click the By Changing Cell box, and then select cell D9.

You might need to drag the Goal Seek dialog box out of the way before you select the cell. You'll reach your goal of a $110,000 loan by changing the house price in cell D9.

5   Click OK or press ENTER.

The Goal Seek Status dialog box appears, telling you that a value has been found. The value appears in cell D9 for you to preview, but it has not been entered in the cell.

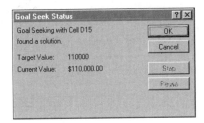

Cells D11, D12, and D13, which depend on the value in cell D9, have changed as well. You might need to move the Goal Seek Status dialog box to see the figures.

6   Click OK.

The value is entered in cell D9, and cells D11, D12, and D13 are updated with the new values. If you don't want to update your worksheet with the new values, click Cancel instead.

   NOTE   If you want to restore the original values in your sheet after seeking a goal, you can use the Undo command on the Edit menu or the Undo button on the toolbar, provided that you have not taken any other actions. You can also click the Undo button on the toolbar repeatedly to switch between the original and new values.

Looking at Alternatives with Data Tables

After you have entered formulas on your worksheet, you might want to perform what-if analyses to see a range of possible values for your formulas. *Data tables* can provide a shortcut by calculating all of the values in one operation. A data table is a range of cells that shows the results of substituting different values in one or more formulas.

Perhaps you have several possible combinations of data that you'd like to compare. For example, you might need to compare loan payments for different interest rates or for different terms. Or, you might need to compare the effect of different sales growth figures on your operating income. Rather than using goal seeking, which determines a single input required to produce a single value, you could use a data table to compare several values. You can create data tables to list as many values as you need for one or two variables. For example, you could find out what the loan payment would be for interest rates between 6 and 12 percent, or you could see the effect of 2, 3, 4, or 5 percent sales growth on your operating income.

There are two types of data tables: *one-input data tables* and *two-input data tables*. With a one-input table, you enter different values for one variable and see their effect on one or more formulas. With a two-input table, you enter different values for two variables and see their effect on one formula.

Creating a One-Input Data Table

Suppose you want to know what the payments on a specific loan amount would be at different interest rates. You can create a one-input data table to show all the different interest rates and their corresponding payments.

To set up a one-input data table, you can list the input values down a single column or across a single row. Then you create the formula that will use the input values to fill in the table. To create a data table, you use the Table command on the Data menu.

Before you can set up a data table to find values, however, you need to decide on a formula to use. In this case, you want a formula to find the actual payment amount for a loan.

Enter the formula for the data table

In this exercise, you add a formula to your worksheet that calculates payments based on a varying interest rate with a constant term and loan amount. You use the Function Wizard to create a formula that calculates the payments for a loan based on its interest rate, term, and present value, and you use named cells so that the formulas will be easy to read.

1 Switch to the Payment Amounts sheet.

Cells D8:D10 have already been named, using the Create Names command and the labels in cells C8:C10. To see the cell names, select each cell in the range D8:D10 and look at the Name box, where you'll see the cell name.

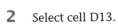

Function Wizard

2 Select cell D13.

You will enter the payment formula in this cell.

3 Click the Function Wizard button on the toolbar.

The Function Wizard dialog box opens.

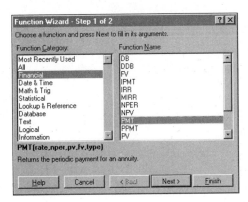

4 In the Function Category list, select Financial.

5 In the Function Name list, select PMT, and then click the Next button.

PMT is a standard function for calculating payments in loans. The next step in the Function Wizard dialog box appears.

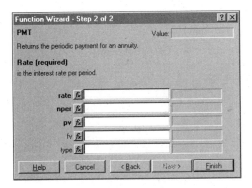

When you enter an argument in the Function Wizard dialog box, the value of the argument you entered is displayed in the gray box to the right of the argument.

6 Click in the rate box, then click the Name box down arrow on the worksheet, and select the name Interest_Rate from the list of names.

The rate option refers to the monthly interest rate for the loan. The cell named Interest_Rate contains the yearly percentage rate. To find the monthly percentage rate, you must divide the yearly rate by 12.

7 In the rate box, type **/12** after Interest_Rate.

The entry in the rate box should read Interest_Rate/12.

8 Click in the nper box, and then select the name Number_of_Months from the Name box list.

The nper label refers to the total number of payments in your loan, or the value in the cell named Number_of_Months.

9 Click in the pv box, then type a minus sign (–), and then select the name Loan_Amount from the Name box list.

The arguments "fv" and "type" are optional arguments, which is indicated by the non-bold format. To learn about them, click the question mark button in the upper-right corner of the dialog box, then click the argument you want to learn about.

The pv label refers to the present value of your loan. Since you have not made any payments, the present value of your loan (from your perspective) is negative. The Function Wizard should look like the following.

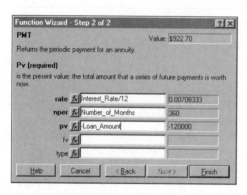

10 Click the Finish button.

The PMT function is entered into cell D13 and returns the monthly payment of $922.70, based on an 8.5-percent interest rate. Your worksheet should look like the following illustration.

	D13		=PMT(Interest_Rate/12,Number_of_Months,-Loan_Amount)				
	A	**B**	**C**	**D**	**E**	**F**	**G**
1	Title		Kris Mueller Mortgage Loan Analysis - Monthly Payments				
2	Date		6/13/95				
3	Created by		Kris Mueller				
4							
5	Purpose		To determine the monthly payment amounts on an $120,000.00 mortgage				
6			loan, depending on the interest rate and term of the loan.				
7							
8	Initial Data		Interest Rate	8.50%			
9			Number of Months	360			
10			Loan Amount	$120,000.00			
11							
12	Interest Rate Model Area			Monthly Payment	Interest Paid		
13				$922.70			
14			6.00%				
15			6.25%				
16			6.50%				
17			6.75%				

Down Payment \ **Payment Amounts** \ Loan Scenarios

Next, you need to set up a data table so that the interest rates in column C (the *input values*) are each substituted for the value in cell D8 (the *input cell*), and the resulting monthly payments appear in the cells below the formula in cell D13. When the input values are in a column, as it is in this case, you enter the formula that refers to the input cell in the row above the first input value and one cell to the right of the column of input values. This is why you entered your formula in cell D13 in the previous exercise. (If the input values are in a row, you would enter the formula one cell below and to the left of them.)

Create the one-input data table

In this exercise, you create a data table that uses one variable to fill in the payment amounts for loans at percentages between 6 and 9 percent.

1   Select cells C13:D26.

2   On the Data menu, click Table.

The Table dialog box appears.

3   Click in the Column Input Cell box, and then click cell D8.

Cell D8 (the input cell) contains the original interest rate. You use the Column Input Cell box because the values you are substituting for the input cell are in a column.

4   Click OK.

The values in cell C14:C26 are each substituted for the Interest_Rate argument in the payment formula, and the table is filled in with the results. Your worksheet should look like the following illustration.

	A	B	C	D	E	F	G
11							
12	Interest Rate Model Area			Monthly Payment	Interest Paid		
13				$922.70			
14			6.00%	$719.46			
15			6.25%	$738.86			
16			6.50%	$758.48			
17			6.75%	$778.32			
18			7.00%	$798.36			
19			7.25%	$818.61			
20			7.50%	$839.06			
21			7.75%	$859.69			
22			8.00%	$880.52			
23			8.25%	$901.52			
24			8.50%	$922.70			
25			8.75%	$944.04			
26			9.00%	$965.55			
27							

Down Payment \ **Payment Amounts** \ Loan Scenarios

Adding Formulas to Existing Data Tables

Now that you have the data table in place, you can compare the values and make some decisions. But what if you need to find out how the different values will affect another formula? How will the different interest rates affect the overall amount of interest paid, for example? You can add a formula to a data table and see exactly how the values in the data table affect the results of the formula.

Calculate the total interest paid

In this exercise, you add a formula to the table to calculate the interest paid over the life of the loan.

1 In cell E13, type =($D$13*Number_of_Months)–Loan_Amount

This formula calculates the total amount of interest you would pay (beyond repayment of the basic principal). You can select the names from the Name box list instead of typing them.

2 Press ENTER.

Microsoft Excel calculates the total interest paid based on an 8.5-percent interest rate ($212,170.62).

3 Select cells C13:E26.

4 On the Data menu, click Table.

5 Click in the Column Input Cell box, then click cell D8, and click OK.

Each value in column C is substituted for the input cell value, as before, and the data table is filled in with the results of the formulas.

	A	B	C	D	E	F	G
11							
12	Interest Rate Model Area			Monthly Payment	Interest Paid		
13				$922.70	$212,170.62		
14			6.00%	$719.46	$139,005.83		
15			6.25%	$738.86	$145,989.83		
16			6.50%	$758.48	$153,053.39		
17			6.75%	$778.32	$160,194.38		
18			7.00%	$798.36	$167,410.68		
19			7.25%	$818.61	$174,700.15		
20			7.50%	$839.06	$182,060.67		
21			7.75%	$859.69	$189,490.09		
22			8.00%	$880.52	$196,986.30		
23			8.25%	$901.52	$204,547.17		
24			8.50%	$922.70	$212,170.62		
25			8.75%	$944.04	$219,854.58		
26			9.00%	$965.55	$227,596.97		
27							

Down Payment \ **Payment Amounts** \ Loan Scenarios

Creating a Two-Input Data Table

If you want to see how changes in two variables affect one formula, you can use a two-input data table. For example, you could see how your loan payments change depending on both the interest rate and the term of the loan.

Calculate loan payments based on both interest rate and term

In this exercise, you create a data table with two variables to calculate the loan payments.

Copy

Paste

1 Select cell D13, and then click the Copy button on the toolbar.

Because you need to use the same formula to find the payments, and because you created it with named cells, you can save time by copying and pasting the formula into the new data table area.

2 Select cell C30, and then click the Paste button on the toolbar.

The PMT function and all of its arguments are pasted into cell C30.

To find the loan payments based on both interest rate and term, you would set up a data table so that interest rates entered in column C are substituted for one input cell (D8) and loan terms entered in row 30 are substituted for a second input cell (D9).

To create a data table with two variables, you need to put one set of values in a single column and one set in a single row. For example, you'd place the interest rates in column C and the terms in row 30. With two variables, you can use only one formula in your data table, and you must enter the formula in the cell at the intersection of your row and column of possible values. You already placed the formula in cell C30 in the previous exercise. When you perform calculations using the Table command, the resulting monthly payments are entered in the cells below row 30 and to the right of column C.

Fill in a two-input data table

1 Select cells C30:I43.

2 On the Data menu, click Table.

3 Click in the Row Input Cell box, and then click cell D9.

You use the Row Input Cell box because the values for the number of months are in a row. Cell D9 contains the term (number of months) of the loan.

4 Click in the Column Input Cell box, and then click cell D8.

You use the Column Input Cell box because the values for the interest rate are in a column. Cell D8 contains the value of the interest rate.

241

5 Click OK.

6 If necessary, scroll to display cells C29:I43.

Microsoft Excel substitutes each of the values in the input cells and fills in the data table with the results of the formulas. Cell C30 contains the formula on which the data table is based. Your two-input data table should look like the following illustration.

	C	D	E	F	G	H	I
29			**Monthly Payment**				
30	$922.70	180	240	300	360	420	480
31	6.00%	$1,012.63	$859.72	$773.16	$719.46	$684.23	$660.26
32	6.25%	$1,028.91	$877.11	$791.60	$738.86	$704.49	$681.29
33	6.50%	$1,045.33	$894.69	$810.25	$758.48	$724.99	$702.55
34	6.75%	$1,061.89	$912.44	$829.09	$778.32	$745.70	$724.03
35	7.00%	$1,078.59	$930.36	$848.14	$798.36	$766.63	$745.72
36	7.25%	$1,095.44	$948.45	$867.37	$818.61	$787.76	$767.61
37	7.50%	$1,112.41	$966.71	$886.79	$839.06	$809.09	$789.68
38	7.75%	$1,129.53	$985.14	$906.39	$859.69	$830.61	$811.94
39	8.00%	$1,146.78	$1,003.73	$926.18	$880.52	$852.31	$834.37
40	8.25%	$1,164.17	$1,022.48	$946.14	$901.52	$874.19	$856.97
41	8.50%	$1,181.69	$1,041.39	$966.27	$922.70	$896.23	$879.71
42	8.75%	$1,199.34	$1,060.45	$986.57	$944.04	$918.44	$902.60
43	9.00%	$1,217.12	$1,079.67	$1,007.04	$965.55	$940.79	$925.63
44							
45							

Down Payment \ **Payment Amounts** / Loan Scenarios

Editing and Deleting Data Tables

If you decide that the data table does not give you the information that you need, you can edit the input values or formulas in the top row or the left column. Microsoft Excel recalculates the table after you edit any cells that affect the table results. If you decide that you don't need the data table at all, you can delete the entire table. In the next exercises, you change the loan amount in your data table to $135,000.00 and then delete the data table.

Change the loan amount

1 Select Loan_Amount from the Name box list, then type **135000**, and press ENTER.

2 Scroll downward to view both tables.

Your tables are updated to reflect the new loan amount. Your tables should look like the following.

You can click the Undo button on the toolbar repeatedly to switch back and forth between the original tables and the new tables and see the changes.

	Monthly Payment	Interest Paid
	$1,038.03	$238,691.95
6.00%	$809.39	$156,381.56
6.25%	$831.22	$164,238.56
6.50%	$853.29	$172,185.06
6.75%	$875.61	$180,218.67
7.00%	$898.16	$188,337.01
7.25%	$920.94	$196,537.67
7.50%	$943.94	$204,818.25
7.75%	$967.16	$213,176.35
8.00%	$990.58	$221,609.58
8.25%	$1,014.21	$230,115.57
8.50%	$1,038.03	$238,691.95
8.75%	$1,062.05	$247,336.40
9.00%	$1,086.24	$256,046.59

	Monthly Payment					
$1,038.03	180	240	300	360	420	480
6.00%	$1,139.21	$967.18	$869.81	$809.39	$769.76	$742.79
6.25%	$1,157.52	$986.75	$890.55	$831.22	$792.55	$766.45
6.50%	$1,175.99	$1,006.52	$911.53	$853.29	$815.61	$790.37
6.75%	$1,194.63	$1,026.49	$932.73	$875.61	$838.91	$814.53
7.00%	$1,213.42	$1,046.65	$954.15	$898.16	$862.46	$838.93
7.25%	$1,232.36	$1,067.01	$975.79	$920.94	$886.23	$863.56
7.50%	$1,251.47	$1,087.55	$997.64	$943.94	$910.23	$888.40
7.75%	$1,270.72	$1,108.28	$1,019.69	$967.16	$934.44	$913.44
8.00%	$1,290.13	$1,129.19	$1,041.95	$990.58	$958.85	$938.67
8.25%	$1,309.69	$1,150.29	$1,064.41	$1,014.21	$983.46	$964.09
8.50%	$1,329.40	$1,171.56	$1,087.06	$1,038.03	$1,008.26	$989.68
8.75%	$1,349.26	$1,193.01	$1,109.89	$1,062.05	$1,033.24	$1,015.43
9.00%	$1,369.26	$1,214.63	$1,132.92	$1,086.24	$1,058.39	$1,041.34

NOTE Curly brackets { } around the formulas in the data table indicate that the cells contain an *array formula*. Because the resulting values in a data table are an array, you cannot edit or clear them individually. If you try to edit the data table values, a message appears telling you that you cannot change part of a table. If you want to edit data table results, you can convert the results into a range of constant values. To do this, use the Values option in the Paste Special dialog box.

You can also copy and paste values from a data table, just as you did in Lesson 2 when you copied values to another worksheet. When you do this, only the values are copied, not the formulas for those values. To recalculate, move, or delete a data table, you must first select the entire table, including the formulas and the input values.

Delete a data table

In this exercise, you select and then delete an entire data table.

1   Select C30:I43.

2   Use the right mouse button to click anywhere within the selected range, and on the shortcut menu, click Clear Contents.

Creating a Data Table Using AutoFill

The data tables you created use array formulas. One of the drawbacks of array formulas is that you cannot edit or delete individual cells that share the array formula—the entire array formula (all the cells sharing the formula) must be edited or deleted. But you can create the same comparison table by using AutoFill, and then each cell can be edited or deleted individually.

Use AutoFill to complete a data table

If you are using AutoFill to fill a column of cells adjacent to an existing table, you can double-click the fill handle instead of dragging it. AutoFill will fill the column down to the bottom of the table.

1   Select cells C14:C26, and then copy the cells and paste them to F14.

2   Copy the formula in D13 and paste it in G14.

3   Double-click cell G14, then double-click the name Interest_Rate.

4   Click cell F14, then press ENTER.

In the formula, Interest_Rate is replaced with F14, and the value of the formula is $809.39.

5   Double-click the fill handle on cell G14.

The comparison table is filled in with individual formulas rather than an array formula.

Using Scenario Manager to Analyze Data

Occasionally you might need to examine possible results on a larger scale than either goal seeking or data tables can manage. If you need to see a collection of input values to substitute into your worksheet, and you need to maintain several sets of these collections, you can use Scenario Manager. For example, if you want to find out the result that a different down payment and a different interest rate would have on your purchase price, but you want to see each result separately, you could create separate scenarios to store different combinations of data. Or, if you want to see whether hiring another salesperson or increasing advertising would have the greatest effect on your sales growth, you could compare the scenarios. With Scenario Manager, you can set up each collection of data separately to examine when making your decision.

To set up separate scenarios, you need to begin with a worksheet that already contains the data and formulas that you want to use. Then you can use the Scenario Manager to name the scenarios and to substitute different values in the cells you specify. In the following exercises, you'll name input cells and then create three scenarios to compare three combinations of price, interest rate, and down payment for a home. If you will need to show the original (current) values in your worksheet again, create your first scenario by using the current values in the worksheet.

Name input cells

1   Switch to the Loan Scenarios sheet.

2   Select cells C8:D12.

3   On the Insert menu, point to Name, and then click Create.

4   Be sure that Left Column is checked, and then click OK.

The cells in column D of the selected range have been named using the labels in column C.

Create a current scenario and a new scenario

1   On the Tools menu, click Scenarios.

The Scenario Manager dialog box opens.

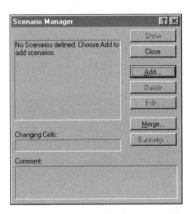

2   Click the Add button.

The Add Scenario dialog box opens.

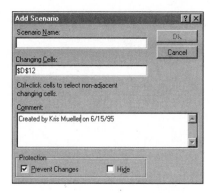

3 In the Scenario Name text box, type **Current**

Your first scenario will use current values in the worksheet, so you will be able to show the current values again after you create and show other scenarios.

4 Delete the existing entry in the Changing Cells box, and then select cells D8:D10 in the worksheet.

Cells D8:D10 contain the values that you will change to create different scenarios. You might need to move the dialog box out of the way first.

5 Click OK.

The Scenario Values dialog box opens. The cell names appear because you had named the cells in the previous exercise.

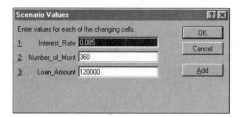

6 Leave the current values in place, and click OK.

The Scenario Manager appears again, and your scenario of current values, Current, is listed in the Scenarios box.

7 Click the Add button to add a new scenario.

8 In the Scenario Name text box, type **Low Rate**, and then click OK.

The Scenario Values dialog box opens.

9   In the Interest_Rate box, type **6%**, and then click OK.

The Scenario Manager appears again, and your new scenario, Low Rate, is listed in the Scenarios box.

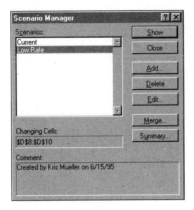

Create additional scenarios

1   Click the Add button.

The Add Scenario dialog box displays the set of changing cells previously specified.

2   In the Scenario Name box, type **Low Rate, Low Term**, and then click OK.

3   In the Interest_Rate box, type **7%**, and then press TAB. In the Number_of_Months box, type **240**, and then click the Add button.

The Add Scenario dialog box appears again.

4   In the Scenario Name box, type **Low Rate, Low Term, Low Amount**, and then click OK.

5   In the Interest_Rate box, type **7%**, and then press TAB. In the Number_of_Months box, type **240**, and then press TAB. In the Loan_Amount box, type **110000**, and then click OK or press ENTER.

The Scenario Manager dialog box reappears with all four scenarios listed.

NOTE   You can also create a scenario by using the Scenarios box on the Workgroup toolbar. Make changes to the cells on the worksheet, and then select the changing cells and enter a new name in the Scenarios box. To display the Workgroup toolbar, use the right mouse button to click on any toolbar, and then click Workgroup on the shortcut menu.

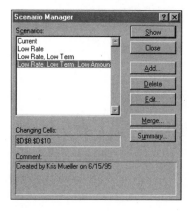

6 Click Close.

Show a scenario

In this exercise, you use Scenario Manager to show the scenarios you had created in the preceding steps.

1 On the Tools menu, click Scenarios.

2 In the Scenarios box, select Low Rate.

3 Click the Show button.

Microsoft Excel substitutes the values from the Low Rate scenario in your worksheet. You might need to move the Scenario Manager dialog box out of the way first.

4 Click Close.

To show your original worksheet data again, show Current, the scenario you created using the original data.

NOTE You can also show a scenario by selecting it from the Scenarios box on the Workgroup toolbar. To display the Workgroup toolbar, use the right mouse button to click on any toolbar, and then click Workgroup.

Editing Scenarios

After you create a scenario, you can change or add input values. You use the Scenarios command to edit the values. In the Scenario Manager dialog box, you select the name of the scenario you want to edit, and then click the Edit button.

Edit a scenario

1 On the Tools menu, click Scenarios to display the Scenario Manager dialog box.

2 In the Scenarios list, select Low Rate, Low Term, Low Amount, and then click the Edit button.

The Edit Scenario dialog box opens.

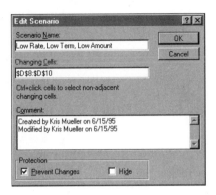

3 In the Scenario Name box, type **Low Rate, Low Term, High Amount** and then click OK.

The Scenario Values dialog box opens.

4 In the Loan_Amount box, replace the existing number with **140000** and then click OK.

5 Click the Show button.

The new scenario appears in your worksheet. You can switch between scenarios easily by selecting them in the Scenarios box on the Workgroup toolbar.

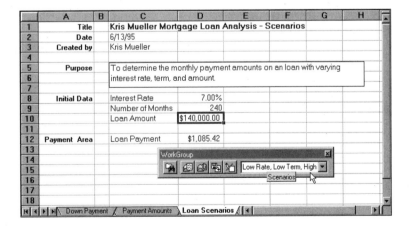

6 Click Close.

The Scenario Manager dialog box closes.

One Step Further: Summarizing Scenarios

If you want to see your scenario data all at once, you can create a report that lists the scenarios you created as well as any input values and any *result cells* that you want to display. A result cell is any cell on your worksheet that is recalculated when you apply a new scenario. Microsoft Excel creates the summary report on a separate worksheet.

Create a scenario summary

In this exercise, you use Scenario Manager to add one more scenario, and then you create a summary report, specifying the cell containing the loan payment (cell D12) as the result cell.

1   On the Tools menu, click Scenarios.

2   Add a scenario named "High Rate, High Term, High Amount."

3   Enter the values 9.25%, 360, and 140000 for the Interest_Rate box, the Number_of_Months box, and the Loan_Amount box, respectively.

4   Click OK.

5   In the Scenario Manager dialog box, be sure that the High Rate, High Term, High Amount scenario is selected, and then click the Summary button.

The Scenario Summary dialog box appears, and Scenario Summary should be selected in Report Type.

6   Be sure that the Result Cells box displays cell $D$12.

Cell D12 contains the loan payment value, which is the result of the changes you make in the changing cells.

7   Click OK.

A new sheet called Scenario Summary appears with a summary of your scenarios already formatted and outlined. Because you named the cells used in the scenarios, the cell names, instead of the cell addresses, appear in column C, which makes the summary much easier to understand. Your scenario report should look like the following illustration.

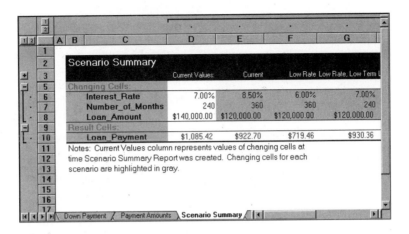

If You Want to Continue to the Next Lesson

1 On the File menu, click Save.

2 On the File menu, click Close.

If You Want to Quit Microsoft Excel for Now

▶ On the File menu, click Exit.

   If you see the Save dialog box, click Yes.

Lesson Summary

To	Do this
Find a specific value to make a formula reach your goal	Select the cell containing the formula that you want to use to reach a specific value. On the Tools menu, click the Goal Seek command, type a goal value in the To Value box, and specify the variable cell whose value you want to change in the By Changing Cell box.

To	Do this
Create a one-input data table	Enter the input values in a row or column. Enter a formula above and to the right of the input values (if they are in a column) or below and to the left (if they are in a row). This formula depends on an input cell. Select the range of cells containing the input values, the formula, and the cells that will contain the table values, and then click the Table command on the Data menu. When prompted, enter the reference of the row or column input cell.
Create a two-input data table	Enter the input values in a row and column. Enter a formula at the intersection of the row and column of input values. Select the range of cells containing the input values, the formula, and the cells that will contain the table values, and then click the Table command on the Data menu. When prompted, enter the references of the row and column input cells.
Edit a data table	Select the formula or the input value that you want to change, and type the new formula or input value.
Delete a data table	Select the entire table. Click the right mouse button in the selected range to display the shortcut menu, and then click Clear Contents.
Create a scenario	On the Tools menu, click Scenarios. Click the Add button. In the Scenario Name box, type a name. In the Changing Cells box, drag to select the cells that will change. Click OK. In the Scenario Values dialog box, type the values that you want, and then click OK. Click Close.
Show a scenario	On the Tools menu, click Scenarios. Select the scenario that you want, and then click the Show button.

To	Do this
Edit a scenario	On the Tools menu, click Scenarios. Select the scenario that you want, and then click the Edit button. Make your changes in the dialog boxes, and then click OK.

For online information about	Use the Answer Wizard to search for
Using financial functions	**function**
Seeking a specific goal	**goal seek**
Finding alternatives with data tables	**data table**
Creating scenarios	**scenario**

Preview of the Next Lesson

In the next lesson, "Linking Your Data," you'll learn how to use the same data in more than one file by using links between worksheets. You'll learn how to create the links, update them when your data changes, and restore links that are broken.

Linking Your Data

Estimated time

20 min.

In this lesson you will learn how to:

- Create links so that you can use the same data in more than one worksheet.
- Update the data when the source information changes.
- Change or restore broken links.

When you are creating a worksheet, you often need to use data stored in a different worksheet or workbook. You can copy and paste the data, but what if the data changes frequently? If you copy and paste, you'll need to copy and paste every time the data changes. There's a solution to this problem: *linking*. You can create a link between a *dependent worksheet* (the worksheet that will use the data) and a *source worksheet* (the worksheet in which the original data resides). Your dependent worksheet will then be updated whenever the data changes in the source worksheet. With Microsoft Excel, you can easily create links between a dependent worksheet and a source worksheet, and Microsoft Excel can update the data automatically when it changes.

In this lesson, you'll learn how to create links that allow you to use the same data for more than one worksheet, update the linked data if the original data changes, and change links or restore lost or broken links.

Start the lesson

Follow the steps below to open the practice file called 12Lesson, and then save it with the new name Lesson12.

Open

To select the folder containing your practice files, refer to "Open a practice file" near the start of Lesson 1.

1 On the Standard toolbar, click the Open button.

2 In the Look In box, be sure that the Excel SBS Practice folder appears.

3 In the file list box, double-click the file named 12Lesson to open it.

4 On the File menu, click Save As.

The Save As dialog box opens. Be sure that the Excel SBS Practice folder appears in the Save In box.

5 Double-click in the File Name box, and then type **Lesson12**

6 Click the Save button, or press ENTER.

7 Repeat steps 1 through 6 for the file 12LessonA, and save it as **Lesson12A**

If you share your computer with others who use Microsoft Excel, the screen display might have changed since your last lesson. If your screen does not look similar to the illustrations as you work through this lesson, see the Appendix, "Matching the Exercises."

Creating Links

Suppose that the Copier division at West Coast Sales is starting a new marketing campaign in January, and you need to include some of the marketing campaign data in the copier division budget. The campaign information resides in one workbook and the division information is in another. Instead of copying the information from the campaign workbook to the division workbook or retyping the information in the division workbook, you can create a link between the two workbooks. To do this, open the dependent (copier division) workbook, which receives the linked data, and use a formula to point to the information in the source (marketing campaign) workbook, which contains the original data. The formula that you use to link the source data and the dependent data takes the form (at its simplest) of an external cell reference. You tell the dependent worksheet the location where the data resides in the source worksheet, and Microsoft Excel does the rest.

The following illustrates the link between the dependent (copier division) workbook and the source (marketing campaign) workbook.

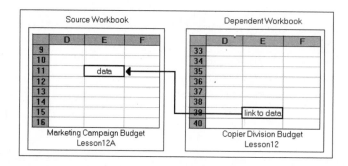

Create a link

In this exercise, you create a link between the marketing campaign workbook in the Lesson12A file and the copier division workbook in the Lesson12 file so that you can track the campaign expenses along with the other division expenses.

1 Be sure that the active file is Lesson12.

You can switch between open files by selecting the workbook name you want on the Window menu.

2 On the Copier Division Budget sheet, click cell E39, and then type =

You'll create a link in this cell to point to the Campaign Allocation amount in the Marketing Campaign Budget sheet in Lesson12A.

3 On the Window menu, click Lesson12A.

The Marketing Campaign Budget sheet becomes the active sheet.

4 On the Marketing Campaign Budget sheet, click cell E11, and then press ENTER.

When you press ENTER, the link formula is completed, and you are returned to the Copier Division Budget sheet in the Lesson12 workbook. The campaign allocation amount appears in cell E39.

5 Select cell E39.

The extension .xls following the filename identifies the file as a Microsoft Excel file.

In the formula bar, the formula in cell E39 refers to cell E11 on the Marketing Campaign Budget sheet in the file Lesson12A. Cell E39 shows the value in cell E11 ($62,000.00). Your worksheet should look like the following.

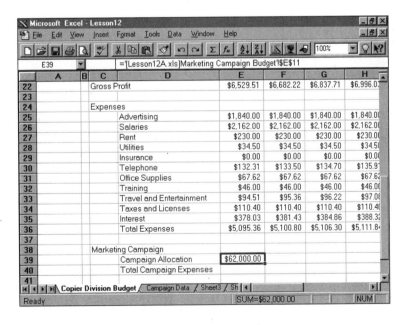

The formula that you created to link the data from the source sheet to the dependent sheet in step 4 uses only an equal sign and the external cell reference, ='[Lesson12A.xls]Marketing Campaign Budget'!$E$11. Just as with any other formula, the equal sign begins the formula, and the cell reference tells the formula which cells to use.

The cell reference for a linking formula contains more than just a cell location, however; it also includes the file name and sheet name of the source worksheet, and sometimes the path name if the source workbook is in a different folder from the dependent workbook. For external cell references, such as this one in the linking formula, workbook names are always surrounded by square brackets [ ], and the cell reference is always preceded by an exclamation point.

NOTE Cell references in linking formulas are automatically created as absolute references because you don't usually want them to change if you move the formula in your dependent workbook.

Now that you have one link, you can easily add several more links to the same sheet. You can simply copy the first link formula into the other cells, but since the formula includes absolute references, you'll need to update the cell references to point to the correct cells. You can also point to the cells you want to reference; however, copying and then updating the formula will generally save you time and help you avoid typing errors.

Add links for the rest of the campaign information

In this exercise, you copy the link formula into the other campaign area cells in the copier division workbook, and then update the references to point to the correct cells.

1	Select cell E39, and drag the fill handle on the cell across to cell H39.

The same formula and value appear in cells F39 to H39.

38	Marketing Campaign				
39	Campaign Allocation	$62,000.00	$62,000.00	$62,000.00	$62,000.00
40	Total Campaign Expenses				

2	Double-click cell F39.

You'll update the reference in cells F39 to H39 to point to the correct cells in the source workbook.

3	In the formula, delete the E, and then type **F** and press ENTER.

The formula is updated to point to cell F39, and the cell now displays the value $62,250.00.

4	Double-click cell G39.

5 In the formula, delete the E, and then type **G** and press ENTER.

6 Double-click cell H39.

7 In the formula, delete the E, and then type **H** and press ENTER.

The updated references should look like the following.

38	Marketing Campaign				
39	Campaign Allocation	$62,000.00	$62,250.00	$62,750.00	$63,000.00
40	Total Campaign Expenses				

Link the campaign expenses data to the copier division worksheet

In this exercise, you create the other links you need in your copier division workbook. First you copy the formula to the other cells, and then you update the references.

1 Drag to select E39:H39.

2 Drag the fill handle on cell H39 down to cell H40, and then release it.

The formulas in E39:H39 are filled into cells E40:H40.

3 Double-click cell E40.

4 In the formula, delete 11, and then type **20** and press ENTER.

5 Repeat steps 3 and 4 for cells F40, G40, and H40.

Your references are changed to point to the Total Campaign Expenses and Campaign Allocation rows on your Marketing Campaign Budget sheet. The updated references should look similar to the following.

38	Marketing Campaign				
39	Campaign Allocation	$62,000.00	$62,250.00	$62,750.00	$63,000.00
40	Total Campaign Expenses	$50,075.00	$49,725.00	$52,750.00	$52,450.00

Updating Links

If the data in your source workbook changes, the information is updated in your dependent workbook. If both workbooks are open when the source data is changed, the update takes place immediately. If you make a change to the source data while the dependent workbook is closed, a dialog box will appear the next time you open the dependent workbook, asking whether you want to update the data. You can also update a link with the Links command on the Edit menu.

Exercise caution whenever you rearrange the data in source workbooks. Sometimes a source worksheet is rearranged, for example, by moving the data or adding a column to the worksheet. If the source data is rearranged while the dependent workbook is closed, the links will be broken because the source data will no longer be in the same cells where the dependent workbook is looking for it.

 NOTE Microsoft Excel has automatic updating, as you will see in the next exercise, which can save you a lot of time when you are working with small workbooks. Automatic updating means that every time you change a value, all the cells affected by the change are recalculated. But automatic updating can slow down your work in large workbooks, because large workbooks require more time to recalculate. If you want to turn off automatic updating, use the Options command on the Tools menu, and then in the Options dialog box, click the Calculation tab. In the Calculation area, select the Manual option, and then click OK. In manual calculation mode, you can either press the F9 key to recalculate the active worksheet or press CTRL+SHIFT+F9 to recalculate all open workbooks.

Update a link

In this exercise, you make changes in the source workbook and then view the updated dependent workbook.

1 On the Window menu, click Arrange.

The Arrange Windows dialog box opens.

2 In the dialog box, select Horizontal, and then click OK.

Arranging your windows will allow you to see both windows at once. You'll learn more about arranging your windows in Lesson 14, "Customizing Your Workspace."

3 Click the window for Lesson12A.

4 On the Marketing Campaign Budget sheet, select cell E11.

5 Type **75000** and then press ENTER.

6 Select E11 again, and drag the fill handle from cell E11 to H11.

All of the cells now show the value $75,000.00, and your links are updated automatically. Cells E39:H39 on the Copier Division Budget sheet show the value $75,000.00. Your worksheet should look similar to the following.

	C	D	E	F	G	H	I
35		Interest	$378.03	$381.43	$384.86	$388.32	$391.82
36		Total Expenses	$5,095.36	$5,100.80	$5,106.30	$5,111.84	$5,226.45
37							
38	Marketing Campaign						
39		Campaign Allocation	$75,000.00	$75,000.00	$75,000.00	$75,000.00	
40		Total Campaign Expenses	$50,075.00	$49,725.00	$52,750.00	$52,450.00	
41							

Copier Division Budget / Campaign Data / Sheet3 / Sheet4 / Sheet5 / Sheet6 / Sheet7 / Sheet8

Lesson12A

	C	D	E	F	G	H	I
10			Jan	Feb	Mar	Apr	Tota
11	Campaign Budget Allocation		$75,000.00	$75,000.00	$75,000.00	$75,000.00	$300,000.0
12							
13	Expenses						
14		Advertising	$25,000.00	$24,000.00	$26,000.00	$25,000.00	$100,000.0
15		Telemarketing	6,250.00	6,000.00	6,500.00	6,250.00	25,000.0
16		Direct Mail	11,500.00	12,500.00	12,500.00	13,500.00	50,000.0

Marketing Campaign Budget / Sheet4 / Sheet5 / Shee

Changing and Restoring Links

If you move the source workbook file to another folder, rename it, or delete it, the links to your data will be broken. If you have a backup copy of your source file, or if your file is in another folder, you can easily change the link so that the linked data will appear in the dependent workbook as before. If you need to move a file into a new folder, you can avoid breaking links by moving any other files that are linked to it to the same folder.

If you break a link between a source and dependent file, you can restore the link with the Links command on the Edit menu. Whether you are restoring a link to a source workbook that was moved to another folder or changing a link to point to a new source workbook, you can use the procedure shown in the next exercise.

NOTE If you want to delete a source file and remove any links to it, you can select the linked cells on the dependent worksheet and clear the linking formulas. If you want to retain the information but not the link, you can copy the cells on the dependent worksheet that contain the linked information and then use the Paste Special command to paste only the values in place of the linking formulas.

Change a link to a backup copy of a file

In this exercise, you change the links to your copier campaign data to point to a backup file.

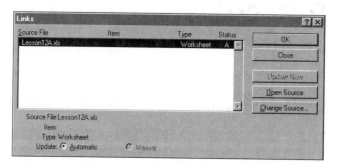

Maximize

1 In the Lesson12 window, click the Maximize button in the upper-right corner.

2 Be sure that the Copier Division Budget sheet in Lesson12 is the active sheet.

3 Select cell E39, and then on the Edit menu, click Links.

The Links dialog box opens.

4 In the Links dialog box, be sure that the file Lesson12A is selected.

5 Click the Change Source button.

The Change Links dialog box opens.

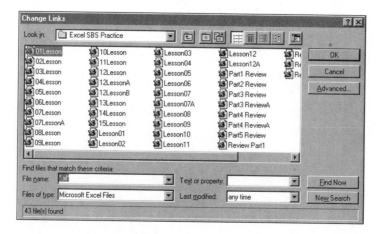

6　In the list of file names, select 12LessonB.

7　Click OK.

The Change Links dialog box closes, and the Links dialog box remains open.

8　Be sure that the file 12LessonB is selected in the Links dialog box, and click OK.

Your Lesson12 workbook is updated with the data from the backup file (the linking formulas have been updated with the new file name). Because the backup file contained old information, the cells in row 39 now contain the old values ($62,500.00). Your workbook should look similar to the following.

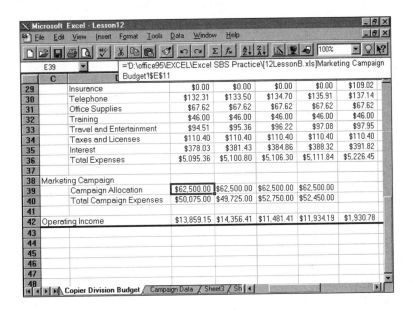

One Step Further: Using Arrays to Link Ranges

You've seen that you can link data easily by using a formula and pointing to the cell you want to link. When you link data with a formula, you can easily change the link or even accidentally erase it if you are not careful. If you have a large range of data that you want to link to another worksheet and you do not want anyone to be able to change the data on the dependent sheet, even accidentally, you can link data by making use of an *array*, a formula that produces multiple results or operates on a range of cells.

263

You can also use arrays for writing multiple-value formulas and improving worksheet efficiency.

An array formula usually occupies only one cell, but it can calculate values in many cells in which you need to do similar calculations. You can greatly improve the efficiency of your worksheet by using array formulas instead of ordinary single-value formulas. In this case, you use a special application of an array, linking a range from a source worksheet to a range in the dependent worksheet. In the sheet, the linked array will occupy several cells on the dependent worksheet, but only use one linking formula. In other words, you only need to create the linking formula once, and the array takes care of the rest. You don't have to copy the formula or update the references.

You can use the Paste Special command to paste and link an array of cells to another sheet. When you use arrays, however, you cannot change anything in the cells of the dependent sheet after you've pasted the data. You cannot move or delete part of an array on a dependent sheet, or use part of an array and leave the rest. You can only use, update, or delete arrays as a whole. You should use arrays only if you need all of the data in exactly the same format on another sheet and if you will not need to change any individual cell.

Link all of the campaign information to the copier budget worksheet

Because you want to be able to view all of the marketing campaign budget information in the copier division budget worksheet, you can use an array to link the data to a range of cells in the copier budget worksheet. In this exercise, you use an array to link data from the campaign budget worksheet (the source) to the copier budget worksheet.

1 Switch to Lesson12A.

2 Select cells D14:H19.

3 Click the Copy button on the toolbar.

4 Switch to Lesson12, and then click the Campaign Data sheet.

5 Use the right mouse button to click cell D14, and on the shortcut menu, click Paste Special.

The Paste Special dialog box opens.

Copy

6 In the dialog box, click the Paste Link button.

The campaign information is pasted as an array into the Campaign Data sheet (the curly brackets around the formula indicate that it is an array). Your workbook should look similar to the following.

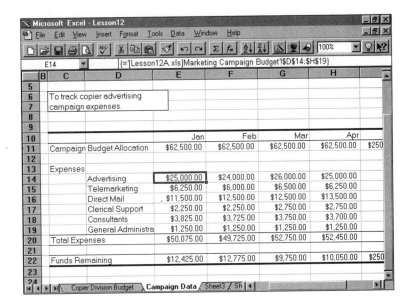

7 Click cell D14 and press DEL.

A dialog box appears, notifying you that you cannot change part of an array.

8 Click OK.

The dialog box closes.

If You Want to Continue to the Next Lesson

1 On the File menu, click Save.

2 Hold down SHIFT, and then on the File menu, click Close All.

If you see the Save dialog box, click Yes.

If You Want to Quit Microsoft Excel for Now

➤ On the File menu, click Exit.

If you see the *Save* dialog box, click Yes.

Lesson Summary

To	Do this
Create a link between two worksheets	Click the cell in the dependent sheet where you want the data to appear, and type = in the cell. Switch to the source sheet, and click the cell that contains the data. Press ENTER.
Update a link	Open the dependent file. If you are prompted to update the links, click Yes.
Change a link	On the Edit menu in the dependent workbook, click Links. Select the source filename of the link that you want to change, and click the Change Source button. Select a new source file in the File Name list, and then click OK.

For online information about	Use the Answer Wizard to search for
Linking your data	**link**

Preview of the Next Lesson

In the next lesson, "Sharing Your Data with Other Applications," you'll learn how to import graphics, how to link information between programs, and how to embed information into a worksheet from another program. You'll also learn about the efficiency you can gain by using Microsoft Excel and Microsoft Word together.

Sharing Your Data with Other Applications

Estimated time
25 min.

In this lesson you will learn how to:

- Incorporate text and graphics from another program into a Microsoft Excel sheet.
- Take advantage of the similarities between Microsoft Word and Microsoft Excel.

As you create reports, prepare presentations, or distribute information to other people, you will probably need to share your Microsoft Excel data with other programs. You might need to include a portion of a Microsoft Excel database in a letter to a potential contact, or you might need to use a Microsoft Excel table in a larger presentation. Sharing with other programs can go the other way as well, when you use text or graphics from other programs in your Microsoft Excel sheets. With OLE, you can link data from the sheet it resides on to another program, or vice versa. And working with Microsoft Word and Microsoft Excel together has never been easier—you can copy and paste between Microsoft Word for Windows 95 and Microsoft Excel for Windows 95 without having to learn a new set of menus or buttons on the toolbar.

Start the lesson

Follow the steps below to open the practice file called 13Lesson, and then save it with the new name Lesson13.

Open

1   On the Standard toolbar, click the Open button.

2   In the Look In box, be sure that the Excel SBS Practice folder appears.

To select the folder containing your practice files, refer to "Open a practice file" near the start of Lesson 1.

3 In the file list box, double-click the file named 13Lesson to open it.

4 On the File menu, click Save As.

The Save As dialog box opens. Be sure that the Excel SBS Practice folder appears in the Save In box.

5 Double-click in the File Name box, and then type **Lesson13**

6 Click the Save button, or press ENTER.

If you share your computer with others who use Microsoft Excel, the screen display might have changed since your last lesson. If your screen does not look similar to the illustrations as you work through this lesson, see the Appendix, "Matching the Exercises."

Sharing Data

You've already seen how linking data between worksheets can make your work more efficient. You can apply this same principle to other programs, which makes sharing data between programs efficient as well. You can copy and paste information between other programs and Microsoft Excel, or you can link the information so that the information will be updated whenever it changes. You can also *embed* the information so that you can make changes to the copy of the information in your worksheet without altering the original file. For example, if you have a graphic that you created in Paint, you can simply place the graphic in your Microsoft Excel worksheet. Or, you can create a link in your worksheet so that any time you change the graphic, it will be updated in the worksheet. You can also embed the graphic so that you can alter the graphic in your worksheet easily, without changing the original file.

Placing Graphics into Microsoft Excel

If you just want to put a copy of a graphic into a Microsoft Excel worksheet, you don't need to link or embed it. You can simply copy and paste, or you can use the Picture command on the Insert menu to place the picture in your sheet. The graphic will not retain any links to its original program; it will instead become an object like the text boxes and other graphic objects you've already used in your sheets.

In the following exercises, you'll place a new logo design created in Paint into your Copier Marketing Budget sheet and then delete it to make room for another version.

Place a graphic in your inventory

1   In the Copier Marketing Budget sheet, select cell F1.

The picture will not actually be inserted into a cell, but you are selecting a cell near where you want the graphic to appear. In this case, the graphic will cover from cell F1 to about cell G8.

2   On the Insert menu, click Picture.

The Picture dialog box opens.

3   In the Look In box, be sure that your Practice folder is the active folder.

4   In the Name list, select Logo1.

5   Click the Preview button if it is not already clicked.

The picture appears in the Preview area, similar to the following.

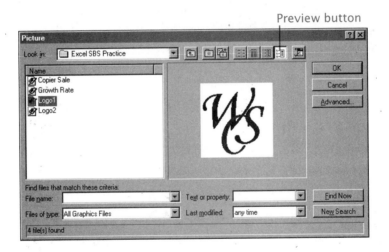

Preview button

6   Click OK.

The Logo1 picture is placed in your Copier Marketing Budget sheet. Your worksheet should look similar to the following.

	A	B	C	D	E	F	G	H	
1									
2									
3									
4									
5	Title			WCS Copier Marketing Budget					
6	Date			6/16/95					
7	Created by			Kris Mueller					
8									
9	Purpose			To show copier advertising campaign expenses					
10									
11	Budget Area								
12				Campaign Budget Allocation	$62,500.00	$62,500.00	$62,500.00	$62,500.00	$2!
13									
14				Expenses					
15				Advertising	$25,000.00	$25,000.00	$25,000.00	$25,000.00	$1(
16				Telemarketing	6,250.00	6,250.00	6,250.00	6,250.00	
17				Direct Mail	12,500.00	12,500.00	12,500.00	12,500.00	!
18				Clerical Support	2,500.00	2,500.00	2,500.00	2,500.00	
19				Consultants	3,750.00	3,750.00	3,750.00	3,750.00	

Copier Marketing Budget

Columns E-H headers: Jan | Feb | Mar | Apr

Delete a graphic

1 Click the Logo1 graphic in your Copier Marketing Budget sheet if it is not already selected.

2 Press DEL.

The graphic is removed from your Copier Marketing Budget sheet.

Linking Information Between Programs

Suppose that the Art department at West Coast Sales has created a library of graphic images for use in company correspondence, reports, and presentations. The Art department maintains this library and makes changes to the images occasionally. If you simply copy and paste or use the Insert Picture command to place one of these graphics in your sheet, you won't know if the original graphic changes or if you have the most current version. To be sure that the image in your sheet is the current version, you can *link* the graphic. When you link information, whether it's data, graphics, text, or another kind of information, you retain an active connection to the source file; the linked information is updated automatically whenever the source file changes.

NOTE To link objects in Microsoft Excel, the other program you want to use must support OLE version 1 or 2. Check the user's guide or online Help system for your program to determine this.

Link a graphic to your inventory sheet

In this exercise, you link the company logo graphic to your Copier Marketing Budget sheet.

1 In the Copier Marketing Budget sheet, select cell G1.

The upper-left corner of the picture will be pasted over cell G1.

2 On the Insert menu, click Object.

3 In the Object dialog box, click the Create From File tab, and click the Browse button.

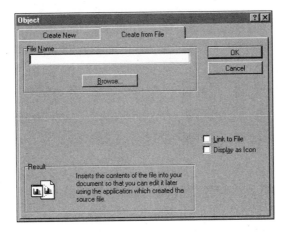

4 In the Browse dialog box, select the Logo2 file, and click the Insert button.

Be sure that the Excel SBS Practice folder is displayed in the Look In box, or you won't find the Logo2 file.

5 In the Object dialog box, click the Link To File checkbox, and click OK.

The picture is pasted and linked to your Copier Marketing Budget sheet. The linking formula in the formula bar is similar to the one you created to link data from one sheet to another in Lesson 12. Your worksheet should look similar to the following.

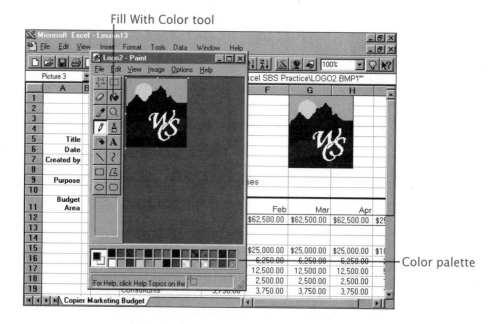

Change a linked graphic from within Microsoft Excel

1 Double-click the linked graphic object on your worksheet.

Paint appears, with the logo open.

2   In the Paint window, select the Fill With Color tool.

3   Click the dark blue color on the color palette, and then click the purple area on the picture in the Paint window.

The purple area is changed to dark blue. The picture is changed in the Copier Marketing Budget sheet, as well as in Paint, as in the following illustration.

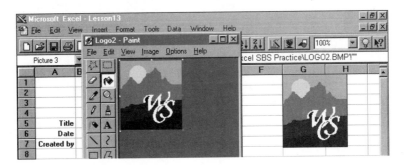

4   In the Paint window, click the Close button.

A dialog box opens, asking whether you want to save the changes to the Paint picture.

5   Click Yes.

Working with Microsoft Word for Windows 95

You probably don't spend your entire day working in Microsoft Excel. You might need to create memos or letters as well, and often you'll need to refer to your workbook data in these documents. If you are creating a report or a memo in Microsoft Word, for example, you might want to insert data from a Microsoft Excel worksheet, such as a budget or personnel report. With Microsoft Word and Microsoft Excel, you can create such combination documents easily. These programs have similar menus, toolbars, and operations, so you don't need to learn a new set of tools when you switch between the programs.

The menu names and the first few commands on each menu are largely the same, so you can quickly find the commands you use frequently. Most of the keyboard shortcuts, such as CTRL+C for Copy and F4 for Repeat, are identical between Microsoft Word and Microsoft Excel. Even the basic dialog boxes look the same, so you don't need to learn a new way to choose among a series of options.

With programs such as these, you can either link or embed information from one to the other. When you embed information from Microsoft Excel, you place the information into Microsoft Word and retain a connection to Microsoft Excel, but not to a specific file (whereas if you link information, you retain a connection to a specific file).

In the following exercises, you start Microsoft Word and open the file 13Lesson. Then you embed part of a Microsoft Excel worksheet into your campaign budget report.

Start Microsoft Word for Windows 95

1 Click the Start button on the taskbar.

If you don't have Microsoft Word, you can use the WordPad accessory on the Accessories menu.

2 Point to Programs, and then click Microsoft Word.

3 In Microsoft Word, open the file 13Lesson in your Excel SBS Practice folder, and then save it as Lesson13.

4 Click the Maximize button on the document window if it is not already maximized.

Your window should look similar to the following.

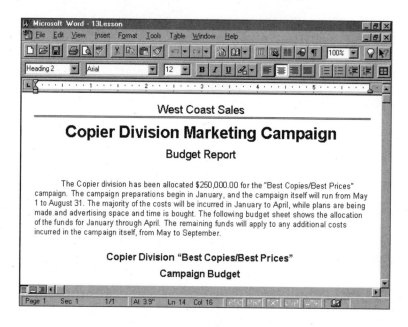

Embed information from a workbook into a Microsoft Word document

1 Switch to Microsoft Excel, and on the Copier Marketing Budget sheet, select cells C11:I23.

2 Click the Copy button on the toolbar.

Copy

To switch between programs, click the appropriate button on the taskbar.

3 Switch to Microsoft Word, and press CTRL+END to place the insertion point at the end of the document.

4 On the Edit menu in Microsoft Word, click Paste Special.

The Paste Special dialog box opens.

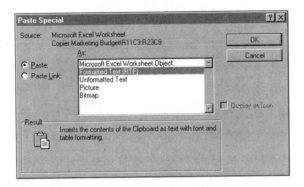

5 In the As list, select Microsoft Excel Worksheet Object, be sure that the Paste option is selected, and then click OK.

The worksheet data is embedded in your Microsoft Word document.

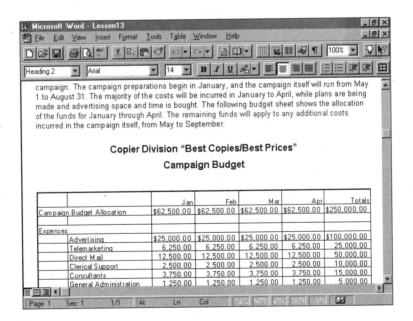

Editing Worksheet Data in Word for Windows 95

If the data that you embedded in your Microsoft Word document needs to be changed, you don't need to open Microsoft Excel before you can make the changes. You can make the changes right in your Microsoft Word document. When you select Microsoft Excel data that's embedded in a Microsoft Word document, the menus change automatically to allow you to make any changes that you need. When you click in the text areas of the document outside of the embedded object area, the menus change back to Microsoft Word menus so that you can continue with your text editing.

NOTE   The ability to edit a Microsoft Excel object in a Microsoft Word document without leaving Microsoft Word is a feature of OLE 2. This feature is available in Microsoft Word version 6 or later, and Microsoft Excel version 5 or later. Many other programs also support OLE 2 features.

Format Microsoft Excel data in your Microsoft Word document

In this exercise, you add formatting to your recently embedded Microsoft Excel data to polish the presentation in your report.

1   In the Microsoft Word document, double-click the Microsoft Excel object.

The Microsoft Word menus are replaced by Microsoft Excel menus. For example, the Table menu is gone, replaced by the Data menu. Also, the Microsoft Word toolbars are replaced by Microsoft Excel toolbars.

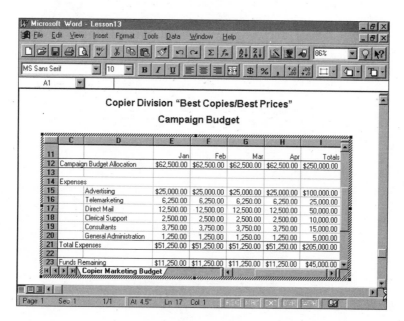

NOTE Because this is an embedded object, the original workbook file is not opened; instead, the Microsoft Excel environment is opened, allowing you to edit the embedded Microsoft Excel object. No changes will be made to the original worksheet.

2 In the Excel object, select cells C11:I23, and then on the Format menu, click AutoFormat.

The AutoFormat dialog box opens.

3 In the list of formats, choose Classic 3, and then click OK.

The AutoFormat dialog box closes, and the data is formatted.

4 Click in the text area of the Microsoft Word document.

The Microsoft Word menus and toolbars appear again. Your document should look similar to the following.

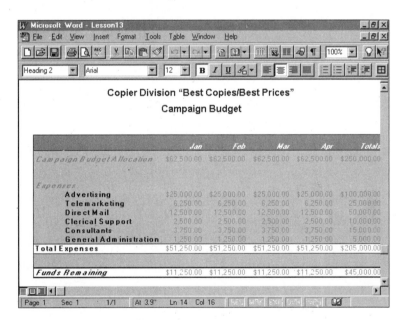

One Step Further: Using an Icon to Link Files

This One Step Further exercise requires Microsoft Word.

If you need to link to another electronic document so that the information will be available, but you don't need to show the entire document in the sheet you're working with, you can link it with an icon. The icon acts as a placeholder that you can double-click to open the actual linked document. When you place only the icon on your sheet, you can save page space and memory while still calling the extra information to another user's attention. Use an icon whenever the information you need to link is not vital to the sheet but is more of a comment or an addition to it.

Try linking your Microsoft Word budget report to your budget sheet with only the icon, and then open the linked information by double-clicking the icon.

Link a Microsoft Word document with an icon

1 Switch back to Microsoft Excel.

2 On the Copier Marketing Budget sheet, select cell C26, type **Double-click this for more information:** and then press ENTER.

3 Select cell F26, and then switch to Microsoft Word.

4 In the Lesson13 document, select all of the text.

Do not include the embedded Microsoft Excel object.

Copy

5 Click the Copy button on the toolbar.

6 Switch back to Microsoft Excel, and on the Edit menu, click Paste Special.

The Paste Special dialog box opens.

7 In the dialog box, be sure that Microsoft Word Document Object is selected, and select the Paste Link option.

8 Click the Display As Icon check box to select it, and click OK.

The dialog box closes, and a Microsoft Word icon appears in your sheet.

	A	B	C	D	E	F	G	H	
14			Expenses						
15				Advertising	$25,000.00	$25,000.00	$25,000.00	$25,000.00	$10
16				Telemarketing	6,250.00	6,250.00	6,250.00	6,250.00	2
17				Direct Mail	12,500.00	12,500.00	12,500.00	12,500.00	5
18				Clerical Support	2,500.00	2,500.00	2,500.00	2,500.00	1
19				Consultants	3,750.00	3,750.00	3,750.00	3,750.00	
20				General Administration	1,250.00	1,250.00	1,250.00	1,250.00	
21			Total Expenses		$51,250.00	$51,250.00	$51,250.00	$51,250.00	$20
22									
23			Funds Remaining		$11,250.00	$11,250.00	$11,250.00	$11,250.00	$4
24									
25									
26			Double-click this for more information:						
27									
28						Microsoft Word Document			
29									
30									
31									

Copier Marketing Budget

9 Double-click the Microsoft Word icon.

Microsoft Word opens with the document displayed. Unlike an embedded object, when you double-click an icon or a linked object, the original file is opened. To close the Microsoft Word file, click the Close button in the upper-right corner of the Microsoft Word window.

If You Want to Continue to the Next Lesson

1 If Microsoft Word is open, on the File menu, click Save.

2 On the File menu, click Close.

3 In Microsoft Excel, on the File menu, click Save.

4 On the File menu, click Close.

If You Want to Quit Microsoft Excel and Microsoft Word for Now

1 If Microsoft Word is open, on the File menu in Word, click Exit.

If you see the Save dialog box, click Yes.

2 In Microsoft Excel, on the File menu, click Exit.

If you see the Save dialog box, click Yes.

Lesson Summary

To	Do this
Insert a graphic into a sheet	Open the sheet, and click a cell near where you want to place the picture. On the Insert menu, click Picture. Select the filename of the picture you want from the File Name list, and then click OK.
Delete an inserted, embedded, or linked object	Select the object, and then press DEL.

To	Do this
Link information from another OLE2 program, such as Microsoft Word, to a Microsoft Excel sheet	Open the file in the source application. Select the information you want, and then on the Edit menu, click Copy. Switch to Microsoft Excel, and select the cell where you want the information to appear. On the Edit menu, click Paste Special. In the Paste Special dialog box, click the Paste Link option button. In the As list, select the type of object, and then click OK.
Embed Microsoft Excel information into a Microsoft Word document	In Microsoft Excel, select the information that you want to embed. On the Edit menu, click Copy. Switch to Microsoft Word, and place the insertion point where you want the information to appear. On the Edit menu in Microsoft Word, click Paste Special. In the As list, select Microsoft Excel Worksheet Object, and then click the Paste option. Click OK.
Edit a Microsoft Excel object embedded in Microsoft Word	Double-click the Microsoft Excel object in the Microsoft Word document, make your changes, and then click outside of the Microsoft Excel object to return to Microsoft Word.
Link information from a non-OLE2 program, such as Microsoft Paint, to a Microsoft Excel sheet	Activate the Microsoft Excel sheet. On the Insert menu, click Object. Click Create From File, then click Browse and select the file you want to link to. Click Insert, then click Link To File, and click OK.

For online information about	Use the Answer Wizard to search for
Placing graphics in Microsoft Excel	**graphic**
Linking information between programs	**link**
Working with Microsoft Word	**word**

Preview of the Next Lessons

In Part 5, you'll learn how to customize the appearance of your worksheets and toolbars on your screen and how to automate complex tasks that you might have to repeat often. In the next lesson, "Customizing Your Workspace," you'll learn how to customize Microsoft Excel to create the working environment that will best suit your needs. You'll learn about toolbars by moving and customizing the buttons where you need them. You'll also learn about options in Microsoft Excel that can make your work easier.

Review & Practice

In the lessons in Part 4, "Analyzing and Sharing Your Data," you learned skills to help you answer what-if questions and to share data between Microsoft Excel and other programs. If you want to practice these skills and test your understanding before you proceed with the lessons in Part 5, you can work through the Review & Practice section following this lesson.

Review & Practice

You will review and practice how to:

- Find a value using goal seeking.
- Use a data table to find a series of solutions to a what-if problem.
- Create scenarios to show several possibilities.
- Link data between workbooks so that the data will always be current.
- Insert a picture to illustrate and emphasize data.
- Link a picture to show the latest version of it at all times.
- Add Microsoft Excel data to a Microsoft Word document to finish a report.

Estimated time
30 min.

Before you move on to Part 5, which covers customizing your workspace, you can practice the skills in Part 4 by working through the steps in this Review & Practice section. You will solve a what-if problem with goal seeking, link information between workbooks, link a graphic to your worksheet, and embed Microsoft Excel data into a Microsoft Word document.

Scenario

You've nearly completed the Sales Journal report. All you need to do is add a few finishing touches. You need to use goal seeking to find the sales growth figure that will allow the Copier division to reach its sales goal, and you need to create a data table and scenarios to show what happens to the sales figure at different growth rates. You also need to link the copier data to an all-division report in another workbook. Then you will insert an illustration to add emphasis to the sales figure in the Copier division part of the report, and link a graphic to your growth rate data. Finally, you'll open a Word document that includes introductory text and then add the Microsoft Excel data and graphic to finish the report.

Step 1: Seek a Value to Reach a Goal

From 1993 to 1995, the copier sales grew from $172,102.76 to $179,161.05, a constant annual growth rate of 2.03%. In 1996, you expect sales to reach at least $190,000.00. Find the percentage of sales growth that would be necessary to reach this sales goal.

1   Open the file Part4 Review, and save it as Review Part4.

2   Use the Goal Seek command to set cell G18 to 190,000 by changing the value in cell D8, and then save the change in your worksheet.

For more information on	See
Finding a specific value	Lesson 11

Step 2: Find a Series of Solutions to a What-If Problem

For your own information, you want to see what kind of sales income you could expect with growth rates between 3 percent and 10 percent. Build a data table to show the sales income that these rates could generate.

1   Copy the formula in cell G18 to cell D23.

2   Use the Table command on the Data menu to create a data table that replaces the column input value in cell D8 with the values in C24:C31.

For more information on	See
Using data tables to find a series of values	Lesson 11

Step 3: Create Scenarios for Different Growth Rates

You need to show how the changing growth rates could affect each product marketer's sales, as well as the company's total sales amounts. Create three scenarios, for Low (2%), Medium (5%), and High (10%) growth rates, to show how the different growth rates would affect each product marketer's sales for 1996.

1   Select cell D36 and use the Scenarios command to add scenarios for 2%, 5%, and 10% growth rates. If you want to be able to show a scenario of current values, add a Current scenario that uses the current changing cell value of 2.03%.

Cell D36 will be the changing cell, as it contains the value that will change for each scenario. It may be helpful to name cell D36 before you create the scenarios.

2   Use the Show button to see the results in each scenario and then to show the current values again.

3   Create a scenario summary sheet so that the different scenarios can be compared side-by-side.

Use the Summary button on the Scenario Manager dialog box, and select the range E40:E46 as result cells. The Scenario Summary will be much more useful if you first name each cell in the Result Cells range with the last name of the salesperson.

For more information on	**See**
Naming cells	Lesson 2
Creating and viewing scenarios	Lesson 11

Step 4:   *Create Links to an All-Division Workbook*

Along with each division's sales records, the Administration department keeps track of the sales for all of the divisions. You need to put the Copier division's sales information into their all-division workbook. If you link the data, you won't have to update it every time the data changes.

1   Open the file Part4 ReviewA, and save it as Review Part4A.

2   In the Total Sales sheet, create a formula in cell D12 to link to cell C12 of the Review Part4 workbook on the Copier Sales sheet.

3   Copy the linking formula downward to D17 and then across to cell H17.

You can either link the cells one by one or copy the formulas to the rest of the total range and then update the references to the proper cells. Your sheet should look similar to the following.

 TIP   You can use the Replace command on the Edit menu to speed up the task of updating the cell references in the linked cells. Select cells E12:E17, and then click Replace on the Edit menu. In the Find What box, type **$c**, and in the Replace With box, type **$d**, and then click the Replace All button. All of the column C references in the selected range will be replaced with column D references. Repeat this procedure to replace the column C references with appropriate column references in each range of linked cells.

You might need to reapply the formatting if your screen does not match this illustration (use the Format Painter button to re-apply formatting quickly).

	C	D	E	F	G	
7						
8	*Sales Growth*	2.03%				
9						
10						
11	*Division*	*Product Marketer*	*1993 Total*	*1994 Total*	*1995 Total*	*1996 P*
12	Copier	Cane, Nate	$22,143.33	$22,592.83	$23,051.47	$
13	Copier	Morton, Sara	$20,957.67	$21,383.11	$21,817.19	$
14	Copier	Sammler, Mark	$26,167.52	$26,698.72	$27,240.71	$
15	Copier	Seidel, Matt	$28,868.66	$29,454.70	$30,052.63	$
16	Copier	West, Cara	$27,834.68	$28,399.72	$28,976.24	$
17	Copier	Wolf, Hilda	$46,130.90	$47,067.36	$48,022.82	$
18	Fax	Barber, Lisa	$119,057.33	$121,474.19	$123,940.11	$1
19	Fax	Bellwood, Frank	$127,521.67	$130,110.36	$132,751.60	$1
20	Fax	Goldberg, Malcolm	$121,667.52	$124,137.37	$126,657.36	$1
21	Fax	Lampstone, Pete	$125,787.66	$128,341.15	$130,946.48	$1
22	Printer	Berwick, Sam	$123,357.33	$125,861.48	$128,416.47	$1
23	Printer	Cortlandt, Charles	$118,579.67	$120,986.84	$123,442.87	$1
24	Printer	Martinez, Sara	$129,956.52	$132,594.64	$135,286.31	$1
25	Printer	Miller, Janet	$127,543.00	$130,132.12	$132,773.80	$1
26	Printer	Samnson, Carla	$123,850.67	$126,364.84	$128,930.04	$1

4 Save and close the Review Part4A file.

For more information on	**See**
Linking Your Data	Lesson 12

Step 5: *Insert a Picture to Enhance the Information*

The Marketing departments for each division have created division logos for different types of reports or correspondence. The logo for use with the Copier division's sales reports is the Copier Sale logo. Insert this logo into your sheet.

➤ Use the Picture command to insert the Copier Sale logo into cell F3 on your sheet.

For more information on	**See**
Inserting graphics into Microsoft Excel	Lesson 13

Step 6: *Link a Picture to Show the Latest Version*

The Art department has also created some logos that are more generalized and are available in the graphics library. The Art department is in the process of reviewing and revising the graphics, so it's hard to tell whether you have the latest version. Link the graphic in the Growth Rate file to your sheet so that the graphic will be updated automatically whenever it changes.

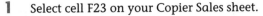

1   Select cell F23 on your Copier Sales sheet.

2   On the Insert menu, click Object, then click the Create From File tab, and then click the Browse button.

3   Select the Growth Rate file, and then click the Insert button.

4   Click the Link To File check box, and click OK.

5   Double-click the graphic object to open Paint.

6   In Paint, change the background color to green, and see the effect upon the linked object in the worksheet.

7   Save the Paint file, and then close Paint.

For more information on	See
Linking information	Lesson 13

Step 7:   *Add Data to a Document in Microsoft Word*

Your Unit Manager likes all reports to have introductory information in Microsoft Word, with data from Microsoft Excel following the introduction. Rather than printing both documents, you will combine them in Microsoft Word to create a professional-looking document.

 NOTE   If you do not have Microsoft Word, you can use WordPad for this exercise.

1   Open the Microsoft Word document Part4 Review, and save it as Review Part4.

     If you are using WordPad, open and save this document in WordPad.

2   In Microsoft Excel, use the Copy button to copy cells A1:G18.

3   In Microsoft Word or WordPad, press CTRL+END to place the insertion point at the end of the report, and then use the Paste Special command to link the Microsoft Excel object.

For more information on	See
Linking information	Lesson 13
Working with Microsoft Word	Lesson 13

If You Want to Continue to the Next Lesson

1 In Microsoft Word, on the File menu, click Save.
2 In Microsoft Word, on the File menu, click Exit.
3 In Microsoft Excel, on the File menu, click Save.
4 In Microsoft Excel, on the File menu, click Close.

If You Want to Quit Microsoft Excel for Now

➤ On the File menu, click Exit.

If you see the Save dialog box, click Yes.

Part

5

Customizing and Automating Microsoft Excel

Customizing Your Workspace

Estimated time
20 min.

In this lesson you will learn how to:

■ Display and customize toolbars.

■ Hide toolbars, menu bars, and the status bar to gain a full screen view of a worksheet.

■ Zoom in or zoom out to see as much of your sheet as you need.

■ Split your worksheets so that you can see more than one section of data at a time.

■ Arrange your sheets within windows so that you can see more than one sheet at a time.

When you are working on a big project with several workbooks full of information, you need some way to arrange your workspace so that the information you need is more accessible. You also need to access any tools you might want to use. In this lesson, you'll learn how to customize the Microsoft Excel screen display to meet your needs. You'll learn how to change your toolbars so that the tools you use most often are easy to find. In addition, you'll find out how to view and arrange worksheets so that you can see the information you need on all of your sheets. You'll view your sheets at different magnifications and split your window into panes to show different parts of your sheet in each pane. Finally, you'll learn how to arrange your windows so that you can see as many files as you need at one time.

Start the lesson

Follow the steps in the next exercise to open the practice file called 14Lesson, and then save it with the new name Lesson14.

Open

To select the folder containing your practice files, refer to "Open a practice file" near the start of Lesson 1.

1 On the Standard toolbar, click the Open button.

2 In the Look In box, be sure that the Excel SBS Practice folder appears.

3 In the file list box, double-click the file named 14Lesson to open it.

4 On the File menu, click Save As.

The Save As dialog box opens. Be sure that the Excel SBS Practice folder appears in the Save In box.

5 Double-click in the File Name box, and then type **Lesson14**

6 Click the Save button, or press ENTER.

If you share your computer with others who use Microsoft Excel, the screen display might have changed since your last lesson. If your screen does not look similar to the illustrations as you work through this lesson, see the Appendix, "Matching the Exercises."

Customizing Your Workspace with Toolbars

Microsoft Excel comes with several built-in toolbars with buttons that can save you time and effort. When you first start the application, you'll see two toolbars by default, the Standard and the Formatting toolbars. You've already used these toolbars, as well as the Drawing, Chart, and Query And Pivot toolbars, in earlier lessons.

In addition to these toolbars, there are several others that you can use as you work with Microsoft Excel. For example, in Lesson 15, you'll use the Stop Recording toolbar. If you use Scenarios often, you'll probably use the Workgroup toolbar. If you work with graphic elements, you'll become more familiar with the Drawing toolbar. If you work with Microsoft Office, you might want to use the Microsoft toolbar to switch to the other programs in the Office package (although you can also customize a Microsoft Excel toolbar to contain a button that starts Microsoft Word, and vice versa). If you are an advanced user of Microsoft Excel, you might use the Auditing and Visual Basic toolbars as well.

Showing and Hiding Toolbars

You've seen how certain toolbars automatically appear when you perform a certain action or choose a particular command. For example, when you created a chart and then activated it to make changes, the Chart toolbar automatically appeared. When you created a pivot table in Lesson 10, the Query And Pivot toolbar appeared so that you could make changes to the table. Other toolbars open automatically when you choose a certain command or activate an object. But what if you need to use a button on a toolbar that isn't open? You can easily open other toolbars, either by using the Toolbars command on the View menu or by selecting the toolbar you want from the toolbar shortcut menu.

Close and then open the Formatting toolbar

In this exercise, you close the Formatting toolbar and then open it again.

1 Move the mouse pointer over any toolbar, and then press the right mouse button.

The toolbar shortcut menu opens, and the Standard and Formatting toolbars have check marks beside their names indicating that the toolbars are currently open.

2 On the shortcut menu, click Formatting.

The Formatting toolbar closes.

3 On the View menu, click Toolbars.

The Toolbars dialog box opens. This is another way to display or hide a toolbar.

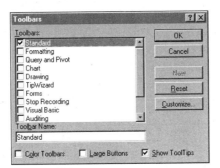

4 In the Toolbars list, click the Formatting checkbox, and then click OK.

The dialog box closes, and the Formatting toolbar appears again.

Customizing and Moving Your Toolbars

You can customize your toolbars to make them work better for you. If, for example, you rarely use the sorting buttons on the Standard toolbar or use only the Sort Descending (and not the Sort Ascending) button, you can remove the buttons you don't need from the toolbar. Or, if you often need to add a new worksheet page to your workbooks, you can add the Insert Worksheet button to the Standard toolbar so it is within easy reach. You can create your own customized toolbars to contain only the buttons that you need to use. You can also move buttons around on your existing toolbar to make them easier to use, or you can move the entire toolbar to a new location.

 NOTE Many toolbar buttons, such as the Sort Ascending and Sort Descending buttons, are multifunctional with the SHIFT key. For example, you can click the Sort Ascending button to sort a list in ascending order, or you can hold down SHIFT while clicking the same button to sort a list in descending order. Some other multifunctional buttons are Save and Open, and Print and Print Preview. The advantage of using multifunctional buttons is that you can reduce the number of buttons on a toolbar and make room for other buttons. To see which buttons are multifunctional, press and hold down SHIFT, and then click a button; if the button is multifunctional, the button face will change to show the alternate function. To avoid activating the button, drag away from the toolbar before releasing the mouse button.

In the following exercises, you'll create a custom toolbar, add some buttons to it, and rearrange the buttons.

Create a new toolbar and add buttons to it

1   On the View menu, click Toolbars.

    The Toolbars dialog box opens.

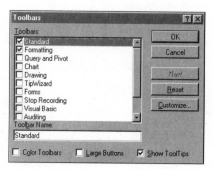

2   In the Toolbar Name box, type **My Tools**, and then click the New button.

The Customize dialog box opens. An empty toolbar appears in the upper-left corner of the screen.

New My Tools toolbar

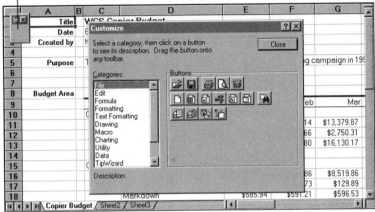

3   In the Categories list, select File if it is not already selected, and then in the Buttons area, locate the Insert Worksheet button.

Insert Worksheet

The toolbar buttons are organized according to the action that they perform. You can click the buttons with your mouse to see their descriptions (but you won't see ToolTip button names until the Customize dialog box is closed).

4   Drag the Insert Worksheet button to your new toolbar in the upper-left corner of the screen.

5   In the Categories list, select Edit, and then drag the Clear Contents, Clear Formats, and Paste Values buttons to your new toolbar.

Clear Contents   *Clear Formats*   *Paste Values*

6   In the Categories list, select Formatting, and then drag the AutoFormat button to your new toolbar. (The AutoFormat button reapplies the last table Autoformat you used.)

AutoFormat

7 In the Categories list, select Drawing, and then drag the Create Button and the Arrow buttons to your new toolbar.

Create Button   *Arrow*

8 In the Categories list, select Utility, and then drag the Freeze Panes button to your new toolbar. (You'll learn about freezing panes later in this lesson.)

Freeze Panes

9 In the Categories list, select Forms, and then drag the Toggle Grid button to your new toolbar.

Toggle Grid

You might need to scroll downward in the list to find the button listing. Leave the Customize dialog box open so that you can rearrange the buttons in the next exercise.

Arrange the buttons on your new toolbar

1 On your My Tools toolbar, click the AutoFormat button, and drag it to the left end of the toolbar.

If your toolbar is vertical, rather than horizontal, drag a border of the toolbar in or out to reshape the toolbar.

The AutoFormat button appears as the leftmost button on the toolbar.

2 Drag the Toggle Grid button to the right of the AutoFormat button.

3 Drag the Toggle Grid button a little to the right to create a space between the Toggle Grid and the AutoFormat button.

A space appears between the Toggle Grid button and the AutoFormat button.

4 Continue rearranging the buttons on your toolbar, creating groups and inserting spaces, until you have an efficient arrangement.

Be careful not to drag buttons off the toolbar. If you drag buttons off the toolbar, you'll need to add them again. Your toolbar might look similar to the following, depending on the arrangement you create.

5 In the Customize dialog box, click Close.

You can move your toolbars to any position on your screen. If you move a toolbar to the top, bottom, or either side of your window, it will *dock* at that location. When your toolbar docks, it changes its shape to a single vertical row of buttons (at the side of your screen) or a single horizontal row of buttons (at the top or bottom of your screen). Toolbars that contain drop-down boxes, such as the Font box or the Size box, cannot dock on the sides of your window, since the boxes will not fit. If you move a toolbar to anywhere near the center of your window, it will float there.

Move the toolbar around on your screen

In this exercise, you move your new toolbar around on your screen to see how it docks at different positions and how it floats in others. Then you dock it at the top of your screen, below the other toolbars.

1 Click the title bar on the My Tools toolbar, drag the toolbar to the far left side of your screen—beyond the row of numbers—and then release the mouse button.

The toolbar moves to the left margin of your window and docks vertically.

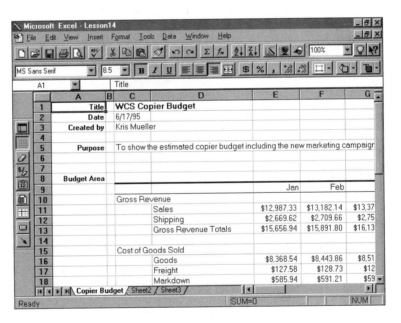

2   Position your cursor in the My Tools toolbar background, and drag downward to the bottom of your screen.

The toolbar moves to the bottom of the Microsoft Excel window and docks again.

3   Using the toolbar background, drag the My Tools toolbar back to the center of the screen.

The toolbar appears near the center of the screen again.

4   Drag the My Tools toolbar to the top of the screen, immediately below the Formatting toolbar and above the column headers.

The toolbar docks at the top of the window, below your other toolbars.

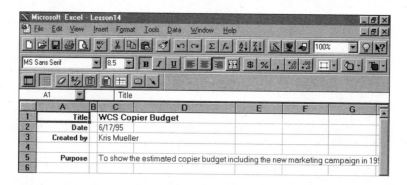

Hiding On-Screen Elements

If you find that you don't use the toolbars often and you want to see more of your data at one time, you can hide the toolbars and other elements on the screen. The Full Screen command on the View menu hides the toolbars, the title bar, and the status bar, showing only your sheet, the scroll bars, and the menu bar. To restore the hidden elements to your view, you can click the Full Screen command again, or you can click the Full Screen button on the Full Screen toolbar.

Arrange a full screen view of a sheet

In this exercise, you arrange a full screen view of your sheet, and then you restore the toolbars, status bar, and title bar to view.

1   On the View menu, click Full Screen.

The title bar, status bar, and any docked toolbars are hidden from view and your sheet fills the entire screen. The Full Screen toolbar appears with the Full Screen button and any floating toolbars.

— Full Screen button

2   Click the Full Screen button.

You can also click the Full Screen command on the View menu again to restore the screen elements to view. The toolbars, title bar, and status bar appear again, and the Full Screen toolbar disappears.

Zooming In or Out to View a Worksheet

You've seen how to make more space to display your sheet by hiding the toolbars, status bar, and title bar, but what if you want to see even more data? To get a wider view of your data, you can zoom out to display more cells in the window. If you want to see fewer cells at a higher magnification, you can zoom in. As with zooming out, you can zoom in to show a certain percentage of the full screen or to fit a particular selection to the size of the window. To zoom in or out, you can use either the Zoom Control box on the Standard toolbar or the Zoom command on the View menu.

Zoom out and zoom in to view a selection

In this exercise, you select part of your worksheet and then zoom out and in to see your data from different perspectives.

1 Select cells C9:G18.

2 On the Standard toolbar, click the down arrow next to the Zoom Control box.

The Zoom Control box opens, showing the standard zoom percentages.

3 In the list, click 50%.

Your window zooms out to show the worksheet at 50% magnification.

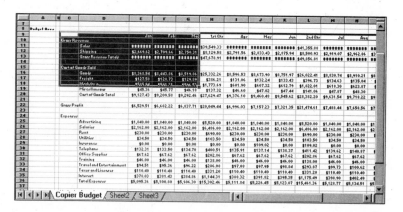

4 Click the down arrow next to the Zoom Control box.

5 In the list, click Selection.

The window zooms in to fit your selection (C9:G18). The percentage in the Zoom Control box adjusts precisely to the required magnification.

Zoom Control

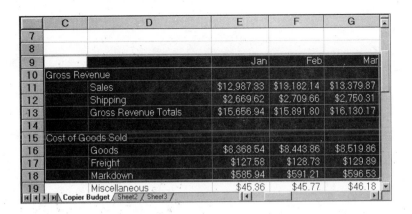

NOTE If your selection is larger than the one screen, either horizontally or vertically, choosing Selection in the Zoom box will zoom out rather than in to display the entire selection.

6 Click the down arrow next to the Zoom Control box, and in the list, click 100%.

Your window returns to 100% magnification of the worksheet.

Splitting Your Worksheets into Panes

With large sheets, you'll often have headings at the top or the left of your sheet with data extending to the right and downward. When you have scrolled past the point where the headings are visible, it can be difficult to remember what they were. If you want to see your headings all of the time while scrolling through your data, you can split your worksheet window into separate sections called *panes* and then freeze the panes so that you can view both headings and data at the same time. For example, if you have headings in row 2 and need to see data in row 55, you won't be able to see the heading and the data at the same time. But if you split your worksheet after row 2 and then freeze the pane with the headings, you can see the headings at all times, no matter where you have scrolled in the data.

To split a window into separate panes, you can use either the Split command on the Window menu or your mouse. You can freeze and unfreeze your window panes or remove the split entirely by choosing commands on the Window menu.

Split a window into panes

In this exercise, you split your worksheet into two panes with the mouse, scroll the top pane to show the headings, and then remove the split.

1   Scroll downward and over until cell C9 is in the upper-left corner of the screen.

Split box

C	D	E	F	G	H	
9		Jan	Feb	Mar	1st Qtr	
10 Gross Revenue						
11	Sales	$12,987.33	$13,182.14	$13,379.87	$39,549.33	$1
12	Shipping	$2,669.62	$2,709.66	$2,750.31	$8,129.58	$
13	Gross Revenue Totals	$15,656.94	$15,891.80	$16,130.17	$47,678.91	$1
14						
15 Cost of Goods Sold						
16	Goods	$8,368.54	$8,443.86	$8,519.86	$25,332.26	$
17	Freight	$127.58	$128.73	$129.89	$386.21	
18	Markdown	$585.94	$591.21	$596.53	$1,773.69	
19	Miscellaneous	$45.36	$45.77	$46.18	$137.32	
20	Cost of Goods Total	$9,127.43	$9,209.58	$9,292.46	$27,629.47	$
21						
22 Gross Profit		$6,529.51	$6,682.22	$6,837.71	$20,049.44	$
23						
24 Expenses						

Copier Budget / Sheet2 / Sheet3 /

Split box

2   Point to the small bar at the top of the vertical scroll bar, and then drag downward and drop the split in the middle of the screen.

This small raised box is called the *split box.* Your pointer changes to look like the illustration to the left, and the window is split into two panes.

⇵

Pointer

3   On the Window menu, click Remove Split.

The split panes are removed from the worksheet. You can also remove a split by double-clicking it.

4   Be sure that cell C9 is the upper-leftmost cell in your window.

You will split your window so that you see only the headings (in row 9 and columns C and D) in one pane and all of the data in the other.

5   Select cell E10, and on your My Tools toolbar, click the Freeze Panes button.

Your window is divided into panes again, but without the extra scroll bars. Rows above and columns to the left of the selected cell E10 are frozen into place, but you can scroll through the data from E10 downward and to the right. Your worksheet should look similar to the following.

	C	D	E	F	G	H	
9			Jan	Feb	Mar	1st Qtr	
10	Gross Revenue						
11		Sales	$12,987.33	$13,182.14	$13,379.87	$39,549.33	$1
12		Shipping	$2,669.62	$2,709.66	$2,750.31	$8,129.58	$
13		Gross Revenue Totals	$15,656.94	$15,891.80	$16,130.17	$47,678.91	$1
14							
15	Cost of Goods Sold						
16		Goods	$8,368.54	$8,443.86	$8,519.86	$25,332.26	$
17		Freight	$127.58	$128.73	$129.89	$386.21	
18		Markdown	$585.94	$591.21	$596.53	$1,773.69	
19		Miscellaneous	$45.36	$45.77	$46.18	$137.32	
20		Cost of Goods Total	$9,127.43	$9,209.58	$9,292.46	$27,629.47	$
21							
22	Gross Profit		$6,529.51	$6,682.22	$6,837.71	$20,049.44	$
23							
24	Expenses						

Copier Budget / Sheet2 / Sheet3 /

> **NOTE** You can also select a row or column and then freeze panes. The window will be split along that row or column, and everything above the row or left of the column will be frozen in place.

6 In the data area, scroll downward and to the right to cell U38.

Even though you are scrolling through the cells in the data area, the headings remain in place. You can scroll anywhere to the right or to the bottom of your worksheet, but you cannot scroll past cell E10 to the left or top of your worksheet.

7 Click the Freeze Panes button on your My Tools toolbar to unfreeze the panes.

You can also use the Unfreeze Panes command on the Window menu. The frozen panes are removed from the worksheet.

Freeze Panes

Arranging Windows

Splitting your windows and zooming in or out can help you see more information on a particular sheet. But what if you have several sheets in a workbook and you need to look at more than one at a time? Or what if you need to compare information that is stored in more than one workbook? You can arrange your windows so that you can see two, three, four, or more windows at a time. Of course, the more windows you have, the harder it will be to see very much information in them. But the biggest advantage in using multiple windows is that you can move and copy cells and sheets between workbooks by dragging from one window to another.

In Lesson 12, "Linking Your Data," you saw how you could arrange your windows horizontally to show smaller, horizontally aligned windows. You can also arrange windows vertically. Alternatively, you can cascade your windows so that only the title bars of the

303

inactive windows show behind the active window. To arrange your windows, use the Arrange command on the Window menu. You can have several workbooks in separate windows or one workbook displayed in several windows.

In the following exercises, you'll open a second and a third window for your workbook and then rearrange the three windows by cascading and tiling. Then you'll move and copy cells and worksheets between two workbooks the fast way, by dragging the cells and sheets between windows.

Open new windows to display different sheets in a workbook

1   On the Window menu, click New Window twice (not a double-click).

    Two new windows open showing your Lesson14 workbook.

2   On the Window menu, click Lesson14:2.

    The Lesson14:2 window appears.

3   Click the Sheet2 tab.

    Sheet2 appears in the Lesson14:2 window.

4   On the Window menu, click Lesson14:3.

    The Lesson14:3 window appears.

5   Click the Sheet3 tab.

    Sheet3 appears in the Lesson14:3 window.

Cascade, tile, and then arrange windows horizontally

1   On the Window menu, click Arrange.

    The Arrange Windows dialog box opens.

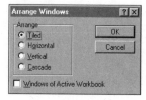

2   Select the Cascade option, and then click OK.

Your windows are arranged so that Lesson14:3 is visible in front and only the title bars of Lesson14:2 and Lesson14:1 are visible. You can click a title bar to make another window active and bring it to the front, as in the following illustration.

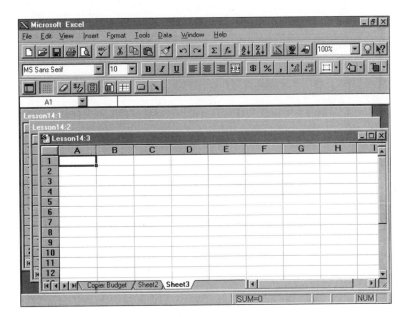

3   On the Window menu, click Arrange.

The Arrange Windows dialog box opens.

4   In the Arrange area, select Tiled, and then click OK.

Your windows are arranged so that Lesson14:3 is on the left, with Lesson14:2 and Lesson14:1 tiled beside it.

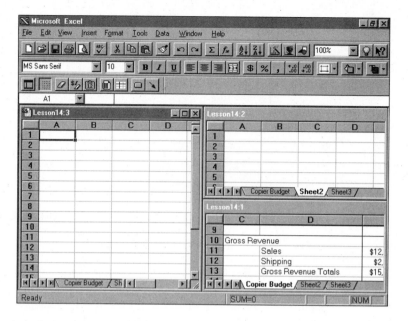

5 On the Window menu, click Arrange.

The Arrange Windows dialog box opens.

6 In the Arrange area, select Horizontal, and then click OK.

Your windows are arranged horizontally, with all three windows visible and the Lesson14:1 window at the bottom.

You can change all of the windows back to full size by maximizing one of the windows. All of the others will be restored to full size automatically, with the inactive windows hidden behind the active window.

Restore your windows

In this exercise, you restore your windows to full size and then close the duplicate windows.

1 Click the Maximize button on the Lesson14:3 window.

All three windows are maximized, but only Lesson14:3 is visible. You can also double-click the title bar to maximize a window.

Minimize
— Close
Maximize

2 Click the Close button on the Lesson14:3 and the Lesson14:2 windows.

The duplicate windows are closed. Your Lesson14 window remains open and maximized.

Drag sheets and cells between windows

In this exercise, you use drag-and-drop editing to copy a range of cells and to move a worksheet between two workbooks.

New Workbook

1   Click the New Workbook button on the Standard toolbar to open a new blank workbook.

2   On the Window menu, click Arrange, then select Horizontal, and click OK.

The new workbook and Lesson14 are arranged horizontally.

3   In the Lesson14 window, select cells A1:C3.

4   Press and hold down CTRL, and drag the border of the selected cells to A1:C3 in the new workbook.

The cells are copied to the new workbook. To move cells without copying, drag the cells without holding down CTRL.

5   In the new workbook, click the Sheet1 tab, drag it down to the Lesson14 window, and then drop it behind Sheet3.

Sheet1 from the new workbook is moved to the Lesson14 workbook. To copy the sheet instead of moving it, hold down CTRL when you drop the sheet.

6   Close the new workbook without saving it, and then double-click the Lesson14 title bar to maximize the window.

The Lesson14 window is restored to maximum size.

One Step Further: Hiding Rows and Columns

In the copier budget sheet in the Lesson14 file, you have columns for every month, as well as summary columns for every quarter and a totals column. In Lesson 9, you saw how you could outline your sheet and hide parts of the outline to show only a summary. If you have some data, however, that you do not need to view at the moment, you can quickly hide the rows or columns that you don't need without outlining your sheet. You can hide rows and columns with the Row and Column commands on the Format menu. To restore your rows or columns, select the rows or columns around the hidden rows or columns, and then use the Row and Column commands on the Format menu again.

Hide columns of data and then restore them

In this exercise, you hide all of the months in your budget so that only the summary columns are visible and then restore them so that you can see all of the data.

1   Switch to the Copier Budget sheet, and then select columns E through G.

2   On the Format menu, point to Column, and then click Hide.

The columns are hidden.

3 Select columns I through K, and then click the right mouse button to display the shortcut menu.

Be sure that your mouse pointer is still over the column header when you display the shortcut menu.

4 On the shortcut menu, click Hide.

Columns I through K are hidden as well.

5 Click the column header for column M, press and hold down CTRL, and select columns N, O, Q, R, and S.

Using the CTRL key, you can select individual, nonadjacent columns, rows, or cells. (Release the CTRL key after you have selected the nonadjacent columns.)

6 On the shortcut menu, click Hide.

All of your month columns are hidden. Only the quarterly summaries and the totals column remain.

	D	H	L	P	T	U	
8							
9		1st Qtr	2nd Qtr	3rd Qtr	4th Qtr	Totals	
10	venue						
11	Sales	$39,549.33	$41,355.88	$43,244.95	$94,010.75	$218,160.90	
12	Shipping	$8,129.58	$8,500.93	$8,889.24	$19,324.43	$44,844.19	
13	Gross Revenue Totals	$47,678.91	$49,856.81	$52,134.19	$113,335.19	$263,005.09	
14							
15	ods Sold						
16	Goods	$25,332.26	$26,022.41	$26,731.35	$58,111.64	$136,197.65	
17	Freight	$386.21	$396.73	$407.54	$885.95	$2,076.42	
18	Markdown	$1,773.69	$1,822.01	$1,871.65	$4,068.80	$9,536.14	
19	Miscellaneous	$137.32	$141.06	$144.90	$315.00	$738.28	
20	Cost of Goods Total	$27,629.47	$28,382.20	$29,155.44	$63,381.39	$148,548.50	
21							
22	fit	$20,049.44	$21,474.61	$22,978.75	$49,953.80	$114,456.59	
23							

Copier Budget / Sheet2 / Sheet3 / Sheet1 /

7 Select columns D through T.

You can redisplay a column by selecting the columns on either side of it, or you can select the entire worksheet.

8 On the Format menu, point to Column, and then click Unhide.

All of the hidden columns are restored. You can also use the Unhide command on the shortcut menu.

9 On the toolbar shortcut menu, click My Tools to close the My Tools toolbar.

If You Want to Continue to the Next Lesson

1 On the File menu, click Save.

2 On the File menu, click Close.

If You Want to Quit Microsoft Excel for Now

➤ On the File menu, click Exit.

If you see the Save dialog box, click Yes.

Lesson Summary

To	Do this	Button
Display a toolbar	Use the right mouse button to click on any open toolbar. On the shortcut menu, select the toolbar that you want. You can also click Toolbars on the View menu.	
Create a new toolbar	On the View menu, click Toolbars. In the Toolbar Name box, type the name for your toolbar, and then click New. Customize your toolbar by adding tools from the Customize dialog box.	
Customize a toolbar	Display the toolbar you want to customize. On the toolbar shortcut menu, click Customize. Drag the buttons you want to remove from the toolbar away from the toolbar. Drag the buttons you want to add from the Buttons area to the toolbar. Drag buttons you want to rearrange on the toolbar to their new locations. In the Customize dialog box, click Close.	
Gain a full screen view of a worksheet or return to normal view	On the View menu, click Full Screen. To return to normal view, click the Full Screen button on the Full Screen toolbar.	🗖
Zoom in or out to view your sheet	Select the cells you want to view. On the View menu, click Zoom, or click the down arrow next to the Zoom box on the Standard toolbar. In the Zoom box, select a percentage, type in a percentage, or select Selection, and then click OK.	`100%  ▾`

To	Do this	Button
Split a worksheet into panes	Drag the split box. *or* On the Window menu, click Split.	
Remove split panes	On the Window menu, click Remove Split. *or* Double-click the split bar.	
Freeze or unfreeze panes	On the Window menu, click Freeze Panes or Unfreeze Panes. *or* Click the Freeze Panes button.	
Open a new window	On the Window menu, click New Window.	
Arrange windows	On the Window menu, click Arrange. In the Arrange Windows dialog box, select Tiled, Horizontal, Vertical, or Cascade, and then click OK.	

For online information about	Use the Answer Wizard to search for
Customizing your workspace with toolbars	**toolbar**
Viewing a sheet full screen	**full screen**
Zooming in or out to view your sheet	**zoom**
Splitting your worksheet into panes	**split**
Arranging multiple windows	**windows**

Preview of the Next Lesson

In the next lesson, "Automating Repetitive Tasks," you are introduced to Microsoft Excel's macro language and you learn how to create simple macros to save yourself time and effort. You learn how to record keystrokes as a macro, how to add comments to make a macro more understandable, and how to add buttons to your sheets to automatically run the macros you create.

Automating Repetitive Tasks

Estimated time
25 min.

In this lesson you will learn how to:

- Create macros to automate repetitive tasks.
- Add comments to your macro to make it easier to understand.
- Create a macro button to make the macro easier to run.

Some of the data entry and formatting that you do in Microsoft Excel can be repetitive. For example, you might set up most of your worksheets with the same basic headings, or format all of your headings alike. Rather than performing the same sequence of tasks over and over again, you can create a *macro*. Then, instead of typing the same headings, or using the same formatting commands repeatedly, you can run the macro, which will enter and format the headings automatically.

A macro consists of a series of instructions written in a language called *Visual Basic* that Microsoft Excel can follow. To create a macro, you don't need to understand the language that is used—you only need to know what Microsoft Excel commands you want the macro to perform for you. You record the commands in sequence, and then they are translated automatically into the language that Microsoft Excel uses. Recording a macro is similar to recording music on a tape—you don't need to understand how the music is recorded onto the tape—you only need to know what music you want to record.

In this lesson, you'll learn how to automate repetitive tasks by recording macros, add comments to your macros to make them easy to understand later, and create macro buttons so that you can access and run your macros quickly.

Start the lesson

Follow the steps below to open the practice file called 15Lesson, and then save it with the new name Lesson15.

Open

To select the folder containing your practice files, refer to "Open a practice file" near the start of Lesson 1.

1 On the Standard toolbar, click the Open button.

2 In the Look In box, be sure that the Excel SBS Practice folder appears.

3 In the file list box, double-click the file named 15Lesson to open it.

4 On the File menu, click Save As.

The Save As dialog box opens. Be sure that the Excel SBS Practice folder appears in the Save In box.

5 Double-click in the File Name box, and then type **Lesson15**

6 Click the Save button, or press ENTER.

If you share your computer with others who use Microsoft Excel, the screen display might have changed since your last lesson. If your screen does not look similar to the illustrations as you work through this lesson, see the Appendix, "Matching the Exercises."

Creating Macros to Automate Tasks

If you find that you perform certain tasks frequently in Microsoft Excel, such as applying bold, italic, and a large type size to sheet titles, or typing the same categories into every budget sheet, you can save time by automating these tasks. You can record a macro for almost any series of actions that you perform with Microsoft Excel.

To create a macro, you simply turn on the *macro recorder*, perform the sequence of tasks that you want to record, and then turn off the macro recorder. As you record the macro, the commands are automatically translated into the Visual Basic language and stored in a separate *module* sheet in your workbook.

NOTE   You can also use any macros you created in Microsoft Excel versions 3, 4, or 5.

After your macro is recorded, you can run it by choosing the macro name in the Macros dialog box. As you will see later in this lesson, you can also run macros by clicking a macro button or by using a shortcut key combination.

Recording Macros

Before you record a macro, you need to plan out exactly what you want the macro to do and in what order. After you choose Record New Macro, every cell you select, everything you type, and every command you choose is recorded in a manner similar to a tape recorder. You also need to think of a name and a description for the macro to identify exactly what the macro does.

You should name your macro to reflect the actions it performs. In this exercise, the macro you will record adds area headings, a title, and the current date to a new budget sheet. The name of this macro will be "Budget_Info" because it adds the budget headings. Macro names cannot include spaces or periods. If you include more than one word, you need to either separate the words with an underscore, as in Copy_All_Data, or use initial capitals to separate the words, as in CopyAllData.

It's a good idea to run through the steps in your plan before you actually record the macro and then test the macro after you record it. Since you will have exact instructions for creating macros in this lesson, however, you will not need to run through the steps before recording them. In the following exercises, you will record a new macro to enter budget area headings into a sheet.

Start recording a macro

NOTE Macros are automatically set to use absolute references. If you record a macro to enter data or select a cell, you might need to switch to relative references. If the macro is recorded with absolute references, the data will appear in the same cells, no matter what cell you select before running the macro.

1 Switch to Sheet1, and select cell A8.

You want to be able to use this macro anywhere in a sheet, so you need to select the cell you'll start with before you begin recording. If you start recording and then select a cell, that selection is part of the macro.

Record Macro

You can also use the Record Macro button on the Visual Basic toolbar instead of the Record New Macro command.

2 On the Tools menu, point to Record Macro, and then click Record New Macro.

The Record New Macro dialog box opens.

3   In the Macro Name box, type **Budget_Info**

4   In the Description box, type **Sets up budget area headings**

5   Click OK.

The macro has begun recording, and the Stop Recording toolbar appears with one button. You might need to move this toolbar out of the way while you record the macro.

6   On the Tools menu, point to Record Macro, and then click Use Relative References.

Switching to relative references allows you to use your macro wherever you need to, rather than only in a particular cell or range.

 NOTE   A macro is only available when the workbook it is stored in is open. If you want a specific macro to be available all the time, no matter which workbooks are open, you can click the Options button in the Record New Macro dialog box, and then select the "Store In Personal Macro Workbook" option. The Personal Macro Workbook is a hidden file that Microsoft Excel creates when you select the option, and this file opens automatically whenever you start Microsoft Excel.

Record the macro

To disable AutoComplete, click Options on the Tools menu. On the Edit tab, clear the Enable AutoComplete For Cell Values check box.

1   In cell A8 type the following, pressing ENTER or TAB where indicated. If you make a typing mistake, just backspace and retype. The macro recorder will not record what it perceives to be errors.

Budget Area ENTER ENTER TAB **Gross Revenue** ENTER **Sales** ENTER **Shipping** ENTER **Gross Revenue Totals** ENTER ENTER **Cost of Goods Sold** ENTER **Goods** ENTER **Freight** ENTER **Markdown** ENTER **Miscellaneous** ENTER **Cost of Goods Sold Total** ENTER

2   Click the Stop Macro button on the Stop Recording toolbar.

The macro stops recording, and the Stop Recording toolbar disappears. A new sheet called a module, named Module1, is added to your workbook.

Stop Macro

Running Macros

After you've recorded a macro, it's a good idea to test it out before you store it permanently or pass it on to someone else. To run a macro, choose the Macro command and then select the macro's name from the list of available macros.

When you run a macro, it simply carries out all of the actions that you performed while you were recording. For some macros, you need to select the cell or cells that you want the macro to affect before you run it. Since the Budget_Info macro you created does not begin on any specific cell, you need to select a cell before you run it.

Run the Budget_Info macro

In this exercise, you run your Budget_Info macro to add another series of budget titles to your sheet.

1 Select cell E8, and then on the Tools menu, click Macro.

The Macro dialog box opens.

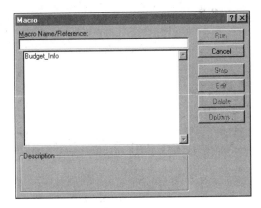

2 Select Budget_Info, and then click the Run button.

The macro runs, and your budget titles are added to the sheet. Your worksheet should look similar to the following.

	A	B	C	D	E	F	G	H	I
6									
7									
8	Budget Area				Budget Area				
9									
10		Gross Revenue				Gross Revenue			
11		Sales				Sales			
12		Shipping				Shipping			
13		Gross Revenue Totals				Gross Revenue Totals			
14									
15		Cost of Goods Sold				Cost of Goods Sold			
16		Goods				Goods			
17		Freight				Freight			
18		Markdown				Markdown			
19		Miscellaneous				Miscellaneous			
20		Cost of Goods Sold Total				Cost of Goods Sold Total			
21									
22									
23									

Copier Budget \ **Sheet1** / Module1

315

Documenting Macros

In Lesson 7, "Organizing Your Workbooks," you learned that it's a good idea to add comments, notes, or headings to your workbooks to describe them. In the same way, you should add comments to, or *document*, your macros so that you or other users can understand how they work. You have begun documenting the macros you created by adding both a title and a description. But what if you need to examine the macro steps at some point and find out what each part of the macro does? You can add comments to the macro steps to do this.

Macros are stored on special sheets in your workbooks called modules. A module is a sheet containing the Visual Basic code that the macro recorder writes when you record a macro. Modules can contain only macros and comments, along with your titles and descriptions. You can edit your macros on the module sheet to add additional comments to explain the particular steps, and you can edit the steps themselves to change or correct them without recording the macro again. For example, if you misspell a word while recording a macro you can edit the spelling in the module rather than re-recording the entire macro.

Examine your macros

In this exercise, you open the module that contains your macros and take a look at them.

If your module sheet displays dots instead of characters, you need to change the font used in your module sheets. On the Tools menu, click Options. In the Options dialog box, click the Module Format tab, and change the font to Courier New. Click OK.

▶ Select the Module1 sheet in your workbook.

The Module1 sheet opens, with the Budget_Info macro displayed. The menu bar changes to include menus and commands specific to modules.

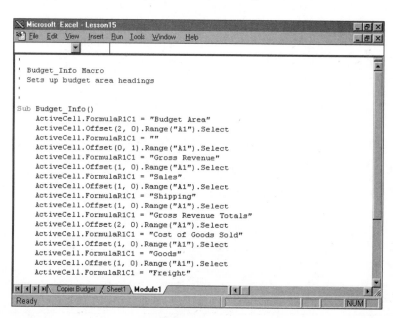

Some text on the module sheet appears in green, some appears in blue, and some appears in black. The green text indicates a comment (and is ignored by Microsoft Excel when a macro is run), the blue text indicates *keywords* that Microsoft Excel recognizes (in this case, the beginning and end of a macro), and the black text indicates a macro step. In your macro, the title "Budget_Info Macro" and the description appear as comments in green. Comments are always preceded by an apostrophe, which tells Microsoft Excel that they are merely comments.

The word "Sub" appears in blue text, followed by "Budget_Info ( )." This line indicates the beginning of a macro called "Budget_Info." After this line, everything else is black, meaning that everything else is a step in the macro, until you reach the line that reads "End Sub" in blue. "End Sub" indicates the end of the macro commands.

NOTE Macros in Microsoft Excel for Windows 95 are written in a language called Visual Basic. If you want to learn more about Visual Basic and the macros in Microsoft Excel for Windows 95, refer to the online Help Contents topic, "Getting Started with Visual Basic."

To document your macro, you'll add comments to each section. You can add a comment that describes a section immediately above the section or immediately following the section. It doesn't matter which you choose, as long as you are consistent. To add a comment, type an apostrophe and then the comment; the comment will turn green automatically after you click away from the line. The apostrophe tells the program that the text is a comment rather than a step. Adding comments will not affect the macro when you run it, as long as you remember to add the apostrophe at the beginning of the line. If you don't, you will see an error message when you try to run the macro again.

Add comments to your Budget_Info macro

In this exercise, you add comments to explain each step of your Budget_Info macro.

1   On the Module1 sheet, click at the end of the Sub Budget_Info ( ) line, after the closed parenthesis.

    Remember that the first action you performed when you created the macro was to label the Budget Area. The "Budget Area" line performs that action.

2   Press ENTER twice, press TAB, and then type **'Adds heading to budget area**

    Remember to type the apostrophe first. Pressing ENTER twice adds extra line spacing, which makes the macro easier to read.

3   Click at the end of the "Budget Area" macro step line.

    The new comment turns green.

4   Press ENTER twice, then type **'Adds budget categories to budget area** and click away from the new line.

    Your macro code should look similar to the following.

```
'
' Budget_Info Macro
' Sets up budget area headings
'
'
Sub Budget_Info()

    'Adds heading to budget area
    ActiveCell.FormulaR1C1 = "Budget Area"

    'Adds budget categories to budget area
    ActiveCell.Offset(2, 0).Range("A1").Select
    ActiveCell.FormulaR1C1 = ""
    ActiveCell.Offset(0, 1).Range("A1").Select
    ActiveCell.FormulaR1C1 = "Gross Revenue"
    ActiveCell.Offset(1, 0).Range("A1").Select
    ActiveCell.FormulaR1C1 = "Sales"
    ActiveCell.Offset(1, 0).Range("A1").Select
    ActiveCell.FormulaR1C1 = "Shipping"
    ActiveCell.Offset(1, 0).Range("A1").Select
    ActiveCell.FormulaR1C1 = "Gross Revenue Totals"
    ActiveCell.Offset(2, 0).Range("A1").Select
    ActiveCell.FormulaR1C1 = "Cost of Goods Sold"
```

Copier Budget / Sheet1 \ **Module1**

Making Macros Easier to Run with Macro Buttons

You can run any macro in your workbook from the Macro dialog box, but this is not always the quickest method. If you have a macro such as the Budget_Info macro you created, which will often be used with a particular sheet, you can add a button to that sheet and assign the macro to the button. That way, you can click the button to run the macro, rather than using a menu command. You can still access the macro through the menu should you need to.

Creating Macro Buttons

When you want a macro button, you can draw a button and assign the macro to it. You draw buttons in the same way that you drew lines and text boxes earlier in this book, by clicking the Create Button button on the Drawing toolbar or the My Tools toolbar, and then dragging on your worksheet to draw the button. You can make the button as large or as small as you like, depending on the amount of space available on your sheet. You can resize or move the button later. When you create the button, you also assign a macro to it from the list of macros in the workbook. After you've created the macro button and assigned a macro to it, it's a good idea to give it a descriptive name so that you can remember what will happen when you click the button.

Add a macro button to run the Budget_Info macro

In this exercise, you add a macro button to run the Budget_Info macro, and you name the button.

1   Switch to the Copier Budget sheet.
2   Display your My Tools toolbar.

Create button

3 Click the Create Button button.

Your pointer changes to a small pair of cross hairs, ready for you to draw a button.

4 Drag to draw a button to cover cells E2:E3.

The button appears, and the Assign Macro dialog box opens.

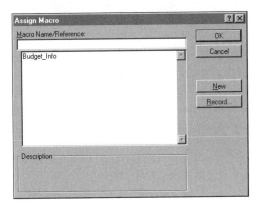

5 Select Budget_Info, and then click OK.

The Assign Macro dialog box closes.

6 Be sure that the button is still selected, and then select the text "Button 1."

7 Type **Adds Budget Titles**, and then click outside the button.

The button is named Adds Budget Titles, although only part of the name might appear. Your worksheet should look similar to the following.

	A	B	C	D	E	F	G
1	Title		WCS Copier Budget				
2	Date		6/17/95		Adds Budget		
3	Created by		Kris Mueller		Titles		
4							
5	Purpose		To show the estimated copier budget including the new marketing campaign in 19
6							
7							
8	Budget Area						
9					Jan	Feb	Mar
10			Gross Revenue				
11				Sales	$12,987.33	$13,182.14	$13,379.87
12				Shipping	$2,669.62	$2,709.66	$2,750.31
13				Gross Revenue Totals	$15,656.94	$15,891.80	$16,130.17
14							
15			Cost of Goods Sold				
16				Goods	$8,368.54	$8,443.86	$8,519.86
17				Freight	$127.58	$128.73	$129.89
18				Markdown	$585.94	$591.21	$596.53

Copier Budget / Sheet1 / Module1 /

When you first create a macro button, you might not place it exactly where you want it, or you might not size it correctly. If the button's label is too long, or if you decide that you need to move the button to a better location on your sheet, you can select it and resize or move it. Unlike most objects on a sheet, however, you cannot simply click the button to select it. (If you simply click the button, you will run the macro.) To select a macro button, you must press and hold down CTRL, and then click the button.

NOTE You can also copy a macro button by holding down CTRL and then dragging the button to a new location. When you copy a button, it retains its connection to the macro, so you can place a copy on several sheets in a workbook and then run the macro from any of them.

Select and resize a macro button

In this exercise, you resize your macro button to fit the size of the button label.

1 Hold down CTRL and then click the macro button, and then release CTRL.

   The macro button is selected, and a border appears around it with small square handles at each side and corner. Be sure that you release CTRL after selecting the button; otherwise, you'll create a copy.

2 Place your mouse pointer over the handle at the right side of the button, and then drag to enlarge the button until its entire label appears on one line.

3 Click away from the button to de-select it.

   The button is resized to fit the text inside it.

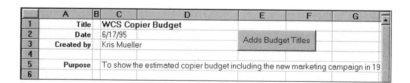

Move a macro button

In this exercise, you move your macro button to where you want to run the macro so that you can see the macro run when you click the button.

1 Hold down CTRL and then click the macro button, and then release CTRL.

   The macro button is selected, and a border appears around it. Be sure that you release CTRL after selecting the button; otherwise, you'll create a copy.

2 Drag the button by a border (not a handle) down to cell A40, and then click away from the button to de-select it.

   This places the button near where you are going to run your macro.

Running Macros with a Macro Button

To delete a macro button, hold down CTRL to select the button, and then press DELETE; or click the macro button with the right mouse button, and then click Clear on the shortcut menu.

To run a macro from a macro button, click the button once. If the macro is one that performs an action on a particular selection, like the Budget_Info macro, you need to select the cell or range that you want it to affect before you click the button. In the next exercise, you'll run the Budget_Info macro using the button you just created.

Run the Budget_Info macro

➤ Select cell C45, and then click the Adds Budget Titles button.

The budget titles are added to cells C45:D56. Your worksheet should look similar to the following.

	A	B	C	D	E	F	G
39				Campaign Allocation	$62,000.00	$62,250.00	$62,750.00
40	Adds Budget Titles			Total Campaign Expenses	$50,075.00	$49,725.00	$52,750.00
41							
42			Operating Income		$13,359.15	$14,106.41	$11,731.41
43							
44							
45			Budget Area				
46							
47				Gross Revenue			
48				Sales			
49				Shipping			
50				Gross Revenue Totals			
51							
52				Cost of Goods Sold			
53				Goods			
54				Freight			
55				Markdown			
56				Miscellaneous			

Copier Budget / Sheet1 / Module1 /

NOTE If you get an error message that you did not see when you ran the macro before, you might have forgotten an apostrophe when you were adding comments to the macro. Look over the macro on the Module1 sheet to add any apostrophes that you might have left out.

One Step Further: Using a Keyboard Shortcut to Run a Macro

You can make your macros even easier to access by assigning a keyboard shortcut to them. You can assign any combination of CTRL+*key* or CTRL+SHIFT+*key*, as long as that particular key combination is not being used to access another command. For example, CTRL+C is already in use as the Copy shortcut, so you would not want to use that key combination. If you used CTRL+C for a macro, you would no longer be able to use it to copy data. To assign a shortcut to a macro, click the Options button in the Macro dialog box.

IMPORTANT When you assign a shortcut key combination to a macro, Microsoft Excel does not notify you whether that combination is already assigned. Exercise caution when you assign shortcut keys so that you don't unintentionally reassign a combination that is already in use.

Assign a shortcut key to a macro

In this exercise, you assign the keyboard shortcut CTRL+SHIFT+I to your Budget_Info macro.

1   On the Tools menu, click Macro.

The Macro dialog box opens.

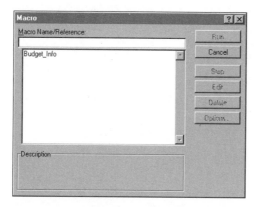

2   Select Budget_Info, and then click the Options button.

The Macro Options dialog box opens.

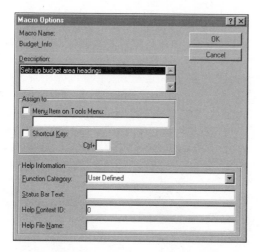

3   In the Assign To area, select the Shortcut Key checkbox.

4   Click in the Ctrl+ box. Hold down SHIFT, and then type **I**

5   Click OK.

6   In the Macro dialog box, click Close.

7   Select cell E45, and then press CTRL+SHIFT+I.

    The Budget_Info macro runs and adds the list of budget titles.

If You Want to Continue to the Next Lesson

1   On the File menu, click Save.

2   On the File menu, click Close.

If You Want to Quit Microsoft Excel for Now

➤   On the File menu, click Exit.

    If you see the Save dialog box, click Yes.

Lesson Summary

To	Do this	Button
Create a macro	On the Tools menu, point to Record Macro, and then click Record New Macro. In the Record New Macro dialog box, type a name and a description for the macro, and then click OK. Perform the keystrokes that you want to include, and then click the Stop Macro button on the Stop Recording toolbar.	
Run a macro	On the Tools menu, click Macro. In the Macro dialog box, select the macro, and then click the Run button.	
Document a macro	Select the module sheet that contains the macro you want to document. Type comments preceded by apostrophes.	

To	Do this	Button
Assign a macro to a button	Click the Create Button button on the Drawing toolbar, and draw a button on your sheet. In the Assign Macro dialog box, select a macro, and then click OK. With the button selected, select the text on the button, and type a button name. Click outside the button.	
Run a macro from a macro button	Click the macro button.	
To assign a shortcut key to a macro	On the Tools menu, click Macro. In the Macro dialog box, click Options. Select the Shortcut Key check box, and then type the shortcut key you want in the CTRL+ box.	

For online information about	Use the Answer Wizard to search for
Creating macros to automate tasks	**create macro**

Review & Practice

In the lessons in Part 5, "Customizing and Automating Microsoft Excel," you learned skills to help you customize your toolbars, modify your screen display, and create macros to automate repetitive tasks. If you want to practice these skills and test your understanding, you can work through the Review & Practice section following this lesson.

Part

5

Review & Practice

Estimated time
15 min.

You will review and practice how to:

- Customize your workspace with toolbars.
- Zoom in to view part of a sheet.
- Arrange windows to show more than one sheet.
- Create a macro to automate a repetitive task.
- Document a macro.
- Add a macro button to make the macro easier to access.

Before you complete this book, you can practice the skills in Part 5 by working through the steps in this Review & Practice section. You will create a new toolbar, zoom in to view part of your worksheet, arrange windows to show more than one sheet at a time, create a macro to save time and effort, document the macro, and then add a macro button to make it easier to run.

Scenario

You're preparing the final version of the 10-year sales history presentation, and you need to do a little more work to make the chart and worksheet even better. You need to get a closeup view of your chart to make sure everything is ready and in place, so you'll zoom in to see separate sections of the data. You also need to compare the values in the data and the chart to be sure that the chart type reflects your point. You'll add a macro to quickly show the chart at full screen and zoomed to 125% size. Finally, you'll document the macro and assign it to a macro button on the sheet. Sometimes, you'll find it's easier to use a button than a menu command. Since many of the buttons you use frequently are not on the default toolbars, first you'll create a new toolbar to make some of your tasks easier.

Step 1: Create a New Toolbar

Create a new toolbar and add the Record Macro button to it, and then move it to the top of the window.

1 Open the file Part5 Review, and save it as Review Part5.

2 Use the toolbar shortcut menu and the Toolbars command to create a new toolbar called "My Macro."

3 Use the Customize dialog box to drag the Record Macro button from the Macro category to your new toolbar, and then close the Customize dialog box.

4 Drag your new toolbar to the top of the worksheet, but do not dock it.

For more information on   See

Opening and customizing toolbars   Lesson 14

Step 2: Arrange the Windows and Zoom Out to See the Chart

You need to see both the data and the chart side by side to be sure that the chart shows the data clearly. Open a new window to show the chart, and tile both windows. Zoom out to show all of the history data in one window and all of the chart in the other. Close the extra window after you have looked over the data and the chart.

1 Be sure the Sales History sheet is the active sheet, and then on the Window menu, click New Window.

2 Tile the windows.

3 In the new window, display the Sales History Chart sheet.

   Click the View menu, and make sure that Sized With Window is checked.

4 Zoom the Sales History sheet to 75%, and then scroll until all of the data is visible in the window.

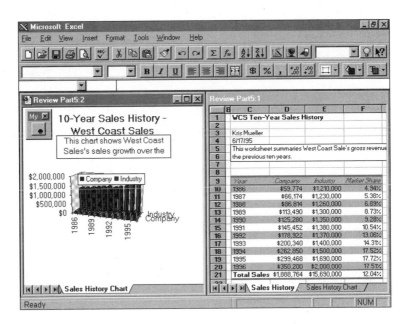

5 Close the new window, then maximize the remaining window and zoom it to 100%.

For more information on	See
Arranging windows	Lesson 14
Zooming in and out to see information	Lesson 14

Step 3: *Create a Macro to Show a Full-Screen View of the Chart*

You find that you often need to select the chart sheet and switch to full-screen view. To save time later, make a macro that first selects the chart sheet and then changes the view to full screen.

1 Be sure that the Sales History sheet is the active sheet, and then use the Record Macro button on the My Macro toolbar to create a new macro.

2 Name the macro "ShowChart" and add the description "Selects chart sheet, changes view to full screen."

3 To record the macro, click the Sales History Chart sheet tab, and select the Full Screen command on the View menu.

4 Use the Stop Macro button to stop recording and finish your macro.

For more information on	See
Recording a macro	Lesson 15

Step 4: *Document the Macro*

You need to document your macro so that others can understand exactly what each step does. Switch to the module sheet, and add comments to the macro to explain each step.

1 After the line "Sub ShowChart( )," press ENTER twice and TAB once, and then type **'Switches to show chart.**

2 After the line "Sheets("Sales History Chart"). Select," press ENTER twice, and then type **'Changes the view to Full Screen.**

For more information on	See
Documenting a macro	Lesson 15

Step 5: *Add a Macro Button and Run the Macro*

Your macro can save you repetitive keystrokes, but only if you can access it quickly. Create a macro button called "Show Chart" to run the macro.

1 Click the Full Screen button to display the toolbars, title bar, and status bar again.

2 Use the Create Button button on your My Tools toolbar to draw a macro button on the Sales History sheet.

3 Assign the ShowChart macro to the button.

4 Name the button "Show Chart."

5 Use the Show Chart button to run the macro, and make sure that the macro works.

For more information on	See
Viewing a sheet full screen	Lesson 14
Zooming in and out to view a sheet	Lesson 14
Creating macro buttons	Lesson 15
Running a macro from a macro button	Lesson 15

To Quit Microsoft Excel for Now

➤ On the File menu, click Exit.

If you see the Save dialog box, click Yes.

Appendix

Matching the Exercises

Microsoft Excel has many optional settings that can affect either the screen display or the operation of certain functions. Some exercise steps, therefore, might not produce exactly the same result on your screen as shown in this book. For example, if your screen does not look like the illustration at a certain point in a lesson, you can turn to this appendix for guidance. Or, if you do not get the outcome described in the lesson, you can use this appendix to determine whether the options you have in effect are the same as the ones used in this book.

Matching the Screen Display to the Illustrations

Microsoft Excel makes it easy for you to set up the program window to suit your working style and preferences. If you share your computer with others, previous users might have changed the screen setup. You can easily change it back so that your screen matches the illustrations in the lessons. The following methods can help you control the screen display.

If you change the screen display as part of a lesson and leave Microsoft Excel, the next time you open Microsoft Excel, the screen looks the way you left it in the previous session.

If the filenames in the File Open dialog box have extensions

A previous user might have changed a display option in Windows Explorer in order to see filename extensions, such as .xls in Microsoft Excel filenames. To hide the extensions, you can change the setting in Windows Explorer, the file management program in Windows 95.

1   On the Start menu, point to Programs, and then click Windows Explorer.

2   On the View menu, click Options, and then click the View tab.

Be sure you click the View menu in Windows Explorer, not in Microsoft Excel.

3   Click the Hide MS-DOS Extensions For File Types That Are Registered option to place a check mark in the box.

4   Click OK, and then close Windows Explorer.

Display toolbars

If toolbars are missing at the top of the screen, previous users might have hidden them to make more room for text. You can easily display the toolbars that contain the buttons you need in the lessons.

1   On the View menu, click the Toolbars command.

2   In the Toolbars dialog box, click the check boxes for the toolbars you need.

Most of the lessons require that the Standard and Formatting toolbars appear.

Hide extra toolbars

To use specific features in some of the lessons, additional toolbars appear in the program window. If, after completing the lesson, you no longer want these toolbars to appear, you can use the Toolbars pop-up menu to hide toolbars you do not want to see. However, most of the lessons require that the Standard and Formatting toolbars appear.

1   Use the right mouse button to click on any toolbar.

2   On the pop-up menu, click the name of the toolbar you do not want to see.

If the vertical or horizontal scroll bars do not appear

If you do not see the vertical or horizontal scroll bars, a previous user might have hidden the scroll bars to make more room for data. You can easily display them again.

1   On the Tools menu, click Options.

2   Click the View tab to display the view options in the dialog box.

3   In the Window Options area, click the Vertical Scroll Bar and Horizontal Scroll Bar check boxes to place a check mark in each box.

If the Vertical Scroll Bar or the Horizontal Scroll Bar option was previously selected, complete step 4 and then see the following procedure, "If the Microsoft Excel program window does not fill the screen."

4   Click the OK button.

If the Microsoft Excel program window does not fill the screen

A previous user might have made the Microsoft Excel program window smaller to allow quick access to another program. You can enlarge the document window by doing the following.

Maximize

➤ Click the Maximize button to the far right of the Microsoft Excel title bar.

If the right edge of the Microsoft Excel window is hidden so that you cannot see the Maximize button, point to "Microsoft Excel" in the title bar at the top of the screen, and then drag the title bar to the left until you see the Maximize button. You can also double-click anywhere on the title bar to maximize the window.

If your chart on a chart sheet does not fill the window

A previous user might have displayed charts at a smaller size. To see your chart at full size, use the Sized With Window command on the View menu.

➤ On the View menu, click Sized With Window.

If the document does not fill the space that Microsoft Excel allows

A previous user might have displayed the workbook in a smaller size to get an overview of a worksheet. To see your workbook at the normal size, use the Zoom Control drop-down list on the Standard toolbar.

➤ Click the down arrow next to the Zoom Control box, and then select 100%.

If the sheet tabs do not appear in your workbook

A previous user might have hidden the sheet tabs to see more of the worksheets. To view the sheet tabs, you use the Options command on the Tools menu.

1 On the Tools menu, click Options.
2 In the Options dialog box, click the View tab.
3 In the Window Options area, click the Sheet Tabs check box, and then click OK.

If you see number signs rather than numbers in your practice files

If you see number signs (#) instead of numbers in your practice files, your column width might not be wide enough. To display the numbers, you resize the columns.

➤ Select the affected columns, and double-click the column header border between two of the selected columns.

333

If gridlines do not appear in your workbook

A previous user might have hidden the gridlines to see a cleaner view of the data. To view the gridlines again, you use the Options command on the Tools menu.

1   On the Tools menu, click Options.
2   In the Options dialog box, click the View tab.
3   In the Window Options area, click the Gridlines check box, and then click OK.

If your columns are identified by numbers instead of letters

A previous user might have changed the reference style to R1C1. To change to the A1 reference style, you use the Options command on the Tools menu.

1   On the Tools menu, click Options, and then click the General tab.
2   In the Reference Style area, select the A1 option button, and then click OK.

If the File Properties dialog box does not open when you save a document

A previous user might have turned off the File Properties option. To turn the Prompt For File Properties option on again, use the Options command on the Tools menu.

1   On the Tools menu, click Options, and then click the General tab.
2   Click the Prompt For File Properties check box, and then click OK.

Changing Other Options

If you are not getting the results described in the lessons, you can follow the instructions in this section to verify that the options set in your program are the same as the ones used in this book.

Review each of the following dialog boxes to compare settings for those options that users change most often and are most likely to account for different results. You can view these dialog boxes by clicking the Options command on the Tools menu. Then you click the tab corresponding to the options you want to see. The following illustrations show the option settings used in this book.

View options

Click the View tab to change options that affect the appearance of the document window.

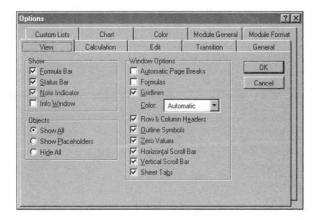

Calculation options

Click the Calculation tab to change options that affect the calculations of your formulas.

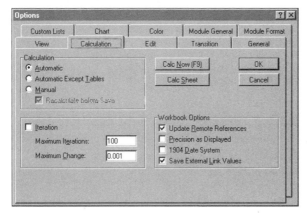

Edit options

Click the Edit tab to change options that affect how editing operations are performed.

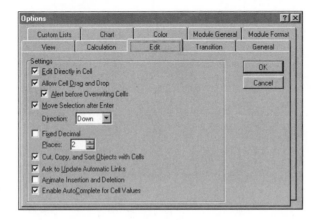

General options

Click the General tab to change options that affect the operation of Microsoft Excel in general.

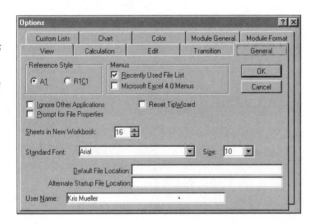

Chart options

Click the Chart tab to change options that affect how charts appear in Microsoft Excel. (Chart tab options are available only when a chart is active.)

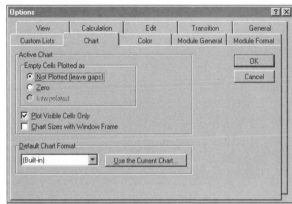

Module General options

Click the Module General tab to change options that affect how module sheets are set up. Module sheets are used to create or edit macros.

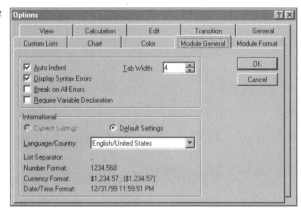

Module Format options

Click the Module Format tab to change options that affect how module sheets are formatted. Module sheets are used to create or edit macros.

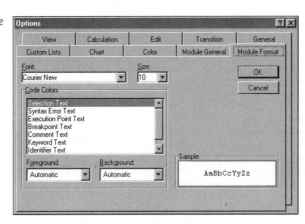

Glossary

absolute reference   A cell reference that refers to the absolute location of a specific cell, rather than to a location relative to the current cell. If a formula containing an absolute reference is moved, the reference remains the same. In an absolute reference, the row and column are each preceded by a dollar sign ($). *See also* reference type.

active cell   The selected cell. When a cell is active, you can type new data or edit the data it contains.

argument   Information you supply to a Microsoft Excel function for calculation.

array   A set of data used to build formulas that produce multiple results or that operate on a group of arguments arranged in rows and columns. There are two types of arrays in Microsoft Excel: array ranges and array constants. An array range is a rectangular area of cells sharing one common formula. An array constant is a specially arranged group of constants used as an argument in a formula.

automatic updating   A form of data exchange in which changes in data are reflected immediately in all documents linked to the data. This form of linking allows you to see any changes to the dependent data immediately, but it gives you less control when shared data changes are incorporated into your document. *See also* link.

axes   Lines bordering the plot area on a chart that provide a frame of reference for measurement or comparison. A two-dimensional (2-D) chart has two axes. A three-dimensional (3-D) chart has two or three axes, depending on the view selected.

block of data   A range of cells that contain data (no blank cells).

cell   The intersection of a column and a row. Each cell can contain text, a number, or a formula, and is named by its position in the row and column.

cell note   A note that explains, identifies, or comments on the information in a specific cell or range of cells.

cell reference   The combination of the column letter and row number for a cell. For example, the intersection of the first column with the first row is a cell called A1. The cell one column to the right of A1 is called B1; the cell one row down from A1 is A2, and so on.

chart   A graphic presentation of data from a worksheet. You can create a chart in a separate chart sheet or embed it on the same worksheet as the data. An embedded chart can be linked to data on other worksheets.

Clipboard   The holding place for information you cut or copy with the Cut, Copy, or Copy Picture command. If you cut or copy worksheet cells, the Clipboard does not display the actual cells. Instead, it displays the action you are taking and the location of the cells you are cutting or copying. Example: "Copy 2R x 3C" or "Cut 2R x 3C."

column   A vertical set of cells. Each column is identified by a unique letter or letter combination (for example, B, F, AD).

comparison operators   There are six standard comparison (logical) operators you can use in Microsoft Excel formulas, as shown in the following table:

Operator	Meaning
=	Equal to
>	Greater than
<	Less than
>=	Greater than or equal to
<=	Less than or equal to
<>	Not equal to

consolidation by category   Consolidates worksheet cells based on their category name. The worksheet cells you want to consolidate must have identical category labels, but the position of the categories within each worksheet can vary.

consolidation by position   Consolidates worksheet cells based on their position. The worksheets that contain the cells you want to consolidate must have identical layouts so that similar categories of data occupy exactly the same location in each source area.

database   A range of cells on a worksheet, also called a *list*. The first row of the database contains the field names. Each additional row of the database is one record; each column in the record is one field.

data series   A group of related data points to be plotted on a chart. Each data point consists of a category and a value. You can plot one or more data series on a chart.

data sheet   A worksheet in which you save input values that you want to substitute in your worksheet cells.

data table   A range of cells summarizing the results of substituting different values in one or more formulas on your worksheet. In Microsoft Excel, there are one-input data tables and two-input data tables.

dependent worksheet   A worksheet that contains an external reference formula or a remote reference formula. When you link two Microsoft Excel worksheets, the dependent worksheet relies on another worksheet for the value in the external reference formula. When you link a Microsoft Excel worksheet to a document in a different program, the worksheet is dependent on that document for the value in the remote reference formula.

embedding   The process by which an object is copied into another document. Embedding can take place between documents within the same program or between documents in different programs, as long as both programs support the embedding process. Because an embedded object maintains "ties" with its original program, you can open that program and edit the embedded object by double-clicking the object.

external reference   A reference to another Microsoft Excel worksheet. An external reference can designate a single cell, a cell range, or a named cell or range.

field   A column or cell in a database. Each column in a database contains a different category of data, and each cell in a database shares a common characteristic with other cells in the same column.

file format   The way information in a document is stored in a file. Different programs use different file formats. You can save documents in a variety of file formats using the Save As command on the File menu.

fill handle   A handle that appears in the lower-right corner of a selected cell or range. By dragging the fill handle to the adjoining cell or range, you can automatically copy or extend a data series into the cells or range.

filtering   A method by which you can extract data that meets certain criteria from a database. You use the field names in your worksheet to filter the data.

floating toolbar   A toolbar that appears in a window with a title bar, stays on top of the other windows, and is not fixed in position.

formula   A sequence of values, cell references, names, functions, or operators that is contained in a cell and produces a new value from existing values. A formula always begins with an equal sign (=).

formula bar   A bar at the top of your Microsoft Excel window that is used to enter or edit values and formulas in cells or charts. It displays the constant value or formula contained in the active cell.

function   A built-in formula that takes a series of values, uses them to perform an operation, and returns the result of the operation. You can use the Function Wizard to select a function and enter it into a cell as part of a formula.

goal seeking   A process in which you enter your goal value, select the variable that you want to change, and then let the program find the value that will allow you to reach your goal. With goal seeking, you can test values and then enter them into your worksheet when you find the ones you need.

graphic object   A line or shape (button, text box, oval, rectangle, arc, picture) you draw using the tools on the toolbar, or a picture you paste into Microsoft Excel.

handles   Small black squares located in the lower-right corner of selected cells or around selected graphic objects, chart items, or text. By dragging the handles, you can perform actions such as moving, copying, filling, sizing, or formatting on the selected cells, objects, chart items, or text.

input cell   A cell into which values from a data table are substituted.

insertion point   A blinking vertical line that shows where text is entered; for example, in the formula bar.

legend   Lists each pattern or symbol that is used as a marker in a chart, followed by the corresponding data series or category name.

link   To create a data connection between a dependent worksheet, the worksheet that will use the data, and a source worksheet, the worksheet in which the original data resides. Your dependent worksheet is updated whenever the data changes in the source worksheet. You can link graphics, text, or other types of information between a source file and your Microsoft Excel file.

linking formula   A formula in a worksheet that contains a reference to a single cell, a cell range, or a named cell or range in another worksheet. A linking formula creates the actual link between Microsoft Excel worksheets.

list   *See* database.

macro   A sequence of commands you record on a module. Later, you can run the recorded macro to automate your work. For easy use, a macro can be assigned to a shortcut key, a button, an object, or a tool.

marquee   *See* moving border.

module   A document that is similar to a worksheet and that contains sets of instructions (macros) for accomplishing specific tasks.

moving border   A moving dotted line that surrounds a cell or range of cells. A moving border appears around a cell or range that has been cut or copied, or around a cell or range you are inserting into a formula.

name   An identifier you create to refer to a cell, a group of cells, a constant value, an array of values, or a formula. When you use names in a formula, the formula is easier to read and remember than a formula containing cell references.

Name box   The box with a down arrow on the left side of the formula bar. You can use the Name box to create names for cells and ranges and to select named cells and ranges.

nested subtotals   Multiple levels of subtotals that provide additional levels of detail in a complex report.

nonadjacent selection   A selection of noncontiguous cells and/or objects.

one-input data table   A table you produce using the Table command on the Data menu. Using a formula containing one variable and a series of values to be substituted for that variable, you can generate a one-row or one-column series of results based on the series of values you entered.

operator   *See* comparison operators.

pane   A separate section of your worksheet window resulting from splitting your window. By splitting your window into panes and then freezing the panes, you can view both headings and data at the same time, no matter where you have scrolled in the data.

paste area   The destination for data you cut with the Cut command or copy with the Copy command.

personal macro workbook   A separate workbook that contains macros that are available every time you start the program. When you record a macro, you can choose to include it in your personal macro workbook.

pivot table   A table, similar to a crosstab, that can display two-dimensional summaries of selected data from a database in different combinations. You create a pivot table with the PivotTable Wizard.

plot area   The area of a chart in which Microsoft Excel plots data. On a 2-D chart, the plot area is bounded by the axes and includes all markers that represent data points. On a 3-D chart, it is defined by the walls and floor of the chart. The walls and floor can be formatted independently.

print title   A heading that you repeat on successive printed pages of a worksheet to identify the data.

range   On a worksheet, a rectangular section containing two or more cells.

record   One row in a database. The first row of the database contains the field names. Each additional row of the database is one record. Each record contains the same categories of data, or fields, as every other record in the database.

reference   The location of a cell or group of cells on a worksheet, indicated by column letter and row number. Examples: C5, A1:D3, R1C1, and R[1]C[3].

reference style   A method of identifying cells in a worksheet. In the A1 reference style, columns are labeled with letters and rows are labeled with numbers. In the R1C1 reference style, R indicates row and C indicates column; both columns and rows are labeled with numbers.

reference type   A relative reference (A1) in a formula indicates the location of another cell in relation to the cell containing the formula. An absolute reference ($A$1) always refers to the exact location of a specific cell. A mixed reference ($A2; A$2) is half relative and half absolute. *See also* absolute reference; relative reference.

refresh   The action of updating the data in a pivot table to reflect changes to the data in your worksheet.

relative reference   A cell reference that refers to the location of a specific cell relative to the current cell, rather than its absolute location. *See also* reference type.

result cell   A cell on your worksheet that is recalculated when you apply a new scenario.

row   A horizontal set of cells. Each row is identified by a number.

scenario   A set of input values you can apply to a worksheet model. You create scenarios with Scenario Manager.

ScreenTip A pop-up Help tip that displays an explanation of a dialog box or screen item. To see a ScreenTip, you can click the question mark button on a dialog box or the Standard toolbar and then click the item you want to know about.

scroll bars Bars along the right and bottom sides of a worksheet or module that allow you to scroll through the document vertically and horizontally, using a mouse. Clicking an arrow moves one column or row at a time. Clicking a shaded area moves one window at a time. The length of the scroll bar represents the entire document. Dragging the scroll box to a different position on the scroll bar and releasing the mouse button displays the part of the document that is in that relative location.

scroll box A box within a scroll bar that you can drag with the mouse to display different areas of the worksheet.

ScrollTips Pop-up tips that display the row or column you will move to when you click and drag the scroll box.

sheet tab A tab at the bottom of the screen that represents a sheet in a workbook. You select sheets by clicking their tabs. By selecting several sheets, you can enter the same information on all sheets at the same time.

sheet tab scroll buttons Four buttons in the lower-left corner of your worksheet that scroll the sheet tabs so that you can display and select the tab you want. You can also click the tab scroll buttons with the right mouse button and then select a sheet name from the shortcut menu.

shortcut menu A menu that appears when you click the right mouse button while pointing to any of several areas on screen. You can display shortcut menus from cells, columns, rows, text boxes, objects, buttons, charts, chart items, toolbars, tools, or workbooks.

sort key The field name or criteria that you use to sort by. To sort a range, you can select any cell within the range and then use the Sort command. When you choose the Sort command, the range around the active cell is automatically selected for sorting.

source worksheet A Microsoft Excel worksheet referred to by an external reference formula or a remote reference formula. The source worksheet is the source of the value contained in the external reference formula or the remote reference formula; it provides source data to the dependent worksheet.

status bar The bar at the bottom of the screen that displays information about the currently selected command, the active dialog box, the standard keys on the keyboard, or the current state of the program and the keyboard.

text box A graphic element that you can place on a worksheet or chart. You can use text boxes to explain or label any part of a worksheet or chart.

toolbar dock The region above the formula bar and below the menu bar, or the regions on the left, right, and bottom sides of the program window, where toolbars can reside.

trendline   A line plotted in a chart that points out the progress of the values in a data series according to a selected regression equation calculated from all points in the series. You can add a trendline to one data series that will clearly show the changes in that series relative to the others in the chart. You can add trendlines to bar, column, area, line, and xy (scatter) charts.

two-input data table   A table you produce using the Table command on the Data menu. Using a formula containing two variables and two series of values to be substituted for those variables, you can generate a two-dimensional matrix of results based on the series of values you entered.

workbook   A Microsoft Excel document in which you can store other documents. A workbook can include multiple worksheets, modules, and charts.

worksheet   A set of rows, columns, and cells in which you store and manipulate data in Microsoft Excel. Several worksheets can appear in one workbook, and you can switch among them easily by clicking their tabs with the mouse.

XY (scatter) chart   A 2-D chart that has numeric values plotted along both axes rather than having values along the vertical axis and categories along the horizontal axis. This kind of chart type is typically used to analyze scientific data to see whether one set of values is dependent on or affects another set of values.

Index

Index

G

Goal Seek dialog box, 235
goal seeking, 234–35, 341
grand totals, in pivot tables, 218–19
graphic objects
    defined, 341
    deleting, 270
    linking, 270–73
    placing in worksheets, 268–70
    updating links, 272–73
graphs. *See* charts
greater-than operator (>), 176, 340
gridlines
    adding to charts, 101, 102–3
    displaying/hiding, 334
    not printing, 139–40
Group And Outline command, 193, 194, 195
Group command, 86, 89, 100

H

handles, defined, 341. *See also* fill handle
Header dialog box, 135
headers and footers
    creating, 134–36
    dates in, 135
    deleting, 132, 133
    fonts in, 135–36
    modifying, 132–34
    overview, 132
    standard, 132–34
headings, row/column
    entering, 9–10
    freezing, 301
    as range names, 32, 33
    repeating on every printed page, 127–28
Help, online, xxxiv–xxxviii. *See also* Answer Wizard
Help dialog box
    Answer Wizard tab, xli–xlii
    Contents tab, xxxv
    Find tab, xxxvii–xxxviii
    Index tab, xxxvi–xxxvii
hiding
    data in pivot tables, 212–14
    filename extensions, 331–32
    gridlines, 334
    outline details, 191, 193

hiding, *continued*
    rows and columns, 307–8
    scroll bars, 332
    sheet tabs, 333
    toolbars, 298–99, 332

I

icons
    arranging, xxxii
    changing size, xxxii
    large, xxxii
    as placeholders in documents, 277–79
importing custom lists, 21
input cells
    defined, 341
    naming, 245
    in one-input data tables, 238–39
    in scenarios, 245
    in two-input data tables, 241, 242
insertion point, 9, 341
Insert Worksheet button, 295
installing practice files, xxiv–xxv
Italic button, 61

K

keyboard
    assigning macros to keys, 321–23
    conventions, xxi
    navigating worksheets with, 7
    selecting cells with, 6, 7
    shortcut keys, xxx

L

labels. *See* headings, row/column; text; titles
landscape orientation, 124, 125
Large Icons button, xxxii
left-aligned cells, 62–63
legends
    adding, 102
    defined, 342
    deleting, 99–100
    formatting, 102–3
    moving, 102–3
less-than operator (<), 176, 340
linear trendlines, 104, 105–6
line charts, 80

Index

Index

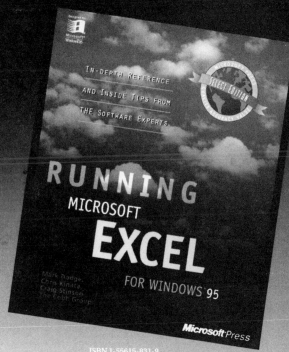

WHO KNOWS MORE ABOUT WINDOWS® 95 THAN MICROSOFT® PRESS?

ISBN 1-55615-816-5
224 pages
$19.95 ($26.95 Canada)

ISBN 1-55615-683-9
320 pages
$29.95 ($39.95 Canada)

These books are essential if you are a newcomer to Microsoft® Windows® or an upgrader wanting to capitalize on your knowledge of Windows 3.1. Both are written in a straightforward, no-nonsense way, with well-illustrated step-by-step examples, and both include practice files on disk. Learn to use Microsoft's newest operating system quickly and easily with MICROSOFT WINDOWS 95 STEP BY STEP and UPGRADING TO MICROSOFT WINDOWS 95 STEP BY STEP, both from Microsoft Press.

IMPORTANT — READ CAREFULLY BEFORE OPENING SOFTWARE PACKET(S).
By opening the sealed packet(s) containing the software, you indicate your acceptance
of the following Microsoft License Agreement.

Microsoft License Agreement

MICROSOFT LICENSE AGREEMENT
(Single User Products)

The
Step by Step
Practice Files Disk

The enclosed 3.5-inch disk contains timesaving, ready-to-use practice files that complement the lessons in this book. To use the practice files, you'll need the Windows 95 operating system.

Each *Step by Step* lesson uses practice files from the disk. Before you begin the *Step by Step* lessons, read the "Getting Ready" section of the book for easy instructions telling how to install the files on your computer's hard disk. As you work through each lesson, be sure to follow the instructions for renaming the practice files so that you can go through a lesson more than once if you need to.

Please take a few moments to read the License Agreement on the previous page before using the enclosed disk.

Register Today!

Return this
Microsoft® Excel for Windows® 95 Step by Step
registration card for:

✔ a Microsoft Press® catalog

✔ exclusive offers on specially priced books

U.S. and Canada addresses only. Fill in information below and mail postage-free. Please mail only the bottom half of this page.

1-55615-825-4A   *Microsoft Excel for Windows 95 Step by Step*   *Owner Registration Card*

_____

NAME

_____

INSTITUTION OR COMPANY NAME

_____

ADDRESS

_____

_____

CITY   STATE   ZIP

Microsoft® Press
Quality Computer Books

For a free catalog of
Microsoft Press® products, call
1-800-MSPRESS

BUSINESS REPLY MAIL
FIRST-CLASS MAIL   PERMIT NO. 53   BOTHELL, WA

POSTAGE WILL BE PAID BY ADDRESSEE

MICROSOFT PRESS REGISTRATION
MICROSOFT EXCEL
FOR WINDOWS 95 STEP BY STEP
PO BOX 3019
BOTHELL WA   98041-9946